The Holy Week Book

By/Edited by

Eileen Elizabeth Freeman

and illustrated by
George F. Collopy

Resource Publications
San Jose, California

The Holy Week Book

Acknowledgements

The music in the music section in this book is used with permission of Sr. Suzanne Toolan, SM.

The music in the chapter entitled *Springs of Water Bless The Lord* is used with permission of Christian Rich.

The Merchants Carol, Mary's Wandering, Love Is Come Again and *My Dancing Day* are taken with permission from the Oxford Book of Carols. *Friday Morning* is used with permission of Sydney Carter.

Cover design and illustration throughout are by George F. Collopy.

ISBN 0-89390-007-9

Library of Congress Catalog Card Number 78-73510

To the two people in the world whom I most admire, Alex and Helen Freeman, my parents. Live long and prosper!

Index Of Crosses

The Holy Week Book includes in its illustrations more than forty different traditional crosses, all of which are presented in a form suitable for adaptation and use in parish banners, liturgy programs or bulletins. Below is an identification and an index to the page on which each of the crosses appears.

Index Of Songs For Holy Week

V:N Issues of *Modern Liturgy* magazine are represented
     by their volume and number (Ex. 6:1 refers to Volume 6
     Number 1).
GR   Gather 'Round Songbook edited by Paul F. Page.
GRT Gather 'Round, Too! Songbook edited by Paul F. Page.
HWB *The Holy Week Book* edited by Eileen E. Freeman.
PTD Picture The Dawning Songbook (accompanying album
     available) by Paul F. Page.
     All of the above are available from Resource Publications,
     PO Box 444, Saratoga, CA 95070.

Table Of Contents

Why A Holy Week Book?

by Eileen E. Freeman

If we are ever going to put our common worship into proper perspective, we must begin by truly believing that the Easter Vigil is the most important celebration of the liturgical year. No other liturgical service can compete with the Vigil, either for solemnity or for centrality of feast. Even the Christmas Eve Mass, with its carols, creches and poinsettias, can never even approach the solemn joy, the anticipation, the wonderment of the Easter Vigil.

Our ancestors in the Faith understood the mystery of the night very well. For them the Easter Vigil was truly a waiting, a longing, an anticipation of the dawn, whose coming celebrated the rising of Christ from the dead. They figuratively died with Christ during the night so as to rise with him in newness of life and light.

Above all else, the Easter Vigil is a celebration of mystery. There have always been "mystery religions" which held secret rites and promised their members hidden rewards and blessings. But the Vigil which culminates our Christian year is more than a shadow; for us, it is the reality. On this night the world seems suspended between order and a return to primeval chaos. Christ in the tomb struggles with the forces of evil and destruction and we wait on the sidelines, vicariously entering into the struggle as we are baptized. We light the candle, proclaiming that Christ has conquered the dark forces and brought light and order into the world again.

Carl Jung, the great psychologist and anthropologist, noted that the images in the Easter Vigil are even more basic than the struggle of life over death. He says that at the moment the Paschal candle is plunged into the font of water, it is a recreating of the primal generative power, the union of male and female, the fulfillment of the Creator's command to "increase and multiply."

Of course, for us much of the Easter Vigil is symbolic. We know that as Saint Paul tells us, Christ having died once, dies no more; death no longer has any power over him. Jesus does not die and rise every year, as the ancients believed about their gods: Baal, Melqart, Adonis. What we celebrate at the Easter Vigil is our own dying and rising and that of the community of which we are a part.

Because the services of Holy Week are so central to our religious experience and heritage, it is vitally important that we let the symbols be what they have always been intended to be. This principle was behind the first reforms of Holy Week made by Pope Pius XII in the 1950's. He saw that it was illogical to celebrate the Vigil on Saturday afternoon, to light candles when the sun was shining, to sing about the beauty of the night when it was still day, etc.

If we are going to celebrate Holy Week in a meaningful way, we must live with the seasons of the year. We must understand what it means that grains of wheat are sown and then die, but rise again in new life. We must understand that some trees' leaves must fall and die, that no one flower lasts in the same way forever, that snow comes or blistering heat, and the plants seem to die away. We must take time to get out of our carefully climate-controlled houses and offices. We must let ourselves become hot or cold; sunburned or snow-blinded, wet or wind-blown. We are a part of nature, its rhythms of death and life. We will never come to understand what Jesus' life and death mean for us if we guard ourselves from living and dying.

Children know all about this instinctively. When it snows, they capture the flakes on their mittens. Then they blow on them and their warm breath makes the flakes disappear. They regret the loss of the flakes, but see also that while the flake is gone, its essential part, the water, is still there and can be seen, tasted, and used. Nature transforms but does not destroy. Children learn about Easter naturally as they watch a caterpillar spin the cocoon and later emerge as a butterfly. If adults never learn this basic paradigm of life while children, they have trouble all their lives with the natural rhythm of life.

The *Holy Week Book* is designed to help parishes that are looking for practical ways to help their communities experience Holy Week in a truly participative, celebrational way. It can help restore the sense of mystery and awe that the rites once held. It is a means of actually implementing the restored liturgy for this holiest of all weeks.

However, *The Holy Week Book* is not a "how-to-do-it manual." It cannot be taken verbatim and used *in toto*. Every idea, every suggestion, every special service is incomplete without local input and should be adapted to the needs of the worshipping community.

Nor is *The Holy Week Book* a historical treatise on the rites of this part of the year. Much background material has deliberately been left out so that the book could have as much space as possible for practical suggestions.

More than anything else, this is a book of practical resources for celebrating Holy Week on the parish level. It includes material for adults, for children; the capable and the incapable; for Catholics and for Protestants. Any of the suggestions it offers is within the power of the community that is interested in trying them.

The Holy Week Book is ministerially oriented. This means that the selections it contains were chosen with the concept of service, of helping and aiding others rather than that of doing, imposing or forcing a program on people. Its contents are designed to foster a climate of common prayer or to make it easier for people to pray at another time.

The Holy Week Book can help make your parish celebrations more fruitful and more enjoyable for your community. It is a very practical resource. But without the understanding of each specific group of parishioners, it can only be a mechanical aid. Without a "personal" touch it must be less than perfect. So these ideas are offered for you to adapt, revise, and change. May your parish community have a more fruitful, awesome and joyful Holy Week.

Eileen E. Freeman
Phoenix, AZ
January, 1979

Part I
Passion
Sunday

Knowledge Of Finality

by Michael E. Moynahan, SJ

Knowledge of finality.
Concluding quickly
what had been,
some short time ago,
begun.

Facing now
those last few days
with what?
A burst of celebration.
A crowd of half-crazed
Roman-riddled Jews
shouting
for all they're worth:
"Blessings on —
whoever comes to save us!"

Just how does one
bow out gracefully?
Useless to explain again
what three years'
word and work
have constantly
moved towards.
Thought by many
possessed, insane;
anticipating unknown pain;
moving with such
stern resolve
to yet another disappointment
for my people —
the last great disaster:
that paschal mystery thing.

Filled with memories
that flood an aching heart
and tired mind.
Every healing, teaching,
contradictory feeling,
tireless reaching out
to simple, hungry people —
all solitary stones.

Pieced together, though,
they paved the way
to this:
confusion's reign,
the frightening recurrence
of sorrow's familiar face,
the loss of those
whose love I knew,
shattered dreams
reluctantly forgotten,
wasted possibilities,
the endless taunt
of haunting questions,
and last, but not least,
that ultimate defeat —
Death —
and whatever lies
beyond death's door:
(That hoped for place
we only dare whisper of
in soft, hushed tones.
A place where all old bones
are catastrophically reborn.)
a New Jerusalem.

Putting The Palm And Passion Together

by Edmund C. Hurlbutt, SJ

During the past several years, Christians have largely restored the celebration of the Paschal Mystery to its original unity.[1] That is, we no longer look on Holy Week as simply a commemoration of the final events of Jesus' earthly life, as separate events leading up to his death and followed by his resurrection. Rather, we now see Holy Week as a single celebration of *one* event: the passage of our Lord Jesus Christ from mortal life to unending risen life, and our participation in that wondrous Passover. The cross and the resurrection are one; every day of Holy Week is Good Friday, and every day is Easter.

In this great restoration of the unity of the Paschal Mystery, however, Palm/Passion Sunday has tended to remain the orphan of Holy Week. Compared to the Easter Triduum — the great feasts of Holy Thursday, Good Friday, and the Easter Vigil — Palm/Passion Sunday pales to seeming insignificance. It seems, at best, no more than preparation, a mere setting of the stage for the more important drama to come. Yet, for two very important reasons, Palm/Passion Sunday has an integral role in the Holy Week liturgy.

First, the very fact that we have two names for the first day of Holy Week — Palm Sunday and Passion Sunday — indicates that this day presents us with perhaps our best opportunity to portray the *unity* of the Paschal Mystery. The suffering (Passion) and the glory (Palms) are one. The Passion is, in fact, the "beata Passio," the happy, the blessed Passion. There is one passage from death to life, and for Christians, the Passion should mean the single wondrous event of Christ's dying, rising, and glorification at the Father's side. Palm/Passion Sunday does far more, then, than simply set the stage; it announces the reason for and the meaning of the entire week long celebration that it begins.

Second, while the Easter Triduum may still remain liturgically more imposing, considered pastorally, Palm/Passion Sunday may rank second only to Easter in the importance of Holy Week celebrations. For while most churches are filled only once on Holy Thursday and Good Friday, those same churches may be filled three, four, or even five times on Palm/Passion Sunday. The simple fact is that while Holy Thursday and Good Friday may be more solemn feasts, more people will actually attend the celebration of "Blessed Passion" Sunday.

This consciousness of numbers becomes particularly important when we consider the great number of people who not only do not participate in the celebration of the Lord's Supper and the Lord's death, but who also participate in the Easter Sunday liturgy rather than the Easter Vigil. For those people Palm/Passion Sunday may be their only opportunity to celebrate the entire Paschal Mystery. For Easter Sunday liturgies (as opposed to the vigil) tend to focus solely on the triumph and joy of the resurrection, on the goal of the Passover, and not on the passage itself. And since to celebrate Easter without celebrating the cross is to distort the Christian message, Passion Sunday becomes extremely important in revealing the Good News of Christ's Passion. Palm/Passion Sunday truly proclaims that just as there is no cross without the resurrection, so there is no resurrection without the cross.

To say that the Paschal Mystery is one event, and that each day of Holy Week should be a celebration of the whole of Christ's Passion, certainly does not mean that every celebration is the same. Each day we celebrate the same mystery under a different aspect. In other words, we might say that while there is only one cause for celebration — the saving mystery of Christ's life, death and resurrection — there are several occasions we use to celebrate that mystery. And on Palm/Passion Sunday, the occasion we use is Christ's messianic entry into Jerusalem.

Certainly, as an occasion for celebration, Palm Sunday is one of the Church's most solemn feasts. Its importance is indicated first by the fact that it is one of the very few events of Christ's life mentioned in all four gospels. Furthermore, it marks the only time in Jesus' public career when he actually accepted public acclaim as Messiah. "If they were to keep quiet," he said of the crowds, "the very stones would cry out." (Luke 19:40). And not only does Jesus accept the acclamation, but he even takes the initiative in organizing his entrance, sending the apostles off to find the donkey he rides upon. And finally, of course, Palm Sunday marks the commencement of Christ's great Passover. He enters the holy city where his Father's will, Christ's own glorification and the salvation of men and women, is to be accomplished.

THE HOLY WEEK BOOK

But how does this solemn entry into Jerusalem serve as an occasion for celebrating the Paschal Mystery? Perhaps the simplest answer to such a question can be found in the acclamation: "Jesus Christ is Lord!" For when we celebrate Christ's dying and rising, we proclaim him as Lord just as surely as if we had stood in the streets of Jerusalem so long ago. Indeed, our hosannas should ring out with a far greater fervor, for we recall and re-enact Christ's entry into Jerusalem with a profoundly deeper understanding of what it means to call Christ our Lord and King. As St. Paul says so beautifully in his great hymn of praise in Philippians, Christ "emptied himself, obediently accepting even death, death on a cross! Because of this, God highly exalted him, so that at the name of Jesus every knee must bend and every tongue proclaim: Jesus Christ is Lord." Jesus is the Lord because he humbled himself and has been raised up by the Father.

And it is not simply a past triumph which we celebrate, but a present and future triumph, too. For the church has always had a marvelous trans-temporal view of all her celebrations. We joyfully recall the events of Christ's earthly life; we gratefully celebrate the present salvific significance of those events; and we look forward in hope to their eschatological completion at Christ's coming in glory. And since Christ's entry into Jerusalem both marked his triumph as Messiah and began the even greater triumph of his Passion, that entry is particularly appropriate to this time-transcending viewpoint. We celebrate a triumph already achieved (Christ's dying and rising), a triumph being achieved (our participation in that saving mystery), and a triumph yet to be achieved (Christ's coming in glory). Seen in this light, the Palm/Passion Sunday liturgy becomes far more than a remembrance of the messianic entrance; it is a celebration of the initial triumph of Christ's death and resurrection, and a call to bring about the final triumph which all creation awaits. For although the initial victory is won and the ultimate victory assured, much remains to be done. Christ, having entered his glory by his own dying and rising, now reigns "until he puts all his enemies beneath his feet." (1 Cor. 15:25) And by our participation in Palm/Passion Sunday we symbolize our commitment to complete that victory. We joyfully join ourselves to Christ, making his Passion our own, so that we may "fill up (in our bodies) what is lacking in the sufferings of Christ, for the sake of his body, the Church." (Col. 1:24) We share his sufferings that we may share and complete his glory. On Palm/Passion Sunday, then, we proclaim in a very special way the death of the Lord until he comes in glory.

Another viewpoint which beautifully combines the Palm and the Passion, the occasion and the meaning, is provided by David M. Stanley, SJ, in his beautiful book *A Modern Scriptural Approach to the Spiritual Exercises*.[2] Stanley quotes the letter to the Hebrews in order to illuminate the meaning of the day: "But when Christ appeared as high priest of the good things which have come to be, he entered once for all into the sanctuary, passing through the greater and more perfect tabernacle not made by hands, that is, not belonging to this creation, by virtue of his own blood, having secured our redemption...For he has entered not a sanctuary made by human hands, but heaven itself, that he might appear before God on our behalf...Now Christ has appeared at the end of the ages, to put an end to sin once for all by the sacrifice of himself...The second time he will appear not to take away sin, but to bring those who eagerly await him to salvation...Since then, brothers, the blood of Jesus assures our entrance into the sanctuary by the new and living path, and since we have a high priest who is over the house of God, let us draw near to God in utter sincerity and absolute confidence, our hearts washed clean from the evil which lay on our conscience and our bodies washed with pure water." (Heb. 9:11-10:22)

When seen from this perspective, Jesus' messianic entrance into Jerusalem becomes a parable-in-action. It symbolizes the whole of Christ's redemptive work, since through his death, resurrection and ascension Christ has entered the Jerusalem, the heavenly sanctuary, in order to intercede for us during the lifetime of the Church. And one day, he shall return in glory, to lead us, his people, processionally into the celestial holy of holies before the throne of God.[3]

Thus celebrated, Palm/Passion Sunday becomes a beautiful symbol of the pilgrim Church, a church on its way. We are moving towards the heavenly Jerusalem, yet wondrously we can only make the journey because it has already been made by Christ in his Passion. "The blood of Jesus assures our entrance into the sanctuary by the new and living path." And even more lovingly, Christ has not only made this journey for us, but now offers to make it with us. For by offering his passion to us as our own, he has made us co-workers in our own redemption. The Palm Sunday procession is not just a procession for Christ, but one with Christ; the Church in procession is Christ in the world. Our Great High Priest is leading his people into the heavenly holy of holies, and we share his entrance into the Father's glory by sharing his passion.

Having seen the Palm and the Passion as one, we can now look at the liturgy with eyes more sensitive to both its opportunities and its dangers. The prime goal of all planning should be to produce a liturgy which celebrates the Paschal Mystery as a unity, as one passage through death to new life and glory. Thus, the procession, the reading of the passion, and the Eucharistic liturgy should be united as closely as possible, with each part illuminating the meaning of the other two, and the whole liturgy revealing the mystery of Christ's Passion. In addition, the liturgy should adequately symbolize — through word, song, and action — our own commitment to participate in Christ's dying and rising. Finally, we should keep in mind that although we celebrate the Paschal Mystery as a whole, we are not attempting to pack all of Holy Week into a single liturgy. Rather, on Palm/Passion Sunday we commence a week-long celebration by announcing its meaning and goal. To this end, the liturgy should be kept simple and brief, and should invite celebration in the rest of Holy Week.

The Procession. The procession is the most distinctive part of the Palm/Passion Sunday liturgy, but it is also the part most likely to be misunderstood. As we have seen, the procession is not simply a re-enactment of Christ's messianic entry to Jerusalem, but is symbolic of our sharing in Christ's dying and rising. Thus, we should never pretend that we participate in the procession unaware of the Passion. Precisely the opposite is true: we participate in the procession because we believe that Christ's own dying and rising make it possible for us to do so. Our participation is a reminder of the unfinished victory, the unfinished journey, and is symbolic of our commitment to complete that victory and that journey, to complete Christ's Passion in our own bodies.

The procession, then, should always be public in nature, in order to make clear both our proclamation of Jesus as Messiah and our commitment to him in his Passion. Second, it should start away from the Church and move for some distance in order to symbolize better both our journey and our dependence on Christ to lead us before the Father in glory. Third, because processing is a symbolic act, a bodying forth of an inner act of love, it should include scripture passages or songs which make clear its meaning. That meaning is found, of course, in the Paschal Mystery, so that passages which speak of Christ's death and resurrection — such as Christ's own predictions — are particularly appropriate. Finally, music — complete with processional instruments (trumpets, trombones) wherever possible — should be used to help express our joy, our gratitude, and our confidence.

THE HOLY WEEK BOOK

The Passion. If the Palm is the symbol of the day, the Passion is its meaning. Thus, the Passion is deserving of a centrality in the liturgy and of a preparation which are unfortunately too often lacking. There should be no jarring shifting of gears between the procession and the Passion, no jump from Palm waving happiness to crucifixion sadness (or, perhaps worse, boredom). The procession and the Passion are one, and the best way to guarantee unity is to plan them as a single liturgy of the word. Furthermore, we should plan the procession around the Passion, and not visa versa. That is, everything in the procession should lead toward the Passion as its meaning and fulfillment. Thus, for example, hearing Christ's own predictions of his Passion, made as he journeyed towards Jerusalem, can help integrate the procession into the Passion. Another means might be to read the first two readings of the Mass for the day during the procession and have only the Passion proclaimed inside the church as the culmination of the liturgy of the word. Or much of the Passion itself could be read during the procession with only the final scene on Golgatha read as the Gospel of the day.

In any event, the Passion should always be proclaimed with dignity, solemnity, and after considerable preparation. The ministers of the word should be conscious of the fact that they are not just reading, but prayerfully proclaiming the drama of salvation. They should also be extensively rehearsed so that they are confident enough of the words and their dramatic expression to concentrate on the prayerfulness of the proclamation. Indeed, it is so important that the Passion be proclaimed well that where time is not available for sufficient rehearsal, or where there are not enough effective speakers, it is best to have just one person read the entire passion. Merely involving even larger numbers of readers does not make the presentation more effective or meaningful. Simple excellence is far more effective in proclaiming God's word than complex mediocrity.

In addition, every effort should be made to involve the congregation in the Passion. Especially effective toward this end is the singing of a refrain by the congregation at various points in the Passion. This refrain should express the triumphant attitude of the celebration and proclaim Christ as Lord. One technique which should be especially avoided is to assign the congregation the negative role of shouting "Crucify him!" Such an activity hardly helps God's people celebrate the meaning of the day.

The Eucharist. Because the reading of the passion on Palm/Passion Sunday concludes with Christ's death, the liturgy of the Eucharist plays an extremely important role in completing the meaning of our celebration. The Passion (Christ's passage to new life, as opposed to the passion — the gospel account of Christ's death) is incomplete without the resurrection, and it is the Risen Christ whom we meet in the Eucharist. Thus, care should be taken to integrate the liturgy of the Eucharist into the entire celebration. During the homily, for example, the impending Eucharist might be portrayed as the heavenly banquet that awaits us when we finish our journey with Christ, a journey made present for us now by the mystery of Christ's own Passion.

Another means of uniting the liturgy would be to have the same refrain sung during the procession, the reading of the passion, and the Eucharistic prayer. Or finally, to use the threefold viewpoint of the Church, we might portray the procession as the victory that has happened (Christ has died), the Passion as our participation in the victory that is happening (Christ is risen), and the Eucharist as the victory that is to come (Christ will come again).

By way of conclusion, the liturgy should end with a simple dispersal, not a recessional. After the blessing and the dismissal, the ministers should simply return to the sacristy, and there should be no concluding song, nor any music played. On Palm/Passion Sunday we have merely begun our celebration, and we will not be finished until we celebrate the glory of Easter.

Footnotes:
1. See especially, Frank B. Norris, SS, "The Real Meaning of Easter," *Modern Liturgy*, Vol. 2 No. 2, February 1975, pp. 4-5, 13. Also, for a history of the development of Holy Week and of a history of the separation of the Paschal Mystery into distinct events, cf. J. Gordon Davies, *Holy Week: A Short History*, Ecumenical Studies in Worship, No. 11 (John Knox Press, 1963).
2. David M. Stanley, SJ, *A Modern Scriptural Approach to The Spiritual Exercises* (Chicago: Institute of Jesuit Resources in cooperation with Loyola University Press, 1967), pp. 79-84.
3. Stanley, p. 82.

Hosanna! Music For The Passion (Palm) Sunday

by Eileen E. Freeman

From a pastoral point of view, Passion Sunday is often viewed as one of three days a year when people come to church who never attend at other times. For some reason, the pageantry of Passion Sunday still attracts Christians who hardly ever go to church. They are our invisible brothers and sisters, whom we rarely see. For the most part, they are people who were baptized into the Body of Christ in infancy, who have never made a personal choice to belong to God's family as responsible adults. Leaders of music should be concerned for these people so as to help them make a mature commitment to Christ and grow in that commitment.

During Holy Week, parish leaders of music have a greater strain put on their ministry than at any other time during the year. There are not only special musical programs, but also additional services. Because of this pressure, it is easy to forget that a ministry exists for the sake and service of people, not for the performance of music. We can become so caught up in choir rehearsals and technical problems that we lose sight of the real goal of liturgical music ministry; to be channels of the love of God to the members of the Body of Christ. Once we lose our vision of what this musical charism is all about, we might as well quit!

Who are the people whom we are trying to serve on Passion Sunday? They are a much more heterogeneous group than at almost any other time during the year. In addition to the people who regularly attend a particular service, there will be others who normally attend other services, but who are there because they like the celebrant, or the type of music. There may be people from other parishes, who either dislike their own parish liturgy, or who especially like the celebration in this parish. There will be the "Easter" church-goers who worship only rarely. There will be curious sightseers who saw the parish's list of special services in the newspaper. There will be out-of-town visitors, relatives and friends of parishioners staying for the holidays. This is quite a disparate group.

Hard as it may be, we have to be concerned for all these people, old friends or strangers, and strive to make all welcome. We must set a tone so that everyone can relax and participate. Our music and our presence should inspire those who are visiting from less liturgically-oriented parishes to go home and work toward change. To those who have never made an adult commitment to Christ, our music ought to give reason to believe; it should help them come to believe in the Lord's love for them. To all those who regularly attend the parish celebrations, our music ministry should offer faith, hope, love, and some continuity. This does not mean that we must consciously gear each piece of liturgical music to fit the needs of every individual present; to do that would be almost impossible. However, if we are aware of special needs, we will be more open to the Spirit and better able to choose proper music.

In any congregation there are people who are still struggling with faith. On Passion Sunday the percentage is likely to go up, since some of the infrequent church-goers include those who do not have a faith-home. This suggests that our music should be especially careful to present what we believe in a clear manner without ambiguities and confusion. This does not mean that every hymn or refrain should have a creedal formulation and end in a doxology, but it means that a hymn should say what it says in such a way as to be easily understood. A song that asks, "Who are You, Jesus?," without ever answering the question, or which presents the question as one of doubtful importance is a bad choice. While a congregation of committed Christians would probably not be hurt by such a song, a group of very "hesitant" pilgrims could be devastated.

There is an important corollary to this; that while faith-filled hymns are an essential part of music ministry, hymns which express an honest search for the truth and a hope for finding an answer are also acceptable music. The best example of this is on Passion Sunday, Psalm 21, the responsorial psalm for the day. The psalmist is clearly troubled, shaken in faith, and makes no pretense of hiding his confusion. But he ends his prayer by hoping in God for an end to trouble and a joyful celebration together with the community of believers.

Liturgy

Continuity of ministry is also important to preserve. We must not be suddenly inconsistent with our music on Passion Sunday, or we will only confuse and perhaps distract our congregation. Of course Passion Sunday is a special day liturgically, with special music. But if we use it as an occasion to teach the congregation six new responses and two new hymns, we will be helping no one to pray. Everyone will be somewhat nervous about being able to sing all the new material, everyone, that is, except the rare individuals who majored in music at Julliard.

There are certain musical difficulties with regard to the Passion Sunday celebration. These are mostly a result of the additional people attending. For instance, the number of hymnals may be suddenly quite inadequate. It may be advisable for pastoral reasons to print up a parish Holy Week booklet so that each person can have one. Naturally this requires prior planning so as to obtain all necessary reprint permissions well ahead of time.

Another problem may be a poor response in singing from the congregation. If a large number of people are present who, for one reason or another, do not attend regularly, they may know little of the music and feel quite hesitant about singing it. Sometimes this difficulty can be bridged by a pre-service rehearsal, but a rehearsal on Passion Sunday is often complicated by the procession. The sensitive music leader will try to provide some congregational responses that are fairly easy to sing.

Just before the liturgy begins, the music minister should remind those who are sitting in the church that the procession will be beginning in another location. Perhaps some of the people will have missed previous announcements, or will be new and unsure of where to go.

Because the Passion Sunday Procession and Liturgy contain some unusual elements, the leader of music needs to give precise directions as to what will be sung and where the music will be found. However, it is more convenient to print up a booklet and only make two or three announcements of music page numbers, than to preface the singing of the Anamnesis or Amen by verbal instruction which completely destroys the rhythm of the prayer.

The Passion Sunday Liturgy has a number of joys which can easily compensate for the difficulties. For one thing, the congregation is generally more aware of what is going on than at other times. They know that the liturgy is different, and hence pay closer attention. The atmosphere of festivity helps many people to participate and to sing enthusiastically, provided directions are given without confusion.

In choosing music for the Passion Sunday Liturgy, the leader of music ought to select music which is clear in its statement of what we believe. It should not be extremely difficult; the lyrics should avoid jargon, which most "occasional" Catholics have difficulty in understanding.

While congregational music may not present many difficulties to the experienced leader of music, suitable choir and organ pieces can prove to be a problem, since many of them are old warhorses which have been done for decades. "The Palms" may have been traditional at one time, but it has been so over used that it deserves a rest. The same can be said about numerous other pieces. People have become so used to hearing them that the music ceases to stimulate anyone's faith, only their emotions. Liturgical warhorses never help people to grow.

There is one choir piece which this writer wholeheartedly recommends: "Ride On, King Jesus," (Augsburg); this is a setting of an old spiritual for SATB which has a certain swing to it. The piece stretches the ranges of all four parts to their limits, but the part-harmony is not that difficult.

Much of what has been said about Passion Sunday congregations can be said about congregations for the rest of Holy Week. If we who are leaders of music allow the liturgy to speak to us, if we grow in faith ourselves, then we will be better prepared to help others grow, too, in their search for God.

Creative Passion Sunday Processions

by Eileen E. Freeman

Creative and inspiring Passion Sunday processions require a great deal of work! Jesus may have entered Jerusalem somewhat spontaneously, riding on a donkey and surrounded by his fans (literally and figuratively), but if we want to recapture some of that intensity of feeling, we must plan, plan and plan.

The more elaborate the procession, the earlier the planning for it must begin. As a rule, the coordination of choirs, leaders, and congregation will take several weeks to orchestrate successfully. The object should be to provide an atmosphere in which people can relax and celebrate. This type of atmosphere has to be created. Usually a congregation in an unfamiliar or unaccustomed place will only be able to relax and pray if everything going on around them is happening like clockwork. Therefore, planning for the procession can begin as early as the beginning of Lent.

A procession can be described as a group of people going on foot from one place to another distinct place. This definition effectively eliminates the custom of marching around the aisles of a church, beginning at the altar and ending up back at the same altar. The so-called "procession" inside the church building is a pitiful shadow of what a procession should be.

There are as many different possibilities for processions as there are parishes; in each case, of course, the end point is the church. The procession can begin in the school gymnasium, in the parking lot, on the sidewalk or lawn. A parish can often obtain permission to use a nearby park; or the street in front of the church may be closed off for the occasion. Since this sort of permission generally takes time to obtain, planning will have to be done as early as possible. In some towns, permission to block off a street or use of a park for religious services requires a permit or approval of the town council.

Wherever the origin point of the procession is going to be, and whatever the route, a few things must be thought out. Very often during a procession there will be people who will not take part, but who will wait in the church. Most of these people are the handicapped, whether temporarily or permanently. The young mother who sits in church with her two toddlers and her infant is "handicapped"; unless someone helps her she cannot manage three children at Mass. The elderly, to whom long walks on uneven sidewalks or flights of stairs are hazardous, will also sit in church instead of participating in the procession. Even the robust college basketball player, who is temporarily on crutches with a broken ankle, may be left out. Handicaps come in all size packages. If we do not want to leave our brothers and sisters out of the celebration, we must think of their needs so they can participate. This may mean not beginning the procession in the school basement, down a steep flight of steps. It may be necessary to offer parents help in watching their children. If the procession is long, wheelchairs or even open-top cars such as are used in the parades ought to be provided. Again, this is something that needs to be planned well in advance.

A parish should have as many full-scale processions as it feels are necessary, despite the general instructions that only one major procession should take place in a parish. The reason for a plurality of processions is that very often within a single parish there are several distinct groups. This writer knows of one Catholic parish in a small city in which the early Mass is still celebrated in Hungarian, the mid-morning Mass in Spanish, and a later one in English. Clearly one procession is not going to meet the needs of three such disparate groups. In such a circumstance, it may be necessary to have three separate planning groups for three very different processions.

Congregations need to be informed about the procession well in advance, particularly if the procession is going to begin earlier than the service usually starts. An announcement in the bulletin is helpful, but it is not enough. An announcement from the lectern the week before is essential to avoid confusion. On the day of the procession, every entrance to the church should have a large bulletin conspicuously posted, saying that the procession will begin at such and such a place, and that all are requested to go there. If there are a few in the congregation whose native language is not English, but who represent too small a minority to have an ethnic procession, these bulletins should be posted in their languages as well. For the benefit of children and those whose ability to read is limited, the bulletins should be kept as simple as possible. At least one should be at a low height, for the sake of the short, the children, and the chair-bound.

Today most churches use palm branches for the procession. This is a tradition which most of us know well. However, the use of palm branches is not obligatory. Their use derives from the account in the Gospels of Jesus' triumphal entry into Jerusalem. Scripture says that the people waved palm branches to greet him. However the Scripture also says that they waved olive branches and spread their cloaks on the ground before him. Today we are perfectly free to use whatever we feel appropriate as a symbol. Green willow, pussy willow, cherry blossom, evergreen are all types of branches that symbolize life or rejoicing. People should be encouraged to bring their branches or flowers from home, if they wish to do so. Of course the parish will need to provide palms or other tokens for the great many parishioners who will not bring tokens with them. These tokens are usually placed on a convenient table for people to take as they enter the area from which the procession will begin. A group of helpers, perhaps from the youth group, should go around and make sure everybody has something to wave. Perhaps young children could have helium-filled balloons, particularly if they are too young to know what a palm tree is and why it is special on this day. Some arrangements would need to be made for the balloons to be deposited at the entrance of the church and picked up after the liturgy or the inevitable distractions from bursting or loose balloons will occur.

Banners are especially appropriate to be carried in procession. If possible, each parish society should have a banner; Altar, Rosary, Holy Name, Knights of Columbus, St. Vicent de Paul, etc. Families could make banners with the family name on it and an appropriate symbol. It is better to avoid too much in the way of slogans, but some can be effective. "Ride on, King Jesus," "Hosanna!," "I.N.R.I.," etc. are typical motifs. Even paper placards can be utilized.

One especially effective decoration is to take several dozen palm branches and to tie them to the top of poles so that they hang down and look like palm trees. There should be at least a dozen of these with people to carry them. These people may be divided into two groups, one for each side of the procession. As the procession enters the church, they take their places at designated pews, slipping the poles into holders provided at the ends of the pews. The effect is to make the church aisle seem as though it were lined with palm trees. "Palm trees" might also be placed in the sanctuary, especially around the pulpit and behind the altar.

People should be encouraged to mix and speak freely during the time before the procession begins. This relaxes them and enables them to take part in the procession with a greater degree of ease. There should be a distinct place for the ministers to stand when they arrive, as well as some sort of aisle for them to approach by. However the atmosphere should not be that of a church. Perhaps the folk group could provide some happy, but quasi-liturgical music in the background.

There is a short ritual before the procession begins. In order for people to hear what is going on, there should be some sort of podium or platform for the ministers to stand on, so they can be seen and heard. In very few cases will the celebrant and deacon have microphones. They must practice speaking clearly, slowly, distinctly and loudly, long before the service begins. If the procession begins inside a school or other building, it will help the situation if their backs are to some kind of wall; this will help sound projection.

The ministers are vested in red for this occasion. The celebrant may wear a cope. Perhaps people from the parish might try designing a vestment for the occasion. If so, be careful to measure lengths carefully. Few celebrants have the knack for walking long distances while wearing floor-length robes. If your celebrant is changed at the last minute, someone may need to be nearby to pin up a robe which has suddenly become too long!

Music for the procession is an extremely important part of the whole celebration, and needs to be planned and rehearsed carefully. Musicians may not be able to carry music with them, especially guitarists, and must know it by heart. As a rule, it is difficult to hear instruments out-of-doors, unless there is a large group of them. Amplification will be next-to impossible. Often the best solution is either to use pre-recorded accompaniment, or to utilize a brass choir. Perhaps the local Salvation Army might be willing to help out, if a church cannot get together a good brass group to accompany the singing. Naturally a great deal of rehearsal will be necessary. Some percussion to accompany the brass of other instruments will also help a great deal.

When the ministers arrive an opening hymn is sung. It may well be preceded by a trumpet fanfare to call people's attention to the fact that the ceremony has begun. The song leader should stand on the platform with the musicians so as to lead the music better and provide direction for the assembly.

The congregation should have programs with the music printed in them. This is one occasion when it is better not to do antiphonal or responsorial singing, unless an entire choir takes the cantor's part. A single voice is almost inevitably lost in a procession, while the continuity of a hymn can be maintained. Hymns which celebrate the kingship of Christ are appropriate, as are unusually festive versions of the "Holy, Holy" from the Mass. The opening hymn must not be too solemn, but should strike a happy and festive note. After all, the Palm Sunday Procession is a joyous one; it is not a funeral procession.

The procession of ministers should also be festive. They should not come forward with sober expressions and eyes to the ground, in rigid formation. It is good to have a number of ministers, carrying the cross, candles, holy water, and thurible. The cross and candles can be draped with palms or flowers or other greenery. (Under *no* circumstances should dried or artificial materials be used!). The ministers should also carry branches or flowers. After the greeting and blessing of branches, they are sprinkled with holy water. They may also be incensed. Certainly incense should be used to honor the Gospel Book and in the procession. One or two passageways should be opened up so the celebrant or deacon can go throughout the crowd and sprinkle all the people's tokens with holy water. Even the most athletic of priests cannot wield an *aspergillum* in such a way that the holy water in it can fly thirty feet away. Instead of using a metal sprinkler, try using a small bunch of evergreen branches bound together with ribbon at one end. This symbolizes the life-giving properties of water better than stainless steel does.

After the blessing, the Gospel is proclaimed. This must be done from a place where the congregation will be able to see and hear what is being proclaimed. Of course the Gospel is normally to be proclaimed by a priest or deacon. However, in many areas, no one on the rectory staff is going to have a suitable voice which projects well. In such circumstances a parish ought not to hesitate to have its best lay reader proclaim the Gospel. Liturgically, the entrance hymn in which all join approximates the priest's greeting; while the blessing prayer is concretized for all in the sprinkling. But there is no congregational substitute for the clear, audible proclamation of the Gospel.

Even in these more informal circumstances, the Gospel must be proclaimed from the Lectionary, not from a sheet of paper or missalette. In fact, since visibility is likely to be less than in church, the Lectionary should be highlighted as much as possible, perhaps with a bright red, ornamented cover. Candles and incense are appropriate; the deacon should ask the customary blessing. It is not necessary to have a homily after the Gospel; in fact, since the people are standing, it may be better to omit it. If the right atmosphere has been created, it should not be necessary for anyone to exhort the congregation to relax, rejoice, sing, or anything else; they should be doing it naturally, as would anyone else at a parade.

At this point, the celebrant announces, "Let us go forward in peace," or something similar. The procession begins to move. The ministers should go first, with the cross leading the way. A couple of people with "palm trees" could also go ahead to lead the way. The procession should wait until the musicians have started the hymn. It is probably best for the musicians to follow the ministers, especially if there is a brass choir; the singing choir can follow them. It is also possible to have the choir in the middle of the procession. However, unless the procession is short, it is generally inadvisable to have the choir bring up the rear; this means they will be last into the church and by then, perhaps a beat or two behind everyone else, as often happens in processional singing. There should be some discreetly-placed ushers or "movement facilitators" to keep the procession moving evenly.

During the procession hymns may be sung and repeated ad lib. It is no crime to have a few minutes when nothing is sung, or to have a brass choir play an instrumental selection to break up the singing. If the choir and/or brass choir are going to be ultimately located in the choir loft, they should not go up there until the procession is completely inside the church. Rather, a place should be cleared for them in the rear of the church. The cantor or song leader can proceed to the front of the church and lead from the microphone there. When everyone is in, the choir can silently take its place upstairs.

The sight of banners and branches waving is a delightful sight. The smell of flowers mixing with incense is joyful and refreshing. Perhaps a church might also try, as did the Jews, spreading rugs and things for the party to walk on. Those who are carrying the "palm trees" might stand on either side of the procession and hold their fans crossed over the heads of all as a canopy. Children might be given baskets of flower petals to scatter on the way.

Only a blizzard the night before should prevent a Passion Sunday procession from taking place. Cold weather should not deter plans for an outside procession. A procession can even be held in the rain, especially if there is time to set up a canopy. If the procession absolutely must be held inside the church, then all who want to should be encouraged to march around the aisles. The procession should go, as the psalm puts it, "right up to the horns of the altar," in other words, into the sanctuary and around the altar. To facilitate this, easily knocked-over furniture and free-standing candlesticks should be removed.

Jesus was greeted by a horde of disciples and well-wishers, who waved their branches and shouted his name. It was a spontaneous, joyous occasion. If we wish to do the same, we must plan our processions so that the greatest amount of spontaneity and relaxation can take place. We must involve as many people and groups as we possibly can. To do all this requires that a parish commit itself to building up a parish tradition or traditions. It will take several years to accustom a parish to a joyful, spontaneous procession acclaiming the Lord; and it will take at least two months every year to prepare for the procession. If that commitment is made, then it will begin to be a source of joy and unity for the parish, which will remind them that they are one body, in the midst of which lives the Lord Jesus.

A Passion Sunday Parade

by Eileen E. Freeman

The typical parish Passion Sunday procession is a quiet, inhibited, solemn and ritualistic march, done by a small group of serious-faced people. It should be a joyful, spontaneous parade of people, praising the Lord.

We are very fond of parades in America; we have them on every possible occasion: Independence Day, Veteran's Day, Thanksgiving, New Year's, St. Patrick's Day. Our year would hardly be complete without the Rose Parade and the many others that are similar to it. It seems that a ten-story, inflatable Donald Duck is necessary for our national happiness. Marching bands and floats, clowns and placards are all part of our common heritage.

Parades have wonderful effects on people. First of all, they draw us together; they pry people out of their homes and back yards and bring them nose to nose for an occasion. They give us a chance to relax, to forget about worries and cares for a while. They also seem to promote goodwill and helpfulness and humor. They give beauty to our eyes and pleasant sounds to our ears. They give us a common pride in something. That is quite a lot for anything to do, let alone a group of people marching down a city street.

That is probably what it was like the day Jesus rode into Jerusalem on a donkey. He did not plan to do so, although He knew the prophecy about the Messiah. No, it appears that as He and his disciples went on their way, the crowd around them just grew until it had reached sizable dimensions. There were no organized bands or floats, but people undoubtedly danced and sang the psalms as they approached the holy city. Jesus probably joined in as well. The crowd must have stripped every tree along the roadside for impromptu banners of branches. What a joyful sight it must have been! What a parade!

There is no reason at all why the Body of Christ cannot continue to celebrate his triumphal entry into Jerusalem with a parade. The rite for the usual procession not only was designed to accommodate the minimum celebration, but allows for a great deal of leeway as well. The parade described below is an example of one way the minimum can be turned into a maximum.

The Passion Sunday Parade is designed as an ecumenical Christian venture, celebrated in the afternoon on Palm Sunday, and not necessarily followed by a Mass. It could also be planned by a group of Catholic parishes, with a large Mass following the parade. However it is planned, it will take a whole year to organize if it is being done for the first time. It is worth the effort for what it does to give witness to Christ before a whole town, and what it does to promote understanding and love among different groups of Christians is amazing.

The person who decides to undertake the venture will have to determine whether it is more feasible to limit the planning and participants to a local group of Catholic parishes, or whether other churches should be invited to participate. The Lutheran and Episcopalian congregations usually celebrate Palm Sunday in some fashion and may be interested. If there is a United Religious Community in the area, they may be contacted as well.

After there has been a meeting of interested groups, the route of the parade will have to be determined. Perhaps the parade could begin in a local park, parade down the main street, and end at an amphitheatre, auditorium, etc. Or, the parade could begin from some large building, proceed through the streets, and end up in a park or field or farm for socializing or a service. In any case, parades usually require a permit from whatever town or city the parade passes through. If streets have to be blocked off from traffic, that will require permission, perhaps the help of local police as well. These permissions should be obtained as early as possible.

The planning group should select a theme which is suitable to the occasion, perhaps "Jesus is Lord of his People" or something similar. All the floats, bands, and other entries would be required to use their entry to interpret that theme as they understand it. The Salvation Army band might play "All Hail the Power"; a flatbed truck from the Episcopal church might have a huge crown on it; the Polish Catholic parish might parade its portrait of Christ the King. A troupe of young people might do portions of "Jesus Christ Superstar." The planning committee should have final say on what is appropriate. After all, ecumenical sensibilities might be offended equally by a life-size Lourdes grotto or someone passing out anti-Catholic leaflets. A parade is not a time to propagandize, but to rejoice, to celebrate common faith in the Kingship of Jesus, to witness without proselytizing.

As many people as possible from the participating churches should walk in the procession, carrying palms, branches, flowers, banners, placards (celebratory, not ideological), balloons or whatever. Bands should be widely separated so the music of one will not run into that of another. There will be enough people watching from the sidelines; the important thing is to be a part of the parade, not a spectator. Transportation should be arranged for the handicapped, the elderly, and all others who cannot walk the length of the parade. Accessible restroom facilities should be arranged as well.

About a block after the beginning of the parade there should be a reviewing stand. At the reviewing stand there should be a delegation of clergy from various groups, all either vested or suited as their different traditions may allow. A large processional cross or a large banner proclaiming the theme of the parade should also be at the reviewing stand. Different local authorities may require the American flag as well; it is necessary to inquire if this is a regulation. The flags or banners of each church participating could also be flown at the reviewing stand, in addition to being borne in procession by each group.

As each float, band or display reaches the reviewing stand it comes to a halt, along with the rest of the parade behind it, and "does its thing." The bands play their music, dancers dance, and so forth. If at all possible, the reviewing stand should have an announcer with microphone, to tell the spectators what is going on and who is doing it. Alternatively, programs can be passed out with the order of the parade. The words to hymns in which all are invited to join can also be printed on programs; this is necessary, since different churches use entirely different words to the same hymn tune. People should be encouraged to cheer, wave, etc. Clapping is appropriate. Perhaps to mark the beginning of the parade, children could release hundreds of balloons on, or in, which are written words from the scriptures about Jesus and his mission, or little cards about the parade or witness cards. Such a project would be looked forward to by many CCD and Sunday School teachers. If there is a local pigeon club, perhaps they can be persuaded to release a flock of doves (homing pigeons!).

Many types of musical participants can be accommodated at a Palm Sunday Parade. School bands can play parade music (with discretion: "Hello Dolly" just wouldn't make it); brass bands can play hymns. Parish choirs can sing, too. Perhaps it would be possible to have them stand on a float where they could be heard better. With some preparation and practice it is possible to use recorded music amplified as a substitute for the non-portable organ, or rig up an old pump organ on a float. The point is not to achieve artistic perfection, which is hard to do while marching along, but to do one's best for the Lord.

Dance troupes can go into their routines to the strains of prerecorded music such as "Superstar" and "Godspell." It would be magnificent if a Gospel choir or two would join in, leading people in some of the marvelous spirituals about Jesus' ride into Jerusalem.

Floats are not as difficult to invent as the Rose Parade might make it seem, nor need they be expensive. Whether they are drawn by car, by horse or by hand, they add a tremendous amount to a parade. A float can be built on the back of a flatbed truck; a platform can be put on wheels and pulled along. Banners, Christian flags and placards can be carried by as many as want to. Everyone should carry something, whether it is a palm, a daffodil, or a sousaphone! Everyone should celebrate, be an example to all who wonder what these crazy Christians are up to!

There is no reason why decorated autos and cycles cannot take part, trailing streamers and flowers. Riders on horseback, clowns handing out palms to the spectators, whatever and whoever can contribute to the theme of the parade should take part, even if their church is not officially participating. The planning committee can decide what float, band, etc. should lead the parade, where it will pause and how long, etc.

As the parade passes the reviewing stand, all banners and the like should be dipped out of respect for the cross or the banner of Christ. The spectators should be urged to follow along at the end of the parade or go by an alternate route to meet the parade when it arrives at its destination. Parades, unlike demonstrations, are rarely heckled by spectators; however, a town usually insists on having a certain number of police officers present, if for nothing else than to help direct traffic. The parade committee should be prepared to pay for the services of these men if they are off duty. Perhaps each church that participates officially in the parade could be asked to pay a modest "entrance fee" to cover such expenses.

When the parade reaches its destination, any one of a number of things may happen. It may simply break up, with all present either going to their churches for services or home to their families. A non-denominational service can be held briefly: a prayer, reading from the scriptures, exhortation, hymn. If the parade participants come from the Catholic parishes, a special Passion Sunday Mass may be held, either out-of-doors, or in a local hall, if none of the parish churches is large enough. If the weather is pleasant, perhaps a picnic lunch can be arranged. Each person could bring a sack lunch, while different churches could provide refreshments, cookies, etc. for a small cost. Perhaps later on the various bands might give a concert. The stage where they perform could have the parade banners as a backdrop.

A parade seems to stand or fall on whether or not it becomes accepted as a tradition, something which the people look forward to every year. The longer a Passion Sunday Parade is celebrated, the easier it is to plan for the next year, to get volunteers, to interest other churches and religious groups. If the parade goes well, if participants are courteous, if the clean-up is done efficiently and quickly, then most towns will welcome back a Passion Sunday Parade year after year.

One of the most serious attacks leveled at liturgy is that it never goes out to where the people are; that it turns in on itself rather than meeting the needs of others. One of the best "side effects" of the Passion Sunday Parade is that it takes a step towards destroying that often justified criticism. It brings different groups together, so that the needs of one can be made known to all. It lets the community know that its churches are not hopelessly divided; that they can stand together. Cooperation on the level of a parade paves the way for cooperation on the level of clinics, job opportunities and the meeting of other needs. And on yet a different level, it even gets us in "practice" for the time when the King finally comes in glory to lead his entire people to the Father in a parade of endless joy!

Staging The Passion

by Eileen E. Freeman

From the time of the Middle Ages, dramatic representations of the passion and death of Christ have been performed. One has only to think of such traditional dramas as the Oberammergau Passion Play, Veronica's Veil and the like. That these and innumerable other plays can go on is largely due to the biblical texts on which they are based. The account in the four Gospels of Jesus' Passion is a true narrative with scenes and actors, dialogue, events and stage directions. We know that the narrative is one of the first pieces of Christian literature to be written and circulated in the early Church, written before the Gospels themselves, antedating even St. Paul's earlier letters.

The Passion is a compelling narrative. It leads us down an inexorable path to death, but, like the stories of O. Henry, gives us the most marvelous of surprise endings. Like an Alfred Hitchcock movie, it tells us from the beginning who is going to be killed, by whom, and how, yet keeps us fascinated until the last scene. Small wonder then that so many passion plays have been created, whether for the stage, the screen or the chancel.

Jesus always had a flair for the dramatic. He was what we would call in this age of psychology an "integrated" man, fully understanding and in control of his entire personality. This being the case, He was never afraid of involvement, of expressing his deepest feelings and thoughts. He could read an audience like a book, and know immediately whether it would be better for Him to speak in parables and stories, or to adopt the haranguing style of a politician.

Jesus expects us to do the same; ultimately to be the same. St. Paul, who seems to have understood this quite well, wrote that he "had become all things to all people, so as to win some of them for Christ." He played whatever role was called for, in order that through him the Spirit of God could touch another person. The "Sons of Thunder," Martha, and Peter began their ministries with rather narrow views of what roles they wanted to play; and Jesus had to take special pains to urge them to open up to their fullest potentials.

We have lost sight of the fact that in the Body of Christ there is really no audience, no group of spectators. All of us are actors with a multiplicity of roles. To be an actor is a good thing nowadays; children are rarely disinherited for expressing a desire to go on stage. Yet the tendency is still for most of us to sit and watch others do the acting, whether it is on television or in the movies or in our daily situations in life, or even in the Mass itself, where we sit like the proverbial "bump on a log" and expect God to do a little dance or something for us in front of the Church. We are passive, not active.

To act is to be active; both are from the Latin *ago, actus,* 'to *do* something.' To be passive is also from the Latin *patior, passus,* 'to have something *done* to you.' In the Gospel narrative of Jesus' death, it is ironic that Jesus, who submits passively (in a physical sense) to all that is done to Him, is nonetheless clearly the most active personality of the whole Passion narrative; that which is called the *Passion* is the very means by which we are *act*ively saved.

The solemn reading or chanting of the Passion on Passion Sunday and Good Friday has always been done with great emphasis on its dramatic qualities. Unlike any other Gospel, it was traditionally divided up into various speaking parts to be recited or sung by the priests and deacons of the Mass. However, there were always problems with this approach. The *recitative*-type melodies had very little dramatic appeal. The text was originally in Latin. Even after the people's acclamation of the Good News had been restored, it was omitted at the reading of the Passion, effectively taking from the people their only form of active participation in the drama.

In recent years several versions of the Gospel "script" have appeared in print, which provide for a much wider use of men and women in the Passion narrative, as well as a few which give a role to the entire congregation. This last effort is a step in the right direction, since the congregation should participate, but it carries along with it one drawback: the need for the congregation to have a printed text to follow so they know when their speaking parts come in. This is inimical not only to the essence of ritual, which is never designed to be read solely from a book, but also to the essence of drama. Who has ever gone to the theatre to watch actors reading from their scripts? Conversely, what actors would want to play to an audience that was reading the dialogue silently out of a book, and not watching what was going on on stage? So, too, a truly effective dramatization of the Passion of Christ must provide the congregation with a means of participating and yet leave their eyes free to watch what is going on in front of them.

The script which follows is designed to be done in an average parish church on Palm Sunday as the Passion Narrative. As with any dramatic happening, it needs coordination and a certain amount of rehearsal. It requires some easily obtainable visual aids, and a few inexpensive props. Each parish will have to adjust the lighting suggestions to conform with the architectural possibilities of that church. This script is that of Matthew's Gospel, which is the "A" cycle reading for Passion Sunday; the interested liturgist, however, should be able to adapt the Mark and Luke Passions, as well as the John Passion which is used on Good Friday.

PERSONNEL NEEDED:

Director: The Director is responsible for casting the different parts (see below) and for directing whatever rehearsals may be necessary. The Director ought to have at least a little bit of experience in drama, even if it is only directing "Hansel and Gretel" in the kindergarten class. It is essential for the Director to be, or get the help of someone, skilled in public speaking, since acoustics, sound systems, echoes, and clarity of words will be important.

Celebrant: If at all possible, the celebrant of the Passion Sunday Mass takes the role of Jesus. Even if the celebrant cannot do this, he needs to be consulted and kept informed about the progress of the production.

Actors and actresses: These people who take the various parts should be adult members of the parish. Children should specifically *not* be recruited for speaking parts. A dramatic presentation of the Passion is not the time to make friendly gestures of getting the teenagers "involved." On the other hand, really mature young people, who request on their own to participate, should be encouraged.

The following parts will be needed:

Jesus: It is usually more effective symbolically if Jesus is the celebrant of the Mass, or another priest, but it is better to have a layperson who reads and acts well than a celebrant who does not.

Narrator: Since the narrator has a large part, the part should be read by the best lector in the parish, if there is no deacon and none of the priests feels qualified.

Judas, Peter, and a group of apostles

Caiaphas the High Priest

A group of about five women

Pontius Pilate the Procurator

A leader for the congregation's part (prompter)

A crowd of women and men: some of these people are called Bystanders, some are called Soldiers and some are called Priests.

A cantor and the organist (or guitarist)

COSTUMES AND PROPS:

Jesus should wear flowing, amply cut vestments, or, if not the celebrant, perhaps a burnoose. **Peter** wears jeans and a sweatshirt, **Judas, Caiaphas** and **Pilate** wear business suits; Judas' suit should be the flashy sort, the others' more conservative. The Narrator, Cantor, and the Prompter for the congregation should be vested in an alb designed for external wear.

All other parts wear appropriate street clothes.

A change purse with coins in it

A drinking glass with a loaf of bread

A purple-red cape

Either a tape recorder with a pre-recorded rooster-crow sound effect, or a parishioner in the wings who can crow like a rooster!

Some kind of reed like a cattail, pampas grass or the like

A crown made to look like thorns

A banner with the words "This is Jesus, King of the Jews" which can be hung or held up behind the altar

A hammer and wood block, or a tape recording of nails being hammered

THE SCENES:

This Passion Narrative is laid out so that the minimum number of movements needs to be made. The Narrator always stands at a lectern (stage right); Jesus stands at the altar as the celebrant normally does; other groups of people speak from the sanctuary floor as directed. The cantor uses a lectern at stage left or shares the Narrator's at the appropriate times. The Prompter (who may also be the cantor) stands facing the congregation from a point outside the sanctuary at stage left.

After the previous reading is finished, the participants enter in procession from the rear of the church, carrying the banner, which is put in the place appointed. Jesus takes his place, with Peter to his left. The other disciples stand on the bottom altar step facing Jesus. Judas, Caiaphas and the Priest are in the middle of the sanctuary floor. Cantor, Prompter and Narrator take their places. The Women and the Crowd move to the back of the sanctuary or to the side for the time being.

While all this is going on, the cantor announces a hymn, for which the people stand. The hymn should have a processional quality and a Christ the King theme, preferably one that everyone will join in on. A hymn from the earlier procession can be repeated. "King of Kings" from Servant Publications is a guitar hymn that would work well, or Proulx's "Song of the Three Young Children" (GIA). When all are ready, the lights in the nave of the church are dimmed and the Narrator announces:

Narrator: The Passion of our Lord Jesus Christ according to Matthew.

(The congregation sings its usual Lenten acclamation, led by the Cantor. The Narrator invites them to be seated for the first part of the drama.)

Scene 1

(Spotlight on Judas' group, if possible)

Narrator: One of the Twelve named Judas Iscariot went to the chief priests and said:

Judas: What will you give me if I hand Jesus over to you?

Caiaphas: We will give you thirty pieces of silver.

Narrator: From that time on Judas looked for the opportunity to betray him.

(Cut spot on Judas and his group; Judas joins the other apostles, stands next to Peter; the rest join the crowd)

Narrator: On the first day of the feast of Unleavened Bread, the disciples came to Jesus and said:

Peter: Where do you wish us to prepare the Passover supper for you?

Jesus: There is a man in the city; go to him and tell him, "The Teacher says: My appointed time approaches. I will celebrate the Passover with my disciples in your house."

Narrator: The disciples then did as Jesus ordered and prepared the Passover supper. When it grew dark, he reclined at table with the Twelve.

(The other apostles come up behind Jesus and face the congregation)

Narrator: During the course of the meal he said:

Jesus: I give you my word, one of you is about to betray me.

Narrator: Distressed at this, they asked him:

Peter: Surely it is not I, Lord!

Jesus: The one who will hand me over is the one who has dipped his hand into the dish with me. The Son of Man is departing as Scripture says of him, but woe to the man by whom he is betrayed. Better for him if he had never been born.

Narrator: Then Judas his betrayer, spoke:

Judas: Surely it is not I, Teacher?

Jesus: Yes, it is you.

Narrator: During supper Jesus took bread, said the blessing, broke it and gave it to his disciples.

Jesus: Take this and eat it; this is my body.

Narrator: Then he took the cup, gave thanks, and gave it to them.

Jesus: Drink from this, all of you, for this is my blood, the blood of the covenant poured out for the multitude for the forgiveness of sins. I tell you, I will not drink this fruit of the vine again until the day I drink it with you in my Father's kingdom.

Narrator: Then they sang psalms of praise.

(The cantor leads the congregation in one of the gradual psalms, or perhaps "For You Are My God" (NAL). Judas leaves and joins Caiaphas and the whole crowd which come forward to the middle of the sanctuary. The apostles except Peter move as far back as they can behind Jesus)

Scene II

Narrator: As they walked out to the Mount of Olives afterwards, Jesus said to the disciples:

Jesus: Tonight your faith in me will be shaken, as the Scripture says: I will strike the shepherd and the sheep will be scattered. But after I am raised up, I will go to Galilee ahead of you.

Narrator: Peter responded:

Peter: Even if everyone else's faith in you is shaken, my faith will never be shaken.

Jesus: I give you my word that before the cock crows tonight you will have disowned me three times.

Peter: Even if I have to die with you, I will never deny You.

Narrator: And all the other disciples said the same thing. Then Jesus went with them to a place called Gethsemane. He said:

Jesus: Stay here while I go over there and pray.

(Jesus moves to one end of the altar and leans on it as if for support, while Peter moves to the opposite end and turns his back to Jesus)

Narrator: He took Peter and Zebedee's two sons along with him and began to experience sorrow and distress.

Jesus: My heart is nearly breaking with grief. Remain here and stay awake with me.

Narrator: He walked on a little further and fell prostrate in prayer.

Jesus: My Father, if it is possible, let this cup pass me by. Still, let it be according to your will, not mine.

Narrator: When he returned to his disciples, he found them asleep. He said to Peter: *(Peter turns around)*

Jesus: So you could not even stay awake for an hour! Be on guard, and pray that you may not undergo the trial. The spirit is willing, but nature is weak.

THE HOLY WEEK BOOK

Narrator: Withdrawing again, he prayed:

Jesus: My Father, if this cannot pass me by without my drinking it, your will be done. *(Peter turns away from Jesus)*

Narrator: Once more on his return, he found them asleep; they could not keep their eyes open. He left them again, and began to pray for a third time, in the same manner as before. Finally he returned to his disciples and said to them:

Jesus: Sleep on now, enjoy your rest! The time has come for the Son of Man to be given into the power of evil men. Get up! Let us be going! See, my betrayer is here! *(Spotlight on the crowd if possible)*

Narrator: While he was speaking, Judas, one of the Twelve, arrived with a great crowd armed with swords and clubs. They had been sent by the chief priests and elders of the people. His betrayer had arranged to give them a signal, saying:

Judas: The man I embrace is the one: seize him.

Narrator: He went over to Jesus at once. *(Judas does so)* and said to him:

Judas: Peace, Teacher!

(Judas embraces Jesus)

Jesus: Do what you are here for, friend.

Narrator: At that moment they stepped forward to lay hands on Jesus and arrested him.

(The crowd goes up behind Jesus who moves again to the center of the altar. The apostles unobtrusively slip off to the sacristy except for Peter (and Judas). Peter makes a gesture towards one of the crowd)

Narrator: Suddenly one of those who accompanied Jesus drew out his sword and attacked the high priest's servant, cutting off his ear.

Jesus: Put back your sword where it belongs. Those who use the sword die by the sword. Do you not suppose that I can call on my Father to provide more than twelve legions of angels at a moment's notice? But then how would the Scripture be fulfilled which says that it must happen this way?

Narrator: Then Jesus said to the crowd:

Jesus: Am I a robber, that you have come out to arrest me armed with swords and clubs? Daily I sat teaching in the Temple precincts, yet you never arrested me. Nevertheless, all this has happened in fulfillment of the prophetic writings.

(Peter leaves the sanctuary and exits via a side door. Judas also leaves. Caiaphas and Jesus face each other across the altar. The crowd faces them from the sanctuary floor. Peter gradually sneaks in again and joins the crowd)

Scene III

Narrator: Then all the disciples deserted him and fled. Those who had arrested Jesus led him off to Caiaphas, the high priest, where the scribes and elders were gathered. Peter followed him from a distance as far as the high priest's residence. He went inside, sat down with the guards, and waited to see the outcome. The chief priests and the whole Sanhedrin were trying desperately to find false witnesses against Jesus so they could ask for the death penalty. Despite all their efforts, they could find no evidence, despite the many witnesses who took the stand. Finally two men came forward and said:

(Someone from the crowd, accompanied by another person, goes up to Caiaphas and says:)

Speaker: This man said: I can destroy God's sanctuary and rebuild it in three days.

Narrator: The high priest stood up and addressed Jesus:

Caiaphas: Have you an answer to this charge against you?

Narrator: But Jesus remained silent. The high priest then said to him:

Caiaphas: I command you to tell us under oath before the living God whether you are the Messiah, the Son of God.

Jesus: Yes, I am. Moreover, I assure you that soon you will see the Son of Man seated at the right hand of God and riding on the clouds of heaven.

Narrator: At this the high priest tore his robes:

Caiaphas: He has blasphemed! What further need have we of witnesses? Remember you heard the blasphemy yourselves! What is your verdict?

Prompter: He deserves to die!

Congregation and Crowd: He deserves to die!

(The crowd moves up and behind Jesus, pushing him, or shoving him a bit. Only Peter and women remain on the floor)

Narrator: Then they began to spit in his face and strike him. Others slapped him, saying:

A Speaker from the Crowd: Play the prophet for us Messiah. Tell us who struck you?

Narrator: Peter was sitting in the courtyard when one of the servant women came over and said to him:

Woman 1: You were with Jesus the Galilean!

Narrator: But Peter denied it publicly:

Peter: I don't know what you're talking about.

Narrator: He went outside to stand near the gate. Another girl saw him and said to those nearby:

Woman 2: This man was a companion of Jesus the Nazarene.

Narrator: But he denied it even more vehemently:

Peter: Damn it! I don't know the man!

Narrator: A little while later some on-lookers came over to Peter and said:

Woman 3: You must be one of them! Even your accent gives you away.

Narrator: At that, Peter began cursing and swore:

Peter: Damn it! I don't know the man!

Narrator: Just then a rooster began to crow *(appropriate sound effects, if possible)* and Peter remembered Jesus' prediction: Before the rooster crows you will deny me three times. He went out and began to weep bitterly.

(Peter exits. Meanwhile the women join the crowd, while those of the crowd who are the priests come forward along with Caiaphas and Judas. Jesus should be standing alone at the altar, with the rest of the crowd somewhat behind him)

Scene IV

Narrator: At daybreak all the chief priests and elders took formal action against Jesus to bring about his death. They bound him and led him away, handing him over to Pilate the Roman governor. Then Judas, who had betrayed him, seeing that Jesus had been condemned, felt deep remorse for what he had done. He took the thirty pieces of silver back to the chief priests and elders and said:

Judas: I did wrong to hand over an innocent man.

Narrator: They retorted:

Caiaphas: What does that matter to us? It is your affair!

Narrator: So Judas flung the money into the Temple and left. *(He does it)* He went off and hanged himself. The chief priests picked up the money, observing:

Caiaphas: It is not lawful to deposit this in the Temple treasury, since it is blood money.

Narrator: After consultation, they used it to buy the potter's field as a cemetery for foreigners. That is why that field, even today, is called Blood Field. On that occasion, what was said by Jeremiah the prophet was fulfilled: They took the thirty pieces of silver, the value of a man with a price on his head as set by the Israelites, and they paid it out for the potter's field, just as the Lord had commanded.

(Judas leaves. Meanwhile Pilate faces Jesus at the altar. Caiaphas and the whole crowd and the women stand in front of the altar on the sanctuary floor, facing Jesus)

Scene V

Narrator: Jesus was arraigned before the procurator, who said:

Pilate: Are you the king of the Jews?

Jesus: As you say, I am.

Narrator: Yet when he had been accused by the chief priests and elders he had made no reply. Then Pilate said to him:

Pilate: Don't you hear how serious the charges are against you?

Narrator: He did not answer to a single charge, much to the astonishment of Pilate. Now on the occasion of a festival the procurator generally released one prisoner, whomever the crowd would choose. At the time, there was a notorious prisoner named Barabbas. Since the crowd was already assembled, Pilate said to them:

Pilate: Which prisoner do you want me to release for you, Barabbas or Jesus, the so-called Messiah?

Narrator: Pilate knew, of course, that it was out of jealousy that the high priest had handed Jesus over to him. While he was still considering the matter officially, his wife sent him a message:

(Someone from the crowd can go up and hand Pilate a sheet of paper)

Pilate: Do not meddle in the case of that holy man. I had a dream about him today which has disturbed me a great deal.

Narrator: Meanwhile the chief priests and elders convinced the crowds to ask for Barabbas and have Jesus put to death. So when Pilate asked them:

Pilate: Which one do you want me to release to you?

Narrator: They answered:

Prompter: Give us Barabbas!

Congregation: Give us Barabbas!

Pilate: Then what am I going to do with Jesus the so-called Messiah?

Prompter: Crucify him!

Congregation: Crucify him!

Narrator: Pilate finally realized that he would get nowhere with the crowd, which was on the verge of open rioting. So he called for water and washed his hands in front of the crowd, declaring as he did so:

Pilate: I am innocent of the blood of this just man. The responsibility is yours.

Narrator: In reply the whole crowd said:

Prompter: His blood be on us and on our children!

Congregation: His blood be on us and on our children!

Narrator: At that, he released Barabbas to them. Jesus, however, he first had scourged: then he gave orders for his execution.

Scene VI

(The Crowd, except for the soldiers, leaves, as does Pilate. The soldiers go up to Jesus, put a reed in his hand, a purple cloak around his shoulders, and a crown on his head. Then they line up on the sanctuary floor and begin genuflecting in mockery)

Narrator: Pilate's soldiers took Jesus inside the praetorium and collected the whole cohort around him. They stripped off his clothes and wrapped him in a scarlet military cloak. Weaving a crown of thorn branches, they pressed it on his head and stuck a reed into his right hand. Then they dropped to their knees and mocked him, saying:

Soldiers: All hail to the King of the Jews!

Narrator: They also spat at him. Afterward they took the reed and hit him on the head. Finally when they had finished their foolishness, they took off the cloak, dressed him in his own clothes, and led him off to be crucified. On their way they met a Cyrenian named Simon, who was coming in from the fields. They pressed him into service to carry the cross beam behind Jesus. *(All of the cast but Judas comes to the sanctuary floor and stands facing Jesus)*

Narrator: When they got to the place called Golgotha, a name which means "skull-place" in Aramaic, they gave wine drugged with gall to drink, which he tasted and refused. Then they nailed him to the cross.

(Offstage hammer-blows are very effective here. At this point Jesus should stretch out his arms in the orante position and hold them there until after his last speech)

Narrator: The soldiers divided his clothes and threw dice for them; then they sat and kept watch. Above Jesus' head they had put the charge against him in writing: This is Jesus, the King of the Jews.

(The banner should be raised at this point)

Narrator: Two radicals were crucified along with him, one on his right, one on his left. Passersby mocked Jesus, shaking their heads and saying:

Speaker: *(Perhaps the same speaker who was the witness from the trial)* So you are the one who was going to tear down the Temple and rebuild it in three days! Save yourself, if you can! Come down off that cross, if you are really God's Son!

Narrator: The chief priests, the scribes and the elders also joined in the jeering:

Caiaphas: He saved others, but he cannot even save himself! So he is the "King" of Israel. Let's see him come down from the cross — then we will believe in him. He trusted that God would deliver him; well, let God rescue him, if he cares to. After all he claimed: I am God's Son!

Narrator: The insurgents who had been crucified with him mocked him in the same way.

(Some of the lights should be turned out here, taking care to keep Jesus in a spotlight)

Narrator: From noon onwards, the whole countryside was darkened until mid-afternoon. Then towards three o'clock Jesus cried out in a loud voice:

Jesus: Eli, eli, lema sabachthani *(pronounced AY-lee, AY-lee, LAY-mah sab-ak-TAH-nee)* My God, my God, why have you abandoned me?

Narrator: This made some of the bystanders who heard it remark:

Speaker: He is invoking Elijah!

Narrator: Immediately one of them went and got a sponge. He soaked it in cheap wine, stuck it on a reed, and tried to make Jesus drink. Meanwhile the rest said:

Speaker: Leave him alone. Let's wait and see if Elijah comes to save him.

Narrator: Once again Jesus cried out with a loud voice, and yielded up his spirit. Suddenly the curtain in the Sanctuary was ripped in two from top to bottom. Many saints who had died were raised, and after Jesus' resurrection they came forth from their tombs and entered the holy city, appearing to many. The centurion and his men who were keeping watch over Jesus were terror stricken at feeling the earthquake and seeing all that was happening, and said:

Soldier: He must have been the Son of God!

(At this point the cantor speaks to the congregation.)

Cantor: Let us kneel in prayer for a moment.

(Meanwhile all the lights in the church are turned out. Jesus goes to a chair placed in front of the altar and to the side and sits down; or he sits on the floor, head falling forward)

Scene VII

(Two women from the crowd representing Mary and the Magdalene, stand on either side of Jesus with their hands on his head or shoulders. All the crowd leaves the sanctuary except for Pilate, Caiaphas and the Priests, who stand together on the sanctuary floor. A few lights are turned on)

Narrator: Many women were present, watching from a distance. Among them were Mary Magadalene, Mary the mother of James and Joseph, and the mother of Zebedee's sons. They had been accustomed to following Jesus from Galilee so as to attend to his needs. When evening drew near, a wealthy man from Arimathaea arrived, named Joseph. He, too, was one of Jesus' disciples, and went to request the body of Jesus. Pilate complied, and issued an order for its release. Taking the body, Joseph wrapped it in fresh linen and laid it in his own new tomb, which had been hewn out of solid rock. Then he rolled a huge stone across the entrance and went away. But Mary Magadalene and the other Mary kept watch there, sitting facing the tomb. The next day following the Day of Preparation, the chief priests and the Pharisees called at Pilate's residence.

Caiaphas: Sir, we have recalled that this imposter, while he was still alive made the claim: After three days I will rise. You should issue an order having the tomb kept under close surveillance until the third day. Otherwise, his disciples may go and steal his body and tell the people, "He has been raised from the dead!" This final imposture could be worse than the first!

Narrator: Pilate told them:

Pilate: You may have a guard. Go and secure the tomb as best as you can.

Narrator: So they went away and kept the tomb under the guard's surveillance, after they had fixed a seal to the stone.

POSTSCRIPT

Those remaining in the front of the church, along with the Narrator, Jesus, Prompter, Cantor, line up, bow to the altar as a group, and return to their appropriate places. The lights are turned up, and the Mass servers remove the extra chairs, lecterns, etc. from the sanctuary area.

Rather than follow the drama with a full length homily, a few words may be more appropriate, perhaps as an introduction to the Prayer of the Faithful. It is essential that this time not be used to make announcements about Holy Week services, collections, or the like. While the table is being set for the Eucharistic celebration, a vigorous hymn in the spirit of the liturgy should be sung. "O Sacred Head" is not really appropriate in this spot, as it is too much on the meditative side, and the congregation will need a definite break. Attentive listening and responding can be quite a strain.

Prior Catechesis: If such a full-scale Passion drama has never been done in a parish before, it will help to have the cantor or celebrant set the scene in a sentence or two, and tell the congregation that they are to follow the Prompter for the cues to their parts.

There is little else to say: the Director in each case will make whatever changes in stage directions need to be made because of unusual architectural or acoustical conditions. However it should be pointed out that the larger the church, the more exaggerated gestures will have to be made for them to be visible to the crowds in the back of the church, many of whom come to church only on Passion Sunday and Easter, and who need to be touched in a particular way by the account of the suffering and death of our Lord and Redeemer, Jesus.

Antiphons For The Gospel Passions

by Dick Hilliard with an introduction by Eileen E. Freeman

INTRODUCTION

There are many ways to proclaim the Passion of our Lord Jesus Christ effectively. The more creative ways try to involve the congregation in the proclamation. The version presented here by Dick Hilliard is designed to be done with one reader, a person to sing the role of Jesus, a choir, songleader and the congregation. Because the parts of all but the narrator are singing parts, it is important to choose participants carefully and to rehearse the proclamation several times. This will insure a proclamation that is both dramatic and joyfully enthusiastic.

Notes on using the ANTIPHONS FOR THE GOSPEL PASSIONS

1. The congregational antiphon is taken from Philippians 2:11, the concluding words of the second reading for Palm/Passion Sunday for Cycles A, B, C. It proclaims the essential meaning of the Passion story, "Jesus Christ is Lord forever!" This should be sung with joy and lively movement.
2. Each of the Gospel narratives has a different emphasis. Thus, the "choir" and "Jesus" refrains attempt to capture the major moods and developments in each narrative, and take their wording from the Gospels. These refrains should be a background response to the congregational antiphon and it is suggested that they be sung in a whispering voice (as though a haunting reminder) by a group ("choir") or by a man ("Jesus") as indicated.
3. The simplicity of one reader of the Passion should be preserved when using these antiphons and refrains for they are intended by themselves to capture the attention and involvement of those hearing the proclamation of the Passion. No text need be provided for the congregation, for they can easily follow the cue of the songleader who would follow a text.
4. This proclamation is most effective in a darkened setting with a light for the reader and a light upon the lone, robed figure of Jesus, standing erect throughout as though on trial, breaking his silence only to sing his assigned refrain when designated. The light upon him could be dimmed to darkness when his death is announced in the reading.
5. Each response is numbered and corresponds to the numbered markings in the texts of the three narratives for Passion Sunday. The Gospel texts are abbreviated here. Refer to your lectionary and make the appropriate corresponding markings as indicated.

Matthew (Year A)

5 *One of the twelve...to hand him over.* **1** *On the first day...Jesus answered, "It is you who have said it."* **1** *During the meal Jesus took bread...And all the other disciples said the same.* **2** *Then Jesus went with them...they stepped forward to lay hands on Jesus, and arrested him.* **1** *Suddenly...Then all the disciples deserted him and fled.* **2** *Those who had apprehended Jesus...He went out and began to weep bitterly.* **2** *At daybreak...just as the Lord had commanded me.* **1** *Jesus was arraigned...But they only shouted the louder, "Crucify him!"* **3** *Pilate finally realized...then he handed him over to be crucified.* **3** *The procurator's soldiers...and led him off to crucifixion.* **3** *On their way out...kept taunting him in the same way.* **3** *From noon onward...and then gave up his spirit.* **3** *Suddenly the curtain...and said, "Clearly this was the Son of God!"* **4** *Many women...after fixing a seal to the stone.* **5**
This is the Gospel of the Lord.

Mark (Year B)

5 *The feasts of Passover...will be told in her memory.* **5** *Then Judas Iscariot...for an opportune way to hand him over.* **6** *On the first day...It were better for him had he never been born.* **6** *During the meal...They all said the same.* **6** *They went then to a place...See! My betrayer is near.* **6** *Even while he was still speaking...they laid hands on him and arrested him.* **6** *One of the bystanders...With that, all deserted him and fled.* **6** *There was a young man... while the officers manhandled him.* **6** *While Peter...He broke down and began to cry.* **6** *As soon as it was daybreak...he handed him over to be crucified.* **3** *The soldiers now led Jesus...and led him out to crucify him.* **3** *A man named Simon...likewise kept taunting him.* **3** *When noon came,...Then Jesus, uttering a loud cry, breathed his last.* **3** *At that moment... "Clearly this was the Son of God!"* **4** *There were also women...Meanwhile, Mary Magdalene and Mary observed where he had been laid.* **5**
This is the Gospel of the Lord.

Luke (Year C)

5 *When the hour arrived...as to which of them would do such a deed.* **7** *A dispute arose...three times denied that you know me.* **2** *He asked them...He answered, "Enough."* **7** *Then he went out...this is your hour—the triumph of darkness!* **7** *They led him away...He went out and wept bitterly.* **2** *Meanwhile the men guarding Jesus...We have heard it from his own mouth.* **8** *Then the entire assembly... and delivered Jesus up to their wishes.* **8** *As they led him away..."If you are the king of the Jews, save yourself."* **8** *There was an inscription..."Aren't you the Messiah? Then save yourself and us."* **8** *But the other one..."I assure you: this day you will be with me in paradise."* **9** *It was now around midday..."Surely this was an innocent man."* **9** *After the crowd assembled...They observed the sabbath as a day of rest, in accordance with the law.* **9** then **5**
This is the Gospel of the Lord.

Moderate and lively   Richard J. Hilliard

All   Je - sus   Christ   is   Lord   for - ev - er!   (Jesus/Choir parts)

All 10. Je - sus   Christ   is   Lord   for - ev - er!

Choir 1. ɤ   Thir - ty   pie - ces._____ Thir - ty   pie - ces._____
Jesus 2. You   will   de - ny   me. You   will   de - ny   me._____
Choir 3. ɤ   Cru - ci - fy   Him!_____ Cru - ci - fy   Him!_____
Choir 4. The   Son   of   God._____ The   Son   of   God._____

Choir 5. For - ev - er! For - ev - er!
Choir 6. Not   I,   Lord. Not   I,   Lord.

Jesus 7. ɤ You   will   be - tray   me.____ You   will   be - tray   me.
Jesus 8. You will   not   be - lieve me. You will   not   be - lieve   me.
Jesus 9. ɤ You   will   be with   me.____ You   will   be with   me.

The Passionate Christ

by Michael E. Moynahan, SJ

In all four gospels, the Christ who enters Jerusalem on Palm Sunday is not merely a triumphant Christ, but a passionate Christ. It is his Passion — his death and resurrection — that Christ is intent upon, not simply his popular triumph; for it is his Passion which gives meaning to his Messianic entry. The triumphal entry to Jerusalem culminates a series of predictions that, once arrived in the Holy City, he would "be handed over...to be made sport of and flogged and crucified. But on the third day he will be raised up." (Matt 20:18-19). This liturgy is designed to stress the theme of our participation in the last days of Christ. The Eucharistic meal is a sign of our hope in the promise of our own resurrection, and so is an appropriate setting for us to enact and experience ritually our participation in this central mystery of our faith: Christ's death and resurrection.

Because it is intended to draw the community into the whole of Holy Week, the Passion Sunday liturgy is kept very simple and brief, as befits what is only the commencement of the drama. It relies on song, symbolism and movement, rather than a preached homily, to draw the congregation into the meaning of the scripture readings. The Eucharistic prayer begins immediately after the Liturgy of the Word, powerfully symbolizing the fact that the bread we share is the living fruit of Christ's Passion; food to strengthen us as we share that Passion. And the liturgy ends without a recession. The celebrant and people leave silently after the opening scene, ready to return for the week-long drama of faith.

I. LITURGY OF THE WORD

The Liturgy of the Word is centered on Christ's own predictions of his death and resurrection. Thus, although the evangelist's account of Christ's suffering and death is not read, the Passion is still proclaimed in Christ's own words. The use of Christ's predictions, made as he journeyed toward Jerusalem, also serves to make clear the meaning of our own procession: our desire to pass with Christ through death to life.

Note how the gradual vesting of the celebrant symbolizes our own gradual acceptance of the "doctrine of the cross," a message which may often scandalize and repel us. Because this symbolism is so important, and because several scenes are mimed, care should be taken that all in the congregation can see easily. In addition to the celebrant and deacon, two mimists, three readers, and musicians are required for the liturgy.

The congregation enters to find the celebrant quietly seated in a central position, but without liturgical vestments. When the people have gathered, he stands and greets them, and invites them to introduce themselves to one another and to extend the sign of Christian peace. The deacon then opens with a brief explanation of the theme of the liturgy: we recall the last days of Christ and celebrate the living out of that mystery in our own lives. Then the celebrant prays the opening prayer.

Opening Prayer: Father, we praise you this morning because your name is "faithful one" and your love is everlasting. You have told us that if anyone wishes to be a follower of yours he must leave self behind, take up his cross and come with you. Today you invite us, your Christian people, to enter into the celebration of Holy Week. Send us the Spirit you have promised us so that we may once again enter with Jesus into Jerusalem and recreate the paschal mystery in the pattern of our lives. This we ask through Jesus Christ, your Son our Lord, who lives and reigns with you in the unity of the Holy Spirit, God forever and ever. Amen.

First Reading: Isaiah 49:1, 8-17.

This reading may be read directly from Scripture or proclaimed in song by the singing of *Isaiah 49*, by Carey Landry (NAL) or *Yahweh Called Me* (Stein; see NAL for information) by the musicians.

Response: Vesting of the Celebrant.

Two assistants, made up in clown white-face, enter and help the celebrant into his white alb. The celebrant then gestures silently to the congregation, indicating that all should follow him. This gesture is repeated and reinforced by the two mimists, and all proceed silently out the side door of the church. When all are outside, the celebrant, deacon, and assistants return to the top of the steps, while the congregation remains below.

First Prediction of the Passion: Matthew 16:13-26.

The passage is read in parts by three members of the Chorus. During the reading, the two white-face mimists perform a mime as Jesus and Peter. After the reading, the mimists assist the celebrant in fastening his cincture; the celebrant gestures to the congregation to follow, and all process slowly and silently to the second station in the parking lot.

Second Prediction of the Passion: Matthew 17:1-12.

The second prediction is read in parts as was the first. In this case, however, the celebrant and readers stand on a small raised stage, and the mimists perform on top of two tables, making them easily visible to all in the parking lot. The musicians are clustered around the small stage. When the reading is completed, the mimists vest the celebrant in a stole, and again he silently indicates that the crowd should follow him to the third station, located closer to the front of the church.

Third Prediction of the Passion: Matthew 20:17-28.

Here again the mimists perform on top of tables, and the musicians, readers and celebrant stand on a small raised stage. At the end of the reading, the celebrant is vested in a red cope and leads the congregation to the front steps of the church. The celebrant, readers, assistants and musicians all take their places at the top of the stairs for the proclamation of the Gospel.

Gospel: Matthew 20:1-11.

The celebrant proclaims the triumphant entry of Jesus into Jerusalem. At verse 9 the narrative is interrupted by the singing of *Hosanna* from "Jesus Christ Superstar" (LDS), with one singer standing apart from the other musicians and singing the part of Caiaphas complaining about the noise of the throng, and another musician answering him in the name of Jesus. When Caiaphas and Jesus are finished with their parts, Caiaphas turns his back on the crowd, which continues to sing while the celebrant concludes with verses 10 and 11. The same music then accompanies the procession of the congregation into the church where the table is prepared. At the table, the mimists remove the cope from the celebrant and vest him in a red chasuble. Immediately he begins the Eucharistic Prayer.

II. LITURGY OF THE EUCHARIST

The entire rite for the preparation of the gifts is omitted so that the Eucharist we share may be tied as closely as possible to the Passion we have heard. The entire prayer is sung to the music for Gregory Norbet, OSB's *Hosanna #11* (WES). At each singing of the refrain, the instrumentation is augmented until at the final singing it includes guitars, double bass, tambourine, marracas, flute, and recorder. During the singing of the refrain, the mimists lead the congregation in waving their palm branches and flowers. The prayer is composed by Rev. James L. Empereur, SJ.

Congregation: Hosanna, Hosanna in the highest (repeated)

Celebrant: We give You thanks, O Lord our God / for Christ the Son of David and Israel's King. / Today we honor Jesus Christ, / triumphant King and Messiah, come to his city.

Congregation: Hosanna, Hosanna in the highest (repeated)

Celebrant: The children of Jerusalem / proclaimed him Lord and King, waving their branches. / They spread their cloaks before him / and loudly praised the Lord, shouting Hosannas.

Congregation: Hosanna, Hosanna in the highest (repeated)

Celebrant: Now on the night before Christ died / he came to eat with his friends the passover meal. / He took and blessed and broke the bread / and spoke to them these words: This is my body, / broken for you.

Celebrant: Then after supper he took the cup / he gave You Father, thanks and praise / "This is my blood, poured out for you / the cup of the new covenant.

Congregation: Hosanna, Hosanna in the highest (repeated)

Celebrant: O Father we recall to mind / the death your Son endured for our salvation, / his resurrection from this death, / his glorious exaltation at your right hand.

Congregation: Hosanna, Hosanna in the highest (repeated)

Celebrant: Send over us your Holy Spirit / that we might all be one, the body of Christ. / We praise You, Father, in our song, / your Son and Holy Spirit, now and forever.

Congregation: Hosanna, Hosanna in the highest (repeated)

Hosanna, Hosanna in the highest (repeated)

Fraction Rite: The fraction rite begins immediately upon the conclusion of the Eucharistic Prayer. During the breaking of the bread, all sing *Rise Up, Jerusalem* (NAL), and communion begins immediately following the fraction. During the distribution of communion, the *Didache* (WLP) is sung, the verses sung by the cantor and the refrain by all. There is a short silence after communion.

Meditation: The Choir sings *This is My Body* (NAL) in four part harmony. Then a group of seven dances the Our Father, while the whole congregation sings this prayer to the traditional melody. A period of silence follows.

Final Prayer and Dismissal: St. Paul's hymn of praise to Christ from Philippians 2:5-11 serves as the final prayer. After this prayer, the celebrant simply bows to the altar and walks from the sanctuary, followed by the other ministers. The community disperses.

1. Three letter publisher identification codes are taken from *The Music Locator:* an index of published liturgical music available from Resource Publications, PO Box 444, Saratoga, CA 95070.

Participation Aids For Passion Sunday And

by Thomas Welbers

Commercially produced participation aids ("missalettes") do fulfill a need. They place liturgical texts in the hands of the "person in the pew," and can be particularly useful for study and preparation, as well as for personal, private prayer based on the liturgy. Another very practical value is that they provide an unlimited source of amusement for small children who can fold, tear, and chew them while being subjected to "adult" liturgies.

However, as aids to proper participation in the liturgical celebration, these "missalettes" leave much to be desired. Some try to include all the options given in official liturgical books, which require a layout that is confusing at best and impossible at worst. Others simplify their format by making selections among the options, thereby imposing their own choice upon the celebrating community. Many of these publications print all the liturgical texts, even the prayers and readings that are supposed to be proclaimed by a minister. This encourages participants to "follow along," and focuses their attention away from communal activity toward an individualistic concentration on the printed words. These booklets become a "paper curtain" effectively isolating members of the community from one another. Most of these publications are also characterized by cheap, mass-production materials and methods, giving them a "throw-away" look and feel which militates against the sense of dignity of the celebration. Finally, in their rigid format they simply do not allow for the inclusion of very legitimate areas of creativity, such as can be found in this book.

A parish or other celebrating community that is serious about good liturgy will usually want to find substitutes for these commercially printed "missalettes." One good possibility, if projected visual media are employed, is simply to include slides of needed responses and song texts in what is shown on the wall or screen. Care must be taken that this visual material does not detract from the liturgy by calling undue attention to itself, and yet still is clearly visible and legible for all.

Often, however, printed cards or booklets will be the most practical way to assist participation. Each has certain advantages and disadvantages.

Printing all responses and song texts on a single card is certainly easiest and least distracting. Whatever is needed may be found at a glance, without searching. Card stock or heavy paper should be used because it has a substantial feel to it, and is not easily folded or crumpled. Cards are quieter; the cumulative noise of several hundred sheets of paper being turned over can be quite intrusive.

If the program material runs to more than two sides of a single sheet, a booklet is necessary. Just to staple several sheets together at the upper left corner is flimsy and gives an undesirably cheap impression.

For Holy Week, a single booklet containing all the liturgies can be a visible and tangible sign of the unity of the week. Careful use of commentaries and artwork can show the interrelatedness of the liturgies, emphasizing that they are facets of a unified whole. A well-prepared booklet has a value outside the actual celebration. It can be used to prepare for the celebration, and may become a souvenir, an object of reference for keeping the Holy Week experience alive in memory and heart.

Holy Week

In preparing printed liturgical programs, whether on cards or booklets, some basic principles of liturgy and communication should be kept in mind:

1. Be sure that you have permission to reproduce copyrighted material, and that this is properly indicated in the program.

2. Be sure that the program includes *everything* that is needed for people's participation, but *only* what is needed.

3. Brief, carefully-composed explanatory comments can help, especially at the points of transition from one part to another, and at times of silent prayer and reflection.

4. Do not print the text of readings to be proclaimed. Rather, print the Scripture reference and a one or two sentence thematic summary or meditation. This will be particularly helpful if the person is looking over the program beforehand or if there is a period of silence following the reading.

5. The same is true of the presidential prayers, especially the eucharistic prayer. The theme of the prayer should be expressed very briefly without giving the entire text.

6. Musical notation should be included if there is the least chance that many members of the congregation might be unfamiliar with the melody.

7. The overall structure of the celebration should always be evident. It helps to have a clear picture of the basic structure of the eucharistic liturgy as a guide. Additions and modifications can be made easily where needed, and people's texts and commentary can be inserted.

8. Give clear directions for posture and movement (stand, sit, kneel, etc.).

9. Be sure that the type-style is clear and large enough to be easily read. If possible, participation texts should be in larger type than directions or commentary. If mimeograph is used, take pains to produce a clean final copy without print-through. Often a local printing shop can be found that will do photo-offset work at relatively low cost.

10. If you intend for people to take the programs home, be sure to indicate this clearly — otherwise they might feel they are committing a sin to do so. On the other hand, if you want them left in the church for further use, indicate this on the program also. It would be helpful to place a clearly marked box on a stand or table at each of the exits so that people may deposit their copies as they leave.

A Palm Tree Legend For Children

by Jack Miffleton

It happened once in a far away land,
On an oasis in the dry desert sand,
That fruit trees grew up lush and green,
Awaiting the caravan of a king or queen.
But in the midst of such delight
Stood the tall and shabby sight
Of a palm tree, orphaned by the wind,
Which stormed and carried off her kin.
Her roots were shallow, though she was tall,
And like her father would surely fall.
The other trees would mock and tease,
For she had no dates or low-hanging leaves.

Travelers came from East and West
To this oasis for drink and rest.
They shared their stories by the well,
Including this one of which I tell:
The night was cool with fires bright,
An Angel, then, came into sight.
She tasted each and every fruit;
Then played a tune upon her lute:
She sang, "O palm tree, sad and mute,
Your story is your finest fruit,
Though untold for many years,
Returns tonight to dry your tears.

On your trunk no branches grow,
For in Jerusalem long ago,
A teacher came from Galilee,
Working his signs for all to see.
The crowds laid palms beneath his feet;
A sea of branches lined the street;
So every palm was cropped and chopped,
Except for the branches high at the top,
Where today they form a beautiful ring,
A crown, to remind us of Christ the King.
So stand tall and proud the rest of your days,
Many have served in lesser ways!"

1978 Jack Miffleton. Used with permission.

Friends Meeting

by Michael E. Moynahan, SJ

Friends meeting
one final time
in life as he knew it.
The thought of things
presently to come
weighing heavily
on his heart.
And others seeing
no more nor less
than what wine-dulled sense
can glean from appearances:
something they had done
with predicted regularity
long before this
momentous time arrived.
Gathered with friends,
celebrating that
passing-over event.
My how time flies
when one's having
a good time!
Minutes ticking past.
Too fast!
Too little time left!
Three years walking,
talking, teaching,
reaching out in hope
and calling forth
the good in each:
healing for
the seasoned cynic
in us all.
So it now
comes down to this:
leave-taking.
What to say?
What to do?
So much to say.
So much to do.
All poured into this
last parting gesture:
a sign,
a prayer.
Relying on
memory's gift
and what a transformed meal
can possibly recall
celebrated
miles and years
from here and now
with people gathered
in his name.

Music For The Lord's Supper

by Eileen E. Freeman

Holy Thursday has a richness about it that has satisfied Christian's hunger for many centuries. It is not just the central fact that at the Eucharist Jesus feeds his Body with his Body and Blood. It is the way the Lord's Supper is celebrated on this night which lends the added richness. The themes interwoven throughout the Mass could hardly be more important; the fact that we are the very Body of Christ, sharers in his Priesthood, ministers to each other and to the whole world of his caring love. The Eucharistic celebration of Holy Thursday is, in a special way, a celebration of the whole Church, a day when we celebrate our very "we-ness" through the Body and Blood of the Paschal Lamb.

The symbols of Holy Thursday are especially rich, touching our senses, and through our senses, our hearts. The smell of candles and incense and flowers, absent for six weeks, refreshes us. The sounds of music, of the Word of God proclaimed, of water poured out on the feet of the Body of Christ, all help to say: This day is not like other days. The taste of wine, for many a still infrequent experience, contains the seeds of what the Fathers called *sobria ebrietas,* the spiritual wine that inebriates the soul without leaving drunkenness in its wake. We see elaborate vesture, processions of ministers, light; we respond in song; we touch the Bread of life and the hands of each other.

Holy Thursday should bind us together in a special way. First, like our spiritual ancestors, we celebrate our deliverance from Egypt, at least in a metaphorical way, and the Lord's passing over the homes of the Israelites. But more specifically we celebrate the night when Christ made a new Passover, in his own Blood. Through the first giving of his Body and Blood to the disciples, Christ laid the foundations of our whole worship life.

The musical note for Holy Thursday is really set during the Washing of the Feet. What is commemmorated here is not merely that Jesus washed the feet of his disciples. Nor are we remembering some supposed act of self-abasement on the part of Jesus. The essential part of the foot-washing is Jesus' command that we actively unite in serving one another with the deepest love we can summon for the task. Jesus is not saying that we should be constantly looking for ways to humiliate ourselves in front of others. When we ingenuously show a kindness to someone else out of a real caring for them, it certainly does not humiliate us; in fact, it does not even embarrass us. Today, foot-washing is done as a symbol; in an age of shoes and rugs, it is rarely necessary for us to wash our feet every time we enter someone's house.

Jesus' loving deed can be translated into modern terms. In his day, it was the host's responsibility to see that the guest had water to wash his feet. However, the host did not wash the feet of his guest; he could not even require his Jewish servant to do such a menial task, only a non-Jew. Nowadays imagine that you are visiting friends on a cold and rainy, muddy day. Jesus, in the guise of your host, welcomes you at the door. You hesitate to come in with your muddy boots, but you are cold; your fingers are nearly frozen. Jesus brings you inside, kisses you, takes your soaked hat and coat and hangs them in his closet. Then he sits you down and proceeds, quite naturally, to undo the mud-coated zippers of your boots and take them off while you warm up by the fireplace. He removes your damp socks and puts on a pair of his bedroom slippers. It all seems very natural. Instead of being embarrassed, you are grateful for his thoughtfulness. Yet taking off dirty boots is normally something that only mothers and school teachers do, and then only for the very young children.

So when we celebrate the Eucharist on Holy Thursday, we need to emphasize things like active love, caring, service, in our music. When we sing about Christ's gift of his Body and Blood to us, we should focus on the communality of the gift, not on personal and pietistic devotions. Holy Thursday is a time for "we," not for "I."

Aside from the Washing of the Feet and the transfer of the Eucharist after Mass, the Holy Thursday liturgy follows the same pattern as most Sunday liturgies. Music will follow along familiar lines. Some suggestions for music will be made in this article; but keep in mind they are only examples of hymns and anthems that fit in with the prevailing themes of Holy Thursday, and do not constitute a sample musical "program" for the Mass.

During the entrance procession, a joyful hymn is a good thing to sing. Most of the people at the liturgy will be tired after a typical workday. They may have just finished supper and are not yet fully attentive. Little children may be up past their bedtime. An entrance hymn that is slow, sad and dragging will lull people to sleep. Traditional hymns like "At the Lamb's High Feast" or "Lord Who at Your First Eucharist" are examples of good hymn melodies with generally good texts. Beware of using syrupy registrations on these, especially the latter. Guitar choirs can use Pat Uhl Howard's "Canticle of the Gift," (ACP) with success.

During the Washing of the Feet there are a number of good settings for choir and organ or for choir with congregation: Proulx's setting of the *Ubi Caritas,* (GIA 1983) for SATB with handbells; an Appalachian version from Pro Arte 1240; for guitar choir, Brown's "Foot-Washing Song" *(Keyhole Songbook,* GIA); in this last piece, the rather sexist refrain, "...Serve your brother, wash his feet," is better changed to "...Serve your neighbors, wash their feet." In addition there are the usual settings, "Where Charity and Love Prevail," and "Where Love and Charity Abide" (Deiss, GIA).

Music during the preparation of gifts may be wise at this Mass, even if the parish tradition is not to have music here. On this day there is likely to be a procession with gifts which will take some time. It may be better to have the choir do a very short piece, especially if the congregation has been singing a great deal. The breaking of the bread should be highlighted as much as possible, since it recalls the first time Christ broke the bread for his own disciples. It is to be hoped that there will be real bread for this Mass, and that all present will receive from the chalice as well. All this will require extra time during the fraction. The happy result of this is that the Lamb of God can be sung and emphasized. One could, for instance, begin Mass with "At the Lamb's High Feast" (omitting the last verse, of course), emphasize the Lamb of God with dance, and point up the celebrant's prayer, "This is the Lamb of God..."

During communion, it is vitally important that the congregation join in on the singing. This is no time for quiet organ music or endless choir pieces. Singing about our unity in the Body of Christ, at the time when we receive the Body of Christ is essential. For practical reasons, the congregation can be invited to sing a short refrain from memory, so they will not have to juggle books and chalice at the altar. Settings of Psalms 23, 104, 16 are especially appropriate. Deiss (WLP) has a number of usable pieces, "Where Two or Three are Gathered," "Priestly People" (sing the verse about the Lamb of God). In a guitar idiom, there are many possibilities, too. Some of these include: "The Lord Jesus," Norbet (WES), "I Am the Bread of Life," Toolan (GIA, for guitar or organ, SATB or SSAA), "Look Beyond," Ducote (FEL). "One Bread, One Body" (NAL) is excellent.

Holy Thursday is a time for thanksgiving, not only for our salvation, but especially for the gift of the Eucharist; Jesus immanent, tangible. For this reason, a thanksgiving hymn, sung by all after communion, is appropriate. "Father We Thank Thee" is a traditional hymn usually set to the French tune *Rendez a Dieu.* It is especially appropriate because the words come from one of the oldest Eucharistic liturgies in the Church, written by 100 A.D. If a church is innovative, try singing the Gloria here, instead of at the beginning, where it is really an anti-climatic second entrance hymn. At different times in the Church, the Gloria was a hymn of thanksgiving, and still can be used as such today.

The difference between a well-centered Holy Thursday celebration and a poorly centered one is the difference between "At the Lamb's High Feast" and "Let All Mortal Flesh Keep Silence." The first celebrates our community with Christ, our share in his Priesthood, our being his Body. The second, though suitable at other times, moves us to withdraw into ourselves, contemplating the action of the Spirit in the private life of each Christian. If we are to grow in spontaneous love and service to each other and to those in need, we must celebrate our call to service, to ministry, in the liturgy. Music, more easily than drama, sermons or banners, can get that message across.

We who are ministers of music, who have felt a call from the Lord and our parishes to serve the Body of Christ in this way, must be extremely sensitive to the leadings of the Spirit when we plan our music for Holy Thursday. For many, the music we choose will be what they will remember. We should plan in such a way that our music is tied together by a common thread, but that all the hymns, psalms, responses, etc., do not say precisely the same thing. Four hymns of different styles, but all based on Jesus' prayer in the Gospel of John, are all examples of liturgical "over-kill." However, if we are truly *ministers* of music, whose professionalism is governed by a sense of pastoral responsibility; if we are really concerned with serving our brothers and sisters in this way; then we can probably go ahead and make our musical choices for Holy Thursday prayerfully and confidently, knowing the Lord has given us both skill and grace to plan our celebrations of his Body and Blood, broken that our unity might be accomplished.

Holy Thursday: A Dramatic Proclamation

adapted by Eileen E. Freeman

The following is an arrangement of the readings for the Liturgy of the Word on Holy Thursday. Like dramatic readings elsewhere in this book, the various readings are combined. This proclamation is intended for the whole community, but can be adapted for smaller or younger groups. It is essential that the readers be fully prepared and rehearsed adults. The effectiveness of the proclamation will depend on the skill with which they play their roles.

The dramatic reader requires a Narrator, a Leader for the congregation, and Readers. The Narrator should stand at the pulpit or ambo. The Leader should have a small stand in the front of the sanctuary where he or she can be seen by the assembly. The Readers may stand in various spots on the altar steps. Each should have a microphone. Each should have a script enclosed in a sturdy folder of the same color as the Lectionary. Even if the Lectionary will not actually be used for the reading, it is important that it be carried in procession, with the Narrator's part clipped in, if necessary.

During the presentation, the lights in the body of the church should be turned down and all should be asked to sit.

Narrator: Tonight our readings will be presented in dramatic form. You will be asked to respond at various times, just as you do during the responsorial psalm. Each time this occurs, the Leader will say the response once, then ask you to repeat it.

(There should be a pause while all the participants assemble and stand in silence.)

Reader 1: While the Israelites were still in bondage in the land of Egypt, the Lord spoke to Moses and his brother, Aaron:

Reader 2: You must speak to the entire community of Israel and say this:

Reader 3: On the tenth of this month, each household must take and slaughter a lamb without blemish. You must put some of the blood on the doorposts and lintels of your houses. That night the lamb is to be eaten roasted over the fire. You must not have anything left over; whatever is not eaten must be burned. You shall eat it standing up, with your shoes and coat on, and with your staff in hand. You must eat it quickly.

Reader 1: This is a passover in honor of the Lord.

Reader 3: On that night I am going to go through the whole land of Egypt and strike down every first born in the land, man and beast alike. The blood of the lamb will serve to mark the houses where you live. When I see the blood I will pass over you and you will escape the destruction.

Leader: Blessed are You...

Congregation: Blessed are You...

Leader: Blessed are you, O Lord, our God...

Congregation: Blessed are You, O Lord our God...

Leader: Blessed are You, O Lord our God, who spared our ancestors in faith.

Congregation: *(Repeat leader's response.)*

Narrator: The Lord also told His people:

Reader 1: From now on you are to celebrate this passover as a feast in honor of the Lord.

Reader 2: It is to be kept as a day of festival for all generations to come.

Reader 3: You are to celebrate it forever.

Leader: Blessed are You... Blessed are You, O Lord our God... Blessed are You, O Lord our God, who has given us this feast to celebrate in Your honor.

Congregation: *(Repeat leader's response.)*

Narrator: And so Moses summoned all the elders of Israel, and told them everything that the Lord had commanded him to say. When the Israelites heard the message, they bowed down and worshipped the Lord. Then they hurried back to their homes and did all that the Lord had commanded. And it came to pass that the angel of the Lord struck down the firstborn of all in the land of Egypt, human and beast alike. But when the angel found a house with blood on the lintel and door posts, he passed over and spared those inside.

Leader: Blessed be God. Blessed is His mercy. Just are His judgments. Holy is His name.

Congregation: *(Repeat leader's response.)*

Narrator: And so each year the people of God celebrated this feast in His honor. Parents explained the meaning to their children, and they in turn explained to their children.

Reader 1: Father, what does the Passover mean?

Reader 2: Why do we eat a lamb?

Reader 3: Why do we eat bitter vegetables and unleavened bread?

Reader 1: Why do we eat standing up?

Reader 2: We do these things in honor of the Passover of the Lord. Once we were slaves in the land of Egypt, but the Lord delivered us with His mighty arm. To punish Egypt He slew the first born of the whole country. But He spared us, because He loves us, and He gave us this feast in His honor. The vegetables remind us of the bitterness of slavery. We eat standing up because the Lord led us out of Egypt that night. We eat unleavened bread because there was no time that night to let it raise.

Narrator: For thirteen hundred years our ancestors celebrated the Passover. And at the end of that time Jesus, God's Son, came into the world to celebrate the great feast in honor of the Lord, and to leave it and us changed by His presence.

Leader: Praise to You, Lord Jesus Christ. You are the new Passover lamb. Yours is the blood that saves us.

Congregation: *(Repeat leader's response.)*

Narrator: On the night Jesus was betrayed He celebrated the Passover for the last time with his disciples. He knew that the time had come for him to pass from this world to the Father. He had always loved those who were his, but now he showed how perfect his love was.

(The washing of the feet may take place here.)

Reader 1: They were all seated at supper. Judas had already yielded to the temptation to betray Jesus as soon as an opportunity arose. Jesus knew that the Father had put everything in his hands. He knew that he had come from God and was going to return to God.

Reader 2: He got up from the table, removed his outer garment and tied a towel around his waist. Then he poured water into a basin and began to wash the disciples' feet, and to wipe them dry with the towel around his waist.

Narrator: He came to Simon Peter, who asked him:

Reader 3: Lord, are you going to wash my feet?

Narrator: Jesus answered:

Reader 1: I know you don't understand what I'm doing; but later on you will.

Narrator: Peter exclaimed:

Reader 2: Never! You shall never wash my feet!

Narrator: Jesus answered Peter:

Reader 1: If I do not wash you, you can have nothing in common with me.

Narrator: Peter relented, and said:

Reader 2: Then you must wash my hands and face as well, Lord.

Narrator: Hearing this, Jesus commented:

Reader 1: No one who has taken a bath needs to wash again; he is clean all over.

Leader: Lord Jesus, wash me. Lord Jesus, wash us and we will be whiter than snow.

Congregation: *(Repeat leader's response.)*

Narrator: When he had finished washing their feet, he put on his clothes again and sat down. He asked them:

Reader 3: Do you understand what I have done to you? You call me your master and Lord, and that is what I am. Well, if I, your master and Lord, have washed your feet, then you should wash each other's feet.

Leader: Blessed are You, O Lord our God. Blessed are You, O Lord our God, for teaching us to wash each other's feet.

Congregation: *(Repeat leader's response.)*

Narrator: Then Jesus took bread and gave thanks for it.

Reader 3: Blessed are You, O Lord our God, King of the universe, who hast brought forth bread from the earth.

Narrator: He broke the bread and gave it to his disciples, saying:

Reader: This is my body, which is broken for you. Do this in remembrance of me.

Narrator: Then he took the cup of wine and gave thanks for it.

Reader 2: Blessed are You O Lord our God, King of the universe, who hast created the fruit of the vine.

Narrator: He gave the cup to his disciples and said:

Reader 2: This cup is the new covenant made in my blood. Whenever you drink it, do it as a remembrance of me.

Reader 1: Therefore, every time we eat this bread and drink this cup, we proclaim the death of the Lord until he returns in glory.

Reader 2: We proclaim that Jesus is the new Passover lamb.

Reader 3: We proclaim that as God delivered our ancestors through the blood of the lamb, now he delivers us from bondage by the blood of Jesus.

Reader 1: We proclaim a feast in honor of the Lord. Come to his table, washed in the blood of Jesus the lamb. Share the cup and the broken loaf. Come out of your bondage to sin and death and live, so you may be able to tell your children about the wonders the Lord has done for us.

Leader: Blessed are You, O Lord our God. You have saved and freed us for Your kindness' sake. You have bought us and brought us to life. You have given us this feast in Your honor. We celebrate Your wonders and sing Your praise.

Congregation: *(Repeat leader's response.)*

A Children's Celebration

by Eileen E. Freeman

Holy Week has mostly been a time for grown-ups in the Church. The mysteries of our salvation are awesome and hard for children to understand. And yet, in the face of such truths, even the most intelligent of adults is reduced to the level of a child who keeps asking his father "Why...?", and who wonders more than he understands.

The liturgical rubrics for the Triduum make clear the fact that the principal celebration of Holy Thursday is the Evening Mass of the Lord's Supper. Except in cases of serious pastoral necessity, no other masses are to be celebrated on that day. However, there is no reason why a paraliturgy cannot be celebrated with school children. The following service can be used either on Wednesday or Thursday, depending on when the students are dismissed for Easter break. It combines both prayer and mime and is visually quite effective.

The service requires the following ministers:
Celebrant
Musician/Song leader
Four readers
Twelve older boys and girls to be disciples.

The sanctuary is prepared in the following way: A long table is set with tablecloth, plates, etc., so it looks like an ordinary dinner table. Benches are placed on all four sides. In the center of the table is a large glass goblet, a clear glass pitcher of grape juice, and matzoh. On a nearby stand is a pitcher of water, a large bowl and a fair size towel. These items are for the washing of the feet.

When everything is ready, the three readers come out and take their places at three microphones set up at separate locations in the sanctuary. They should not be crowding the table. The cantor or songleader announces the opening song. A hymn in the folk idiom that the children know can be sung, with a service or Body of Christ theme. Meanwhile, the celebrant enters, leading the twelve disciples. The celebrant is vested in alb, stole and cope; the twelve are not vested. They sit on the back and side table — benches facing the congregation with Jesus standing in the middle. For the mime the celebrant takes the part of Jesus. The person who plays Jesus should have a microphone as well.

After the opening song is finished, the celebrant invites the congregation to be seated.

1: Good morning. Today our celebration is different than on other days. We are going to hear the story of the Passover; how God saved our ancestors, the Jews, when they were slaves in Egypt. Today we hear the story of the Last Supper of Jesus with his disciples. We have heard these things before. But today they have a special meaning, because today is the Day of Passover and the day of the Last Supper.

(There is a short interlude of instrumental music. The celebrant sits down, and the lights in the body of the church are dimmed, so that only the sanctuary is well lit.)

1: Our story begins hundreds of years ago, in the land of Israel. In every Jewish home on the day of Passover, the family would gather together at sunset for a meal; a very special meal. The youngest child would ask the traditional question:

2: Why is this night different from all other nights? Why is this meal so special?

1: And the father of the family would answer:

3: This night is the Passover of the Lord. On this night the angel of the Lord passed over the land of Egypt, striking down the first-born of the Egyptians, but sparing the children of Israel. On that night we ate quickly, as the Lord told us, so that we could leave Egypt at once. The Lord himself led us from slavery to freedom. He went ahead of us, a pillar of cloud during the day, and a towering fire by night. He drowned our enemies in the sea, but held back the waters so we could pass through safely. The Lord led us through the desert to Mt. Sinai, and there he made a covenant, that is, an agreement with us. He promised to be our God, and we promised to be his people. He gave us a holy law to follow, and led us toward a wonderful land which he promised to give us. After forty years of wandering, we came to that land and made it our own. And so we celebrate the Passover meal tonight, because this is the night the Lord delivered us from prison and made us a free people.

2: But surely there must be more to tell. Why is this night different for those who follow the Lord Jesus?

1: Let us go back in time almost two thousand years to a city named Jerusalem. It is crowded with visitors who have come to celebrate the Passover. Among them is a group of men, mostly fishermen, led by a man named Jesus, a carpenter from the small town of Nazareth. Earlier on that day, Jesus had sent two of the men, Peter and John, ahead of the rest, so they could prepare the Passover meal for the group. Peter and John bought a lamb and had it slaughtered as the Jewish law prescribed. They also bought unleavened bread, wine, bitter salad greens and lettuce, for these are the traditional passover foods. When everything was ready, Jesus and his followers came into the house and sat down around the table. Then Jesus spoke to his followers and said:

4: I have longed to eat this Passover with you before I die. I am not going to eat another Passover meal until it is fulfilled in the kingdom of God.

(As the speaker says this, Jesus (the celebrant) stands up, turns first to the disciples on the left, then on the right, then faces forward with outstretched arms.)

1: And so they ate the Passover meal.

(Jesus lowers arms, clasps hands together.)

2: But why do we share a single loaf of bread tonight?

1: Don't you know what Jesus did on this night? He took the loaf of bread, said the grace, broke the bread, and gave a piece of the loaf to each of his disciples, saying:

4: Take this, all of you, and eat it. This is my body, which shall be given up for you.

(During these last two speeches, the celebrant takes the matzoh, breaks it into pieces, and hands it around to the disciples, who eat it.)

1: And so the bread we break is a communion in the body of Christ. The fact that there is only one loaf means that all of us who share the one bread, even though there are many of us, are one body.

2: And why do we drink wine tonight?

1: We drink wine because on that night, Jesus took a glass filled with wine, gave thanks for it, and passed the glass around to his disciples, saying:

4: Take this, all of you, and drink it, for this wine is the new covenant, the promise that I seal with my blood. Do this, whenever you drink it, to remind yourselves that I am in your midst. I tell you, I shall not drink wine again, until the day I drink it new in the kingdom of my Father.

(During these last two speeches, Jesus pours the wine from the pitcher into the glass and holds it up as if asking a blessing. He gives it to the disciple on his right who passes it around, then back to Jesus, who gives it to the disciple on his left, who passes it to his side.)

1: And so this wine that we bless is a communion with the blood of Christ. Every time we eat this bread and drink this wine, we proclaim that Jesus died and rose from the dead, that he is our Lord, and dwells among us.

2: But one last question...why do we wash feet on this night? *(At this time the disciples seated with Jesus get up and move to the bench in front of the table, so that the foot-washing can more easily be seen. They sit facing the congregation, and take off their shoes and socks. This part can be simplified by either having them slip off their shoes while they are seated at the other side of the table, or by urging that they wear slip-on shoes rather than sneakers or shoes with ties.)*

1: We wash feet because that is what Jesus did. He knew that the time had come for him to leave this world and go to the Father; that he had very little time left to teach his followers how to live. He had always explained to them what it means to love others, but that night he wanted to show them how himself. So he got up from the table, took off his cloak, picked up a towel and began to wash the feet of his disciples and dry them with the towel.

(Jesus takes off the cope and stole, pours water into the bowl from the pitcher, and takes the bowl and towel around to the front of the table. He kneels in front of Peter, and takes his foot as though to wash it.)

1: Jesus came to Simon Peter; Peter said to him:

(Jesus looks up at Peter)

3: Lord, are you going to wash my feet?

(Peter looks horrified)

4: You may not understand now what I am doing, but later on you will understand.

3: You shall never wash my feet!

(Peter stands up, and holds arms out to Jesus, with palms outward, as though pushing him away.)

4: If I do not wash you, you will have no share in my kingdom.

(Jesus looks up at Peter and holds out his hands to grasp Peter's wrists gently. Peter relaxes his stance, takes Jesus' hands and sits down.)

3: Then wash not only my feet but my hands and my head, too, Lord.

(Peter loosens his hands, touches his head with both hands, then stretches them out to Jesus again.)

4: The one who has bathed has no need to wash again; all he needs to do is wash the dust from his feet, and then he is clean all over, just as you are.

(Peter lowers his hands and Jesus washes his feet.)

1: And so Jesus washed the feet of his disciples.

(Jesus now washes the feet of all twelve of the disciples.)

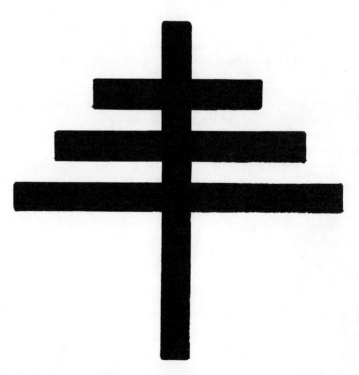

THE HOLY WEEK BOOK

Cantor: While the washing of the feet is going on, we will sing together.

(See "Music for the Lord's Supper" and the "Music Index" in this book for appropriate selections. After the foot-washing is finished, Jesus puts the bowl and towel away, and puts on the stole and cope again. He stands to the front and side of the disciples, so his face can be seen both by the congregation and by the disciples. As the following lines are spoken, he reaches out his hands to the disciples first, and then reaches out to the congregation.)

4: Do you understand what I just did for you? You call me Teacher and Lord, and this is right, because that is what I am. But if I, your Teacher and Lord, have washed your feet, then you must follow my example and wash one another's feet. As I have done, so must you do. *(Pause)*

All speakers together: This is the word of the Lord!

Everyone: Thanks be to God!

(The speakers leave their places and go and stand over by the sanctuary wall, or where the servers usually sit. The celebrant goes to a podium, or out into the congregation where he can be heard, and leads everyone in a prayer, perhaps the Lord's Prayer; or he can compose a prayer spontaneously and have the children repeat it line by line.)

Cantor: *(The Cantor announces a final hymn.)*
(The celebrant leads the twelve apostles out, followed by the four readers, and the service ends.)

Because this reading and mime encompass the three readings of the Holy Thursday Mass of the Lord's Supper, it has been used successfully as the nucleus for the Liturgy of the Word at the Eucharist on that day. When it is used at Mass, the parts are taken by men and women. The celebrant or other priest who plays the part of Jesus may need to be vested differently. Because of space limitations, the elaborate table setting may be replaced by a simple and portable stand on which are placed the bread, wine, etc., and folding chairs which can be moved after the drama is finished.

From Selfishness To Servanthood

by Dennis O. Kennedy

Context

Footwashing conveys at least four meanings: 1) Jesus revealed what it means to be Messiah in washing the disciples' feet; 2) our participation in footwashing shows our image of church to be a servant-people obedient to the Master's mandate; 3) the relationship bonded in footwashing is one of close and mutual service; and 4) the physical and spiritual posture of Christ's followers is humility.[1] On another level, this symbolic gesture is an *upholding* — a lifting to God of something worthwhile and noble that is usually degraded; namely, human feet. In treating feet with holy reverence and a caressing touch, we turn upside down the common perception of feet as filthy, smelly, and untouchable. An example: nursing home owners will tell you that one of the most appreciated gestures to the sick and elderly is to clip their toenails. It is also the one task even the most generous volunteers try to avoid.[2]

The footwashing event also strikes at two other root attitudes: status in the church community, and the taboo of touch. One cannot kneel before another in the posture of a shoe-shine boy, bathe and towel someone's feet, and retain the aloof distance of a bank president. Footwashing is a naked, liminal occasion — all status, high or low, is wiped away. Nor is it any less engaging to have one's feet washed; to realize the person kneeling to your needs gives the service freely, without payment, as a gift, a gesture of humility, makes one aware this is one gift often easier to give than receive. Neither is easy, really, in part because of our reluctance to touch each other's nakedness. We cannot usually be proud to expose our feet to another's gaze and hands. It is something we have practically to give permission for, to let others touch us, to let ourselves touch and be touched. We could all do with a greater respect for, and freedom with, our bodies.
respect for, and freedom with, our bodies.

A final paragraph of context: why do footwashing with the physically disabled? I propose three reasons. First, some churches unconsciously exclude physically disabled from active participation in the life and worship of the local church by means of architectural barriers. Other churches exclude by means of psychological and prejudicial barriers. This service says, "You are welcome." Second, since physically disabled people are often at the bottom of our list, either because we pity or ignore them, doing this service together with them emphasizes the status reversal of footwashing. Notice, this is a service *with* the disabled, not for, to, or at the disabled. We all are invited to the bowl and the table, able-bodied and not so. And third, one of the most crippling handicaps is to be so passive in living that we begin to expect everything to be *done for* us. Giving the physically disabled person a chance to wash another places him or her in the ranks of those who have gifts to serve the community, as well as to be served, which is where we Christians need to be.

Practical Considerations

1) Depending on the size of the crowd, you will need lots of clean, warm water in portable basins (cheap plastic 6" high ones are not as ugly as they sound). You will also need a good amount of towels and some washcloths.

2) The facecloths and some towels are for people who have no feet. They may like their face and/or hands washed instead. Or perhaps others who cannot reach someone else's feet might like to wash faces and hands. However, don't let braces put you off — it may take a few minutes to wash someone's feet who wears leg-braces, but with cooperation between the two of you, it can happen. It's worth it.

3) Let me introduce you to the bane of footwashing — pantyhose (I *said* this would be practical)! Let the women know in advance that they may be asked to get their feet wet; or they may want to have their faces and hands washed instead.

4) I have found soft music, usually one good guitarist, alternating instrumentals with vocals, to be a good cover for the ritual action. You don't want anything too loud, or people will start talking over it. The mood needs to be a quiet, sober joy. Besides the traditional "Ubi Caritas," use your own judgement. Tapes can be suitable if you are sure there will be no technical snafus.

5) Lead the people in the action of footwashing, but that doesn't mean you have to dominate it. After washing the feet of one or two people, spend your time encouraging, watching, or praying. Let the deacons and ushers do the legwork (excuse the pun). You may want to ask some disabled person if he or she would like to move around to someone in particular, and if you can be of help. Don't be surprised if embraces or tears occur. This is a very powerful ritual event.

6) Obviously, planning and practice of logistics are necessary. You and your ministers (deacons, musicians, ushers, lectors, basin bearers) have to provide a structure without stricture so that people can feel at ease to be a little spontaneous.

7) The place is important. Whether you are having the footwashing in conjunction with Holy Thursday Eucharist or not, most of our church buildings are not suitable for this service. You need room to move around in, a warm, good-sized place without architectural barriers such as fixed pews, steps, and narrow doors. You need a place where quiet is possible but not oppressive.

8) Risk taking seriously what you do.

Outline Of Service

I've usually done this with groups of 70 to 80 people. Larger groups may be possible, though the rite then becomes more representative (the Pope washes the feet of twelve) than participative (I wash you). The Holy Thursday scripture texts are most appropriate for that day. I will offer here other possible passages for use on other occasions. The rite can be done in conjunction with Eucharist, or it can stand on its own.

I. Opening Song

II. Greeting, Opening Prayer

III. Word Service

    A. Philippians 2:6-11 or 1 John 4:16-21

    B. Response: silence, song or possibly a poem such as "Feet," by William T. Joyner, in *Ritual in a New Day* (Nashville: Abingdon, page 29).

    C. John 13: 1-17

    D. Homily. It need not be long, but does need to provoke an action, namely, the washing of feet.

Other possible themes are in the context above.

IV. Footwashing (music)

V. Transition to Eucharist, or Blessing, Dismissal, Closing hymn, and Agape meal.

Footnotes

1. *Ritual in a New Day: An Invitation* (Nashville: Abingdon Press, 1976), p. 26.

2. *Ibid.*, p. 28.

After The Mass: Some Principles And Ideas

by Eileen E. Freeman

It is customary in many places to leave the church building open until midnight on Holy Thursday, so that people may spend some time in prayer and Eucharistic devotion. Since most celebrations of the Lord's Supper are finished by nine or nine-thirty in the evening, this usually means that the church is open for about three hours.

The reservation of the Eucharist takes place at the close of the Holy Thursday Eucharist. The consecrated bread for communion on Good Friday is carried in a formal procession through the church, usually to a side altar which has been decorated for the occasion. During this time the congregation sings a hymn. The Eucharist is simply placed inside the temporary tabernacle; then the ministers retire quietly.

This process of reservation of the Eucharist should be done with dignity, of course, but it also should be done as simply and quietly as possible. Using a monstrance or having a benediction service, as is done in places, is just not a good idea. Liturgically the important part of Holy Thursday is, of course, the celebration of the Lord's Supper; the custom of venerating the reserved elements is a much later devotion.

For this reason the procession to the place of repose ought to be a fairly simple one. It is not as full a procession as the Passion Sunday Procession or the communion procession at every Mass. These are true processions which involve most of the community. Unless the place of reposition is elsewhere than in the body of the church, the simpler the procession, the more dramatic it will be. The celebrant carrying the Eucharist, preceded by crossbearer, acolytes and thurifer, is enough.

To be visually effective, even a small procession needs to cover some distance. After all, who would be interested in a Rose Bowl parade that was only a block long? This means that the procession should cover most or all of the aisles in the church before it arrives at the place of reposition. The Holy Thursday Procession is a more subdued one than, for instance, the procession on Corpus Christi. It would help create an intimate atmosphere if during the procession the lights in the main sanctuary area were dimmed or turned off, as well as any other superfluous lights in vestibule, choir loft, etc. The blaze of lights, flowers, fanfares and the like that characterize Corpus Christi are out of place on Holy Thursday. They dwarf the celebration of the Eucharist, which is the only important and necessary event.

During the procession the congregation traditionally sings a hymn, often the *Pange Lingua* — the Eucharistic one, not the Passiontide one. It is a traditional choice because its last verses are used during other Eucharistic devotions like Benediction. There is a certain inconsistency in this. A procession, like a parade, is a visual thing, something which people watch. Sometimes the spectators cheer, as a way of participating, but they never do so out of a "cheer" book. To ask a congrega-

tion to pay attention to a procession while their noses are buried in a hymnal is illogical. It is better to have a cantor lead a responsorial piece and have the congregation respond with the antiphon. If desired, the organ can switch to the *Pange Lingua* when the procession reaches its destination, but this should not be deemed essential. A piece such as Deiss' *Without Seeing You* (WLP) can be very effective, since it proclaims our faith in a Lord whom we cannot see, but whom we believe died and rose for us and dwells in our midst. (See the "Music Index" at the back of this book for other suggestions.)

The place of repose is usually a side altar in the church, or if it is a very large church, a side chapel. However, a parish ought to consider seriously whether another place might be used instead, a place which would require a full procession with the congregation participating instead of watching. Perhaps a room off the church or in the school could be used. Since the procession would take place at night, this should be taken into consideration, as well as whether the elderly and handicapped would have access to the place of reposition.

Normally the place of reposition, particularly when it is a side altar or chapel, looks like a chapel in a funeral parlor. Everything is covered with white satin and lilies. Great banks of candles burn all over the place. The only color scheme considered is white and gold. Eucharistic banners are set up. To be sure, we want to honor Christ in the Eucharist. But on Holy Thursday at least, such a display is inappropriate. It should be kept in mind that the exuberance of Corpus Christi is out of place here. Then, too, the proliferation of white satin and flowers is at times much too feminine and fussy. While being grateful to the numerous altar societies who make the tabernacle veils and order the flowers, it should be noted that rarely are the opinions of the man (male) in the pew considered. Perhaps more of our brothers in the faith would remain to pray if Jesus did not look like little Lord Fauntleroy.

A few discreet flowers and some dramatic lighting can do more to highlight the presence of the Eucharist than all the white satin and gold net in the world. Use spring flowers in strong, bold colors of red and purple and gold. Repeat the flower motif and colors in a simple banner to hang behind the small altar or table. The banner helps act as a focal point, and also serves temporarily to hide the statue of St. Joseph or the picture of St. Rose of Lima or parish patron that often surmounts side altars. The banner ought to be extremely simple, and yield its message without any words. A red sanctuary light hung from a ceiling beam can say more than a dozen other candles. If a mass of candles are used, try for an esthetic placement of them. Rank on rank of candles is not only dull, but hurts the eye and makes one squint. During the time for private devotion, the rest of the church should be as dark as is feasible and safe. If

THE HOLY WEEK BOOK

For Holy Hours

the church's lighting system is not that sophisticated, it may be possible at least to rig a spotlight.

Although the time from about nine until midnight is basically a time for private devotion, it is often a good thing to invite one or two parish groups to lead communal devotions. A scriptural rosary can be recited. The Nocturnal Adoration Society could lead in the recitation of the Office of the Blessed Sacrament. Monastic Compline (Sunday Night Prayer in the revised Liturgy of the Hours) can be recited or sung. The parish ought to be given a schedule of organized devotions. For example: Scriptural Rosary at 10 p.m.: Office of the Blessed Sacrament at 11: Night Prayer at 11:45. This sort of a schedule not only allows people time for private prayer, but also allows them to "tune in" to the prayers of those around them. It is also a good way of getting a parish community used to the common celebration of the Liturgy of the Hours, so that the Hours can be introduced at some later time on a parish-wide scale.

These common forms of prayer should be done with as little ceremony as is necessary. The leaders need not be priests. Vestments and servers are not needed. A table in the rear of the church with the appropriate books or service sheets, and perhaps a kneeler for the leader are all that are needed. The object is not to schedule "mini-services," but to provide time for Christians to pray together on a less formal basis than in a liturgy or a parish-wide paraliturgy.

Eucharistic devotions only last until midnight of Holy Thursday. At midnight the Eucharist is quietly removed to the sacristy or another suitable place, and the candles, flowers, banners, etc., are removed from the place of reposition. All present leave without ceremony, and the church is closed until the Good Friday service.

Dayenu

by Michael E. Moynahan, SJ

Dayenu is a Hebrew word which means "It would have been enough." It is the refrain of a traditional Hebrew hymn sung at the Passover Seder. Like many hymns and religious songs which come out of a folk tradition, it is a cumulative hymn; each verse builds on the one before. Examples from the Christian tradition are: *The Twelve Days of Christmas, Children Go Where I Send Thee,* and *Green Grow The Rushes.*

The Jewish *Dayenu* describes all the wonderful things God did for the Israelites and praises God with deep gratitude for them. This adaptation for the Christian liturgy follows exactly the same pattern, but uses different events. It may be used liturgically as a responsorial text after the reading, or as a form for the Prayer of the Faithful. The verses may be done by one person or by a group. If they are done by a group, rehearsals must be held so that the text is proclaimed clearly.

It Would Have Been Enough!

Prayer Leader: To each verse we shall respond by saying: "It would have been enough!"

Verses

If God had created us and not revealed Himself in all his marvelous works...

"It would have been enough!"

If God had revealed Himself and not made a covenant with his people...

"It would have been enough!"

If God had made a covenant with his people and not breathed his Spirit into us...

"It would have been enough!"

If God had breathed his Spirit into us and not shared with us his heart...

"It would have been enough!"

If God had shared his heart with us and not watched over us when we strayed from his love...

"It would have been enough!"

If God had watched over us when we strayed from his love and not delivered us from the bonds of slavery...

"It would have been enough!"

If God had delivered us from the bonds of slavery and not led us into a land of freedom...

"It would have been enough!"

If God had led us into a land of freedom and not sent us holy men and women to speak to us of his love...

"It would have been enough!"

If God had sent us holy men and women to speak to us of his love and not promised us a Savior...

"It would have been enough!"

If God had promised us a Savior and not sent us his own beloved Son...

"It would have been enough!"

If God had sent us Jesus, his own beloved Son, and he had not become our very brother...

"It would have been enough!"

If Jesus had become our very brother, and not shared our joy and sorrows, our laughter and tears...

"It would have been enough!"

If Jesus had shared our life and not taught us how to forgive each other...

"It would have been enough!"

If Jesus had taught us how to forgive each other and not shown us how to love...

"It would have been enough!"

If Jesus had taught us how to love and not taught us how to serve each other...

"It would have been enough!"

If Jesus had shown us how to serve each other and not left us this meal as a reminder of his love...

"It would have been enough!"

If Jesus had left us this meal as a reminder of his love and not revealed to us the Father's love for us...

"It would have been enough!"

If Jesus had revealed the Father's love for us, and not called us to carry on his work in the world...

"It would have been enough!"

But as it is, Father, your Son Jesus has revealed your love for us. His whole life, his death and his resurrection from the dead testify to your deep mercy and compassion. Therefore, Father, we bless and thank You. We praise and worship You with all creation, for You are worthy of our worship, and beyond all the praises of our hearts. To You and to your Son, Jesus, and to the Holy Spirit belong all glory, now and forever.

All: Amen.

Triumph And Tripudium

by Doug Adams

Every day we should move as the resurrected body of Christ. Every Holy Thursday celebration should incorporate the joy of the resurrection even as we remember the crosses ahead; for the cross itself has meaning only in the context of resurrection. The celebrational joy of the Lord's Supper moves us beyond ourselves and out into the world. The following simple historic Jewish and Christian dance patterns may be used with many of the hymns planned for the Maundy Thursday celebration. The Christian Tripudium dance pattern is especially helpful to incarnate the recessional hymn of the celebration. The following descriptive material on the biblical and historical uses of dance in worship could be incorporated in the homily, or presented as instructions just before the congregation is invited to do (or watch) the dances that embody our faithful response to setbacks or hardships.

Dancing is particularly appropriate during Maundy Thursday celebrations because such celebrations are popularly associated with the Jewish Passover. The very word "passover" (*pesach* in Hebrew; pronounced PAY-sock) means leaping or limping. Scholars conclude that such limping dances were a part of the original Israelite celebrations. They recall the Passover conditions prior to the Exodus experience. Such limping or mourning dances were common in near eastern religions and recalled the slavery condition of the people before their exodus to freedom.[1]

This Pesach dance is appropriate for those who are without hope and those who are utterly dependent; people for whom God has not yet acted decisively. A likely recreation of this dance step is outlined by Jewish dance expert Florence Freehof:

1. Step forward with the right foot.
2. Flex the right knee.
3. Draw the left toe up to the right heel as the right knee is straightened.
4. Step forward with the right foot and continue repeating this limping sequence.[2]

Dancers moving in a circle may demonstrate this limping dance as the speaker continues to provide background information such as the following discussion.

In an effort to disassociate themselves from surrounding near eastern religions, Israelites eventually rejected all mourning dances and used only joyful dances in worship. The only other instance of mourning dance *(pesach)* in the Old Testament is the dance done by the priests of Baal mocked by the Prophet Elijah (I Kings 18:28). That Baal dance was mournful for it was based on a belief that the world's problems were traceable to God being asleep or away. Until the return of God, there was little the people could do except the mourning dance. The Israelites' rejection of the Canaanite version of the mourning dance and embrace of the exclusively joyful dance expressed a belief that the world's problems were traceable to the fact that people were asleep in relationship to a God who was very much alive and active for them. The joyful dance was to wake the people up to all that they could do.[3] Christianity followed in the Jewish tradition and stressed a joyful dance pattern used whenever hymns were sung in worship.

The homily or instruction would climax with the introduction of the joyful tripudium dance, which contrasts strongly with the mourning *pesach* step. It is this simple tripudium dance step that all would be invited to join in doing as they move out of the church singing the recessional hymn at the end of the celebration. The tripudium dance step was the most common dance step in Christian church processions and recessions for a thousand years. It fits with any hymn of 2/4, 3/4, or 4/4 time. Tripudium means in Latin literally "three-step" and comes to be translated "jubilation" because of the joy it produces in those who do it. To do this dance, simply take three steps forward and one back, three steps forward and one back time after time.

People did not do this step in a single file or in a circle. Rather they did it in processions with many abreast, with arms linked in row after row. They moved through the streets and into the church, around inside the church during the hymns of the service, and then out through the streets as a recessional. Moving three or five or more abreast with arms linked makes this step much easier to do. One can hardly fall behind. This manner of dance, which has the character of a march that does not simply go in circles, is more reflective of a faith that believes in a God of history rather than of a view that sees the world caught forever in its own cyclical return. Taking three steps forward and one back, three steps forward and one back, time after time, leads to a spirit that sees setbacks in the context of forward progress.[4]

A most effective closing to a Maundy Thursday worship combines a meaningful gesture of benediction within the context of a joyful recessional use of the tripudium step. Through this dance, people sense a heightening of community, repentence, rejoicing, and rededication. The music leaders begin singing the recessional hymn. After the congregation has joined in the singing, and can continue singing without needing to look at any song sheets, then the dancers and music leaders begin moving (with the tripudium step) around and around the communion altar table as they continue singing. They do this not in single file, nor in rows of two or three abreast with arms linked, although the latter method is an alternative way of recessing. Instead, they move as a massed group, placing a hand on the shoulder of the person ahead of them (as a gesture of benediction). After they have moved around the altar this way for a time, one or more of them invite others in the congregation to join them as they continue to move around the altar. After a few more times around the altar, they move through the aisles of the church signalling others to join them in the singing and in the recessional, as all move out of the church.

1. C. H. Toy, "The Meaning of Pesach," *The Journal of Biblical Literature*, XVI (1897), pp. 178-179; and Theodor H. Gaster, *Passover, Its History and Traditions*, (Boston: Beacon Press, 1968), pp. 23-25.
2. Florence Freehof, *Jews Are A Dancing People*, (San Francisco: Stark-Rath Publishing Co., 1954), p. 56.
3. For a detailed study of these shifting emphases in Jewish dance see Doug Adams' *Congregational Dancing In Christian Worship* (Austin: The Sharing Company, 1977), especially pp. 83-94 on "Jewish Rejoiceful Dance and Recognition of Possibility.")
4. For a more complete history of the tripudium step in Christian worship, see Adams' *Congregational Dancing In Christian Worship*, op.cit., pp. 19-20, 96-97, 110-111.

Breaking Bread: An Easter Event

by John P. Mossi, SJ

The resurrected Christ is present in many signs: the assembled community, the Word of God, the eucharistic prayer, and one particular liturgical action that is receiving restored importance, the breaking of the bread. In the post-Easter passage of Luke 24, the two disciples of Emmaus were not able to "recognize" their fellow traveler until he took bread, gave the blessing, broke the bread and gave himself to them in a special way. Only at that point were the disciples' eyes opened and they "recognized him" (Luke 24:31). Upon meeting other disciples, "Then they told what had happened on the road, and how he was known to them in the breaking of the bread" (Luke 24:35).

The disciples knew that this pilgrim was the Lord because he unambiguously celebrated the actions of the Last Supper.

And he took bread, and when he had given thanks he broke it and gave it to them, saying, 'This is my body which is given for you. Do this in remembrance of me' (Luke 22:19).

The disciples thought Jesus was dead; but in the breaking of the bread, they knew he was risen. In the spirit of the Emmaus disciples and following the command of Jesus, "Do this in remembrance of me," we also unite ourselves with Christ in his words and actions. We do what he did and celebrate his life. We take the bread, praise the Father for his constant love and everlasting mercy, we *break bread*, and distribute the bread as spiritual food for all to eat.

The task of restoring in our liturgy the significance of the breaking of the bread (also known as the fraction rite), is not an easy one because over the centuries it has been hampered by various historical events which have diminished its rich meaning and sign value. For example, in the early church, the community made the eucharistic bread which they presented to the celebrant at the presentation of the gifts. The use of real bread in the eucharistic celebration demanded that appropriate attention be given to the breaking of the bread. The celebrant was assisted by other priests and deacons at the fraction. In turn, acolytes helped distribute the broken bread to the assembly.

However, by the tenth century the breaking of the bread became relegated to a position of secondary importance. The fraction rite slipped quietly into insignificance with the introduction of unleavened bread — today, paper thin hosts. Uniform, pre-broken, and mass produced wafers became the accepted bread for use at the Lord's table. No longer did the faithful make the bread for use at the Lord's table. No longer did concelebrants or deacons assist at the fraction. The celebrant's pure white elevated host, instead of the one loaf of bread for the entire assembly, became the main liturgical focus. Gradually the bread was treated as an object to be looked at instead of what it actually was,

food to be eaten. The host continued to receive excessive devotional attention. The faithful no longer received communion in the hand but only on the tongue. In time, the kneeling posture replaced the traditional standing position as the ordinary manner to receive the Lord's bread. By the fourteenth century, the faithful seldom communicated. Attending Mass was reduced to seeing the host elevated. The essential meal actions of the liturgy became hidden and distorted.

In the majority of parishes, the major eucharistic actions of taking (presentation of gifts), blessing (eucharistic prayer), and giving (communion) of the Last Supper are sufficiently celebrated and understood. The breaking of the bread, still recovering from its token recognition in the old liturgy, is the last of the essential eucharistic actions to achieve its due prominence.

Not only is the fraction a liturgical action that is proper to the Lord's meal, it is also very rich in theological meaning. The breaking of the bread is a resurrectional sign of unity and reconciliation. For us, as it was for the disciples at Emmaus, it is a sign of Christ's presence. We associate ourselves with Christ by commemorating this memorial action of his. When the bread is broken, this event is an invitation for all to participate in the nourishment of the bread of life. Everyone by partaking of the one bread is intimately joined in Christ with one another. Likewise, the fraction reminds us that our divisions must cease so that Christ's spirit may visibly reign.

The cup of blessing which we bless, is it not a participation in the blood of Christ? The bread which we break, is it not a participation in the body of Christ? Because there is one bread, we who are many are one body, for we all partake of the one bread.

For Paul the fraction signifies a new relationship between Christ and the members of the assembly. The members of the assembly are no longer individuals but the body of Christ. Christ, as the one bread, is broken as the source of nourishment and unity for the church.

Guidelines

So far this article has treated the history and theology of the fraction rite. The next step is action. How can the parish or liturgy committee proceed in revitalizing the rite of the breaking of the bread? Fortunately, there are documents available that explicitly underscore the importance of the fraction rite in the liturgy.

The *General Instruction of the Roman Missal*[1], section 283, which is located in the front section of the new sacramentary, states:

The nature of the sign demands that the material for the eucharistic celebration appear as actual food. The eucharistic bread, even though unleavened and traditional in form, should therefore be made in such a way that the priest can break it and distribute the parts to at least some of the faithful. When the number of communicants is large or other pastoral needs require it, small hosts may be used. The gesture of the breaking of the bread, as the eucharist was called in apostolic times, will more clearly show the eucharist as a sign of unity and charity, since the one bread is being distributed among the members of one family.

The *Third Instruction of the Correct Implementation of the Constitution on the Sacred Liturgy*[2] sheds further light on the nature of the bread and the fraction rite. Section five of the document states:

The truth of the sign demands that this bread look like real food which is broken and shared among brothers. The need for greater truth in the eucharistic sign is met more by the color, taste and texture of the bread than by its shape.

Out of reverence for the Sacrament, great care and attention should be used in preparing the altar bread; it should be easy to break and should not be unpleasant for the faithful to eat. Bread which tastes uncooked, or which becomes dry and inedible too quickly, must never be used.

Great reverence must also be used in breaking the consecrated bread and in receiving the bread and wine, both at communion and in consuming what remains after communion.

These two documents are remarkable for their specific recommendations which provide the needed green light to go ahead and restore in a clear manner the breaking of the bread in liturgy. Besides referring to the importance of the fraction rite, both sources speak about the qualities of the eucharistic bread (notice that the word "bread" is employed, not hosts!). Bread is the normative food for use at Mass. It is described as "actual food," and "real bread." The bread is also to be made so that it can be broken. Why do the documents give such attention to the eucharistic bread? If the essential action of the fraction is to be restored in the liturgy, bread, and not hosts, has to be used so that the bread can in fact be broken. It is more imperative now than ever before, that hosts be discontinued. A close look at section 283 of the *General Instruction* shows that hosts at present are restricted in their use. Hosts may be used: 1) when the number of communicants is large or 2) other pastoral needs require it. It should be carefully noted that even in these exceptional circumstances, the *General Instruction* says that small hosts "may be used." In other words, in the mind of these Roman documents, small hosts don't have to be used at all. At best, they are pastorally tolerated.

Immediately objections will be raised that to implement fully the spirit of these guidelines will only cause more problems on the parish level. For instance, who is going to make the bread? Won't the people, and perhaps the clergy, only be further confused? Isn't Mass long

enough, do we have to add a fraction rite? And the litany goes on and on. These seemingly insurmontable obstacles should be balanced against some other important considerations. Why does the community gather to celebrate the eucharist? What meaning do the actions of the Last Supper have for the community? How clear are the liturgical signs? How historically faithful and liturgically correct is the celebration?

Here are a few practical steps that parishes can follow in improving the clarity of the fraction rite.

1. Through notices in the bulletin, various CCD and adult education classess, and a special homily on the theology of the eucharist, adequately instruct and prepare the community for the new level of celebrating the breaking of the bread.

2. If in the parish Masses real bread as recommended in the documents is not being used, then start a group of "papal bakers" to provide the eucharistic bread. Not only will this action be in concert with the spirit of the early church but it will bring increased meaning to the local eucharistic celebration. The bread consecrated in the liturgy will truly be the community's bread.

3. Once the people are accustomed to the new bread, the fraction rite may be enhanced. When breaking the bread, the celebrant should hold the bread up for all to see. Break the bread slowly and reverently. It is very important that the assembly can clearly see that the bread is broken. Insure that the breaking action is in no way visibly hindered by ministers or altar items. If needed, other ministers should assist in the breaking of the bread.

4. In order to embellish the meaning of the breaking action, a short and appropriate passage from scripture can be read during the fraction. I Corinthians 10:16-17, John 6:35, Luke 24:30-31, 35 are some possible texts. Other fraction rite prayers and ideas can be found in the Paulist book, *Bread, Blessed and Broken,* edited by John Mossi, SJ. After a scriptural text or prayer, the congregation can then respond with a sung *Lamb of God* or an appropriate song with a bread theme.

5. If the chalice is to be extended to the assembly, the sign of unity can similarly be expressed with the wine by consecrating it in a single decanter. During the fraction rite, as the bread is being broken, wine from the one decanter is poured into chalices. In this way, the wine for the ministers and assembly comes from the same container. Should pouring wine from a decanter prove too difficult to execute, some wine from one chalice can be poured into the chalices as an expression of unity.

1. General Instruction, copyright 1974, International Committee on English in the Liturgy. Used with permission.
2. Third Instruction on the Sacred Liturgy, Congregation for Divine Worship, 1970.

A Parish Bread Baking Ministry

Eileen E. Freeman

Baking bread for the eucharist is a very rewarding ministry in the liturgy. With just a little effort, any parish can start a program of regular bread baking.

Advantages

There are many advantages to using home-baked bread for the Eucharist. The most important of these is that the loaves actually look and taste like bread, as they were meant to. It has been said that with the traditional hosts, one has to make two acts of faith: one, that the bread is the Body of Christ, and two, that it was ever bread in the first place. Another good reason for using real loaves is that it gives more parishioners a chance to share their gifts with the rest of the community. When Saint Paul describes the charisms of the Holy Spirit, he includes all those who show generosity and liberality, who give freely of their time and talents. Few people have the talent to do things like embroider vestments or design hangings. But making a loaf of bread is, to some degree, a simpler job. It is a very satisfying thing to know that the bread which becomes the spiritual food of the whole parish was baked in one's own oven. Another reason, perhaps a bit more materialistic, but nonetheless valid, is that of economy. The costs for traditional flat hosts are rising as is the postage to mail them. Changing to real bread donated by parishioners will either cut or eliminate the cost.

Beginning a Program

The initiation of a parish bread-baking program requires a program coordinator, a man or a woman from the community to organize the volunteers. Usually one or two people are asked to bake bread for a particular Sunday. The coordinator keeps track of the volunteers, so their tasks can be rotated. Each person may be asked to bake bread once every six weeks to two months. The amount of bread needed will vary widely depending on whether the parish uses the bread to replace or to supplement the traditional hosts.

Many parishes elect to begin this kind of program modestly, using only one or two loaves per eucharistic celebration at first, and then increasing the number so that most of the communicants can receive the bread. Since each loaf is scored into a specific number of pieces before being baked, it is usually just as easy to estimate the number of loaves as it is the number of hosts needed; even easier, since individual pieces will not need to be counted.

Practical Advice

When using home-baked unleavened bread, it must be kept in mind that the bread cannot easily be reserved beyond a day or so. Homemade altar bread, unlike commercial leavened bread, contains no preservatives, and so only remains fresh for a few days. It may still be better to reserve a few pieces of traditional flat hosts for the sick, many of whom would have trouble in chewing and swallowing a substantial piece of bread.

Although in some places it is customary to break up the loaves beforehand, and to have each individual put a piece into the basket or ciborium, it is often even more symbolic to leave the breaking of the bread to the fraction rite itself, and simply leave the loaves whole, to be brought forward at the Preparation of Gifts.

Here are a number of tested recipes for unleavened bread suitable for celebrations of the Eucharist. All can be made in the average kitchen. When using these recipes, bakers should keep a few principles in mind:

1. It is better to underbake slightly than to overbake. Because these loaves are thin, they can dry out very quickly in the oven. Very dry altar bread is extremely hard to swallow, especially for children; the elderly, too, often have inadequate saliva to moisten the bread in their mouths.

2. Altar bread looks much better if it is made into fairly large loaves at least the size of an adult hand with fingers spread out. Some bakers have tried to make them the size of the traditional celebrant's host. This not only complicates the fraction rite, but is a difficult size for people to see.

3. Altar bread can be frozen easily for at least a week. In fact, if it is made at the beginning of the week for the following Sunday, it should be frozen; it will stay much fresher that way.

4. Eucharistic bread should not be sugared on top. It should be made of wheat flour, rather than corn, oat, or other grain. Both white and whole wheat can be combined in the same recipe.

5. The loaves should not contain any artificial ingredients or flavorings; nor should they contain nuts, raisins, or the like.

6. Since in the Western Church eucharistic bread is unleavened, yeast cultures should not be used. However, this does not prohibit the use of small amounts of baking soda. Unlike yeast, soda does not work by organic fermentation; rather it achieves a degree of lightness through other means. The Eastern Rites have, for the most part, always used leavened bread in celebrating the Eucharist.

7. If a congregation has a strong ethnic background, it may be more meaningful to use the unleavened bread of their native country. Recipes for various types of ethnic unleavened bread, such as the wheat tortilla, Greek pita or Syrian flatbread can also be adapted for use as unleavened eucharistic bread.

Recipe A

1½ cups white flour
1½ tsp. baking powder
½ tsp. salt
½ cup whole wheat flour
½ tsp. baking soda
2 tsp. molasses
1 cup buttermilk

Combine ingredients and mix well. Knead with white flour to keep from sticking. Shape into six rounds and place on a greased cookie sheet. Bake at 350° for approximately 10-15 minutes in a preheated oven.

Recipe B

4 cups whole wheat flour
½ cup milk
1½ cups warm water
1 tbs. whole wheat germ
2 tsp. salt

Dissolve the salt, baking powder, and wheat germ in water. Add milk. Stir into the flour, saving a little flour for later. Remove the dough from the bowl and knead for ten minutes, adding liquid or flour as needed. Return the dough to the bowl, cover lightly with a cloth, and set aside for four hours. The dough is apt to be very heavy and sticky. Grease hands and cookie sheet; shape dough into six rounds. Bake in a preheated oven at 375° for 10-15 minutes.

Recipe C

3 cups white flour
1 cup + 2 tbs. chilled shortening
2 rounded tsp. baking soda
3 cups whole wheat flour
1½ tsp. salt
3 tbs. sugar
2 cups buttermilk

Mix all ingredients, kneading them together until well blended. Pat out into two rectangles on a lightly greased cookie sheet; the loaves should be about ½ inch thick. Brush the top with milk. Bake in a preheated oven at 375° for 15 minutes. Each loaf will make about 84 pieces if scored prior to baking.

Recipe D

4 cups whole wheat flour
2 tbs. baking powder
2½ cups warm water
2 cups all-purpose flour
1 tsp. salt
2-4 tbs. honey
2 tbs. oil

Mix together liquid ingredients. Sift dry ingredients together. Add liquid to dry ingredients and mix thoroughly. Knead briefly. Roll dough on floured board to ¼-½ inch thickness. Score the loaf at half-inch intervals, deep enough so bread will break apart easily after baking. Bake on a lightly greased cookie sheet at 350° for approximately 30 minutes. Remove loaves to a wire rack and cool bread for another 30 minutes. These loaves can also be shaped as rounds. If so, they should be made as follows. Cut the rounds out with a three-pound coffee can lid. Score the loaves with a two-pound lid, then with a large, then small glass. This will leave a small round in the center. With a small knife, score the loaf in quarters up to but not including the center round. Then score each quarter into thirds.

To make a slightly sweeter loaf:

Recipe E

1 cup whole wheat flour
2 tbs. wheat germ
2 tbs. dark brown sugar
2 tbs. molasses
½ cup white flour
1 tsp. baking soda
2½ tbs. shortening/oil
½ cup of water

Sift together dry ingredients, then add the liquid ingredients. Knead together briefly, then bake in a preheated oven at 360° for 10-12 minutes. This recipe makes three large rounds.

Recipe F

1½ cups whole wheat flour
1 tsp. baking soda
¼ cup shortening or oil
½ cup white flour
½ tsp. salt
¾ cup water
¼ cup honey

Sift and measure the dry ingredients. Cut in the shortening, then add the other liquid ingredients. Knead the dough well. Roll the dough flat, about ½ inch thick. Cut into one or two large rounds, score, and place on a greased cookie sheet. Bake in a preheated oven at 350° for 10-12 minutes.

Recipe G

3 cups white flour
2 tbs. wheat germ
1 cup buttermilk
1 tsp. baking powder
1 tsp. baking soda
4 tsp. honey

Mix the dry ingredients. Mix together the milk and honey and add to the dry ingredients. Knead well. Add more flour if mixture is too soggy. Roll out to a thickness of ½ inch and cut into rounds. Bake in a preheated oven at 350° for 15 minutes. This recipe makes enough for about 80 people.

Recipe H

1 cup Bisquick
4 tbs. honey
1 cup cracked wheat flour
½ cup warm water
¼ cup milk

Mix all the ingredients together. Divide into four sections, shaping each into a round loaf. Score and bake on a greased sheet at 375° for 10-14 minutes, until bottom is lightly browned.

Note: Most of these recipes can be baked in microwave ovens. This will result in a moister loaf, as well as a very light colored loaf, since microwave ovens do not brown. Cooking time will vary, but will be much shorter than with conventional cooking.

The Cup Of The Lord's Supper

by Thomas Welbers

Wine is truly a gift from God. In his infinite good humor, the Creator gave his work a finishing touch by allowing the bloom of yeast to find its home on the tender surface of the grape. The "work of human hands" does nothing more than provide a marriage bed for the two lovers — yeast and sugar — to unite and bring forth ethanol and a host of siblings — other alcohols, glycerol, tannin, and countless esters — to form a family that is happy and whose company is beautiful indeed.

God said, "$C_6H_{12}O_6 = 2C_2H_5OH + 2CO_2$" — and he saw that it was good.

Jesus knew what he was doing when he selected bread and wine to be the effective and abiding sign of his presence among the children of men. This is where he delights to be, and a celebrational meal is at the heart of delight. We can't celebrate with just bread alone. Bread is our nourishment; it is a necessary part of our ordinary lives. Wine delights rather than nourishes. It is the drink of celebration — the person who drinks wine because he needs to is truly in a bad way. The virtue of wine is that it is in no way necessary. Bread is the staff of life; wine enchances that life. Wine is the sign of the transcendent.

In the symbolism of the eucharist, wine points to the spirit. It raises the elements above the level of mere practical necessity. It was eminently unnecessary for Jesus Christ to shed his blood for us. He did so to show the overflowing abundance of his love. The wine of the eucharist, transformed into the "cup of the new covenant in Christ's blood," continues to manifest this same saving love. This cup contains a reality beyond itself, and so is the sign of the fulfillment of that reality, the eternal banquet of the Kingdom of Heaven.

Further, wine was never meant to be drunk alone. It is the lubricant of community; it celebrates our togetherness and relationship with one another as children of one Father. The wine of the eucharist is the proper drink for God's family, and should not be denied them.

Of course, alcohol can be abused. When it is seen for what it is not — a giver of good in itself rather than a gift that proclaims the Giver — its goodness becomes a potential for destruction. This too is part of the symbol. The greater the gift, the worse its perversion. But to condemn or neglect the gift of wine just because care is required in its use is to insult the Giver and to impoverish our own lives as well. Loving respect and grateful use are the most effective safeguards.

True renewal of the eucharist demands that the sharing of both the eucharistic bread and cup characterizes the normal celebration, not just special occasions or small group liturgies. Perhaps our liturgies have become (and remained) so uncelebrational, and our Christian lives often so formalized and joyless, because common participation in the cup of the Lord's joyful covenant has for so long been denied to all who participate. To share the eucharist in only one form may be necessary at times — for some individuals perhaps all the time — but nevertheless it must always be an exception to the rule rather than the rule itself.

Communion should always be from the cup. As the Lord's words, "Take and eat," are a compelling reason for the return to the ancient tradition of receiving the eucharistic bread in the hand, so also we should take it to heart when he says with equal emphasis, "Take and drink." Intinction may be marginally acceptable as a second-best answer to certain practical difficulties. But under normal circumstances, if true bread is broken into irregular pieces and received in the hand, intinction becomes impractical and impossible.

A eucharistic minister should always give the cup to those who wish to receive it. This gesture of giving and taking speaks of the relationship of service that the Lord demands of those who share his table. Simply to have communicants pick up the chalice from a table, or to pass it around among themselves, is a return to the "fast-food-service" liturgies of yesterday, and is quite foreign to the principle of renewal.

There are some practical difficulties in giving communion from the cup, especially in large groups. It takes longer. It requires more space to move about. There should be two or three ministers of the cup for each minister of the bread. The movement of people has to be arranged so that they do not have to devote their entire attention to finding out where to go and avoiding collisions. But properly handled, this disadvantage becomes a true advantage. An efficient yet unhurried sharing of communion is a sign of the dignity and importance of the sacrament. It is truly a sharing of the Lord's Supper rather than a mechanical distribution.

Another objection may be made on the grounds of health. This may be a problem requiring some serious consideration, although I have heard objection voiced more frequently to the *thought* of sharing a common cup than to the actual practice where it does take place! One study in England[1] concluded that the transmission of bacteria is almost completely avoided if the edge of the cup is wiped and turned slightly after each communicant drinks from it. There is not enough alcohol in the wine to have any germicidal effect. However, bacteria can live only within a moist medium and any traces of saliva that might be deposited on the cup would be gone by the time that part of the cup is used again. We may conclude that under normal circumstances and given proper care, sharing from the cup would be at least as safe a practice as most of our other public social contacts.

Concern for health can also be turned into a sacramental element of the eucharistic action — community responsibility. Avoiding the cup if one has a communicable disease is a genuine sign of love — and in this instance would be a better participation in the sacrament than receiving it! On the other hand, overcoming squeamishness to drink from the cup would also be a demonstration of loving trust of one's brothers and sisters.

It has been proposed that wine be consecrated and distributed in small, individual cups for communion, as is done in some Protestant churches. This would be an unfortunate return to an individualistic concept and practice in the sacramental celebration, and would greatly weaken the central "one bread-one cup" symbolism.

Communion from the cup places the option to receive it or not where it belongs — the choice is up to the communicant. He or she is free to receive under only one species if desired for any reason.

Wine for the eucharist should be brought to the altar and consecrated in a single container — perhaps a very large chalice or a suitable flask. Then it may be poured or dipped into smaller cups for communion at the time of the breaking of the bread. This enhances the reality of the gesture. The one bread and one cup are seen more truly as signs of the one body of Christ. Nothing detracts from the visual graciousness of the celebration more than a clutter of chalices and ciboria on the eucharistic table.

The selection of wine is an important consideration for those who prepare liturgies. A fussy limitation to "approved" altar wine only, as well as an uncaring "anything will do" attitude, will equally impoverish the celebration. Attention to the quality of bread should be matched by a careful choice of wine. Quality, appearance, and taste speak of the nature of the celebration.

Choosing a good wine for the eucharist, even from market shelves, is not impossible, but does require a little knowledge of different kinds of wine and how they are made.

The basic criterion is simple: use genuine, naturally fermented grape wine. The actual selection of wine, however, is more complicated. California laws regarding winemaking are as strict as the Church's law. As a general rule, one can feel safe about using any good California commercial wine for the eucharist.

Unfortunately, the laws of most other states, such as New York, permit the addition of considerable amounts of sugar, water, and other ingredients which make the wine less of what it should be and possibly invalid according to Church law. Some imported wines may also have excessive adulterants, and it is impossible to tell this from the label. If possible, a California wine should be selected. Otherwise, make inquiries about the winemaker's methods.

Fruit wines (strawberry, blackberry, apple, etc.) are obviously unacceptable. So are "pop" wines, like Thunderbird, Ripple, Sangria, etc., which are fruit juices added to a wine base for a little "kick." More traditional types of flavored wines are also unacceptable: Vermouth, Dubonnet, May Wine, etc. Wines that have undergone additional processing besides normal fermentation and aging, such as Sherry, should not be used. Sparkling wines (Champagne, Cold Duck, Spumante, etc.) should also be avoided because of additional processing (a secondary fermentation) and because the bubbles call attention to themselves and the sensation they produce rather than allowing the wine itself to be perceived.

Sweet desert wines (Muscatel, Port, Tokay, Angelica, etc.) all contain more than 14% alcohol, usually, though not always, because they are fortified with brandy in order to stop fermentation while there is still a good percentage of sugar in the wine. While not totally unacceptable, the heavy sweetness of these wines really goes better with cake than with bread.

Normally, then, the choice should be limited to good quality table wines, all of which contain 14% alcohol or less. White wines are usually lighter in flavor characteristics than reds, and more people would probably find them agreeable. Most wine producers make one or more generic white wines that are a little on the sweet side, blended from different varieties of grapes, and sold under the name of Chablis, Rhine Wine, or Sauterne. There is no particular difference between one name and another, though the flavor may vary considerably from one winery to another. White wines named for a particular grape, such as Chardonnay, Chenin Blanc, French Colombard, etc., will often be a bit dryer (less sweet) and have some distinquishing flavor characteristics.

THE HOLY WEEK BOOK

Red wines are usually more full-bodied and tart than whites. A person who does not ordinarily drink wine may find the flavor of most reds less agreeable than the whites. In a glass container, a red wine will certainly be visually more impressive than a white. Generic reds, blended from different varieties of grapes, usually go under the name of Burgundy, Chianti, Claret, or simply, Red Wine. Varietals, such as Cabernet Sauvignon, Pinot Noir, Zinfandel, etc., will have a flavor that carries certain characteristics of the predominant grape.

For the eucharist, it is best to consider generic wines first. They are usually cheaper than the varietals, and from a good winery receive just as much care in production. Unless you are celebrating with a community of wine connoisseurs, the added expense for a varietal would be a waste.

Wines produced on the East Coast often have a characteristic "foxy" flavor of concord grapes. California and European wines never do. Some people like the taste, but many find it an unwelcome intrusion on the true wine flavor.

Most people find that white table wines and sweet wines taste better if chilled, while red table wines are preferred at room temperature. These are not absolute rules, but they do seem to bring out the best characteristics of the wines and should be followed as much as possible for the eucharist.

A community may want to consider making its own wine for the eucharist. If so, be careful to use proper methods and quality ingredients, because artificial substitutes are available. Wine is not just grape juice with alcohol added! Books and assistance are available. Pay attention to federal and state laws about making and using home-made wine. Finally, wine making should not be merely the pet project of an individual and then imposed on the community.

Whether purchased or home-made, never use a wine for the eucharist that hasn't been tried. The eucharist is no place for surprises that might prove unpleasant or inappropriate. An occasional wine-tasting party may help a liturgy committee select good wines that are appropriate for various celebrations. Perhaps the liturgy committee would also want to share its developing expertise by sponsoring a wine-tasting party for the rest of the community too.

For those who want to pursue the subject of wines a little more deeply, here is a list of some standard works that may prove helpful:

Frank Schoonmaker, *Encyclopedia of Wine* (Sixth Revised Edition), New York, Hastings House Publishers, 1975; $9.95. A basic and essential book.

Maynard A. Amerine and Edward B. Roessler, *Wines: Their Sensory Evaluation,* San Francisco, W. H. Freeman and Company, 1976; $8.95. A professional guide to wine-tasting and judging.

Bob Thompson and Hugh Johnson, *The California Wine Book,* New York, William Morrow and Company, Inc., 1976. Gives an interesting and detailed description of both the wineries and the wines.

J. R. Mitchell, *Scientific Winemaking Made Easy,* Andover, England, The "Amateur Winemaker" Publishers, Ltd., 1969; $4.00.

M. A. Amerine and M. A. Joslyn, *Table Wines: The Technology of Their Production* (Second Edition), Berkeley, University of California Press, 1970; $25.00. For professionals.

[1] See B.C. Hobbs in *Journal of Hygiene,* Vol. 65, no. 1 (March, 1967). Also E.P. Dancewicz in *Journal of American Medical Studies,* Vol. 225, no. 3 (July 16, 1973). Reported in *Worship Resources Newsletter,* Vol. 3, no. 10 (March, 1975). Available from Worship Resources, Inc., 12461 W. Dakota Dr., Lakewood, CO 90228.

Sharing The Generosity of Jesus

by Eileen E. Freeman

During Lent every year we are urged and we urge others to be more generous with themselves; with money, time, and talent. The Church encourages what used to be called almsgiving. However, the emphasis has fortunately changed; instead of giving from our surplus, we are urged to share what we ourselves need. Isaiah, speaking with the voice of Yahweh, said, "If you share your bread with the hungry... then your own light shall be as bright as the day... You shall call, and I will say, 'Here I am!'."

One could quote statistics forever to suit any purpose, but it is basically true that America, a country with only six percent of the world's people, consumes over forty percent of the world's resources. We live with a staggering surplus of food and basic goods like clothing. Yet we are so used to the availability of these that when one commodity becomes less available, such as coffee or petroleum products, we grumble and complain as though we had a right to them. In a world in which ten thousand die every week from starvation and malnourishment, and thousands of children are doomed to a life of retardation caused by such malnutrition, we can hardly speak of our "right" to waste billions of dollars worth of food, energy and natural resources. This is certainly not to say that we cannot enjoy the rewards of life, only to plead that we cease our selfish waste.

As the Church, we are bound to follow Jesus' example of generosity. When asked for something, Jesus rarely gave the minimum. In addition to his providing food for a multitude or healing the sick, He also gave them food for thought or a healing of spirit. Ultimately He even gave his life. Surely during Lent we can become more aware of our need to follow the Lord in this way, so as to be able to live it out during the rest of the year.

It is curious that we do not have any problems in being generous with our money if the worthy cause is a remote one. Money for the hungry of Africa, Asia and the rest of the third world areas is available. We seem to be easily impressed by huge causes, by immense needs, by suffering on a gigantic scale, often to the neglect of those quite near us who are in desperate straits. It is easier to confine our generosity to "causes"; it saves us from having to get too deeply involved. If we give money, we don't have to think troublesome thoughts like, "Is my lifestyle justifiable? What can I give of myself and my time?" This is not to say that being generous with money is not a good thing; but when it is a substitute for getting involved, it does us no good. We could arrive at the "gate" of heaven, only to be confronted by Jesus saying, "I lived next door to you; I was old and sick and needed someone to take me to the doctor's office; but you ignored me. Instead you stuck a dollar in the poor box to ease your conscience."

Every parish has to be generous in meeting the needs of men and women in trouble or its spiritual life is going to atrophy. Some of the best parishes this writer has seen are those which have felt called to a ministry of total service. Most things in these parishes are in perspective. The liturgy and worship life is strong and alive, because it is in common worship that the parishioners find strength for their daily life and the parish apostolate. Their worship almost compels them to go out to others and give what they can of themselves; it does not turn them too far inwards, as liturgy can do so easily. And as basic needs are met, people are brought into the Body of Christ and come to experience what it means to belong to a Christian community.

Holy Week is far too late in the year to begin a full scale campaign to wake people up to the Lord's command to feed the hungry. If a parish is beginning to feel that restlessness, that dissatisfaction with the status quo which is so often the leading of the Holy Spirit, then a catechesis, a searching for the way the Lord is leading a parish can begin. The following is a very brief sketch of what that call meant to several parishes, and how they acted on it. The parish described below is a composite. of several parishes which have undertaken such a program.

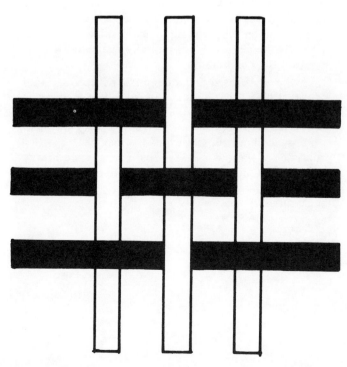

THE HOLY WEEK BOOK

Step One: Assessment of Parish's Current Status

St._____'s parish is not at all unique. Located in a small city, its parishioners come from many ethnic groups and income levels. It has a school which it is trying to maintain, an income not keeping pace with inflation, and a fair turnover of parishioners. There are still petty squabbles over whether the school children should wear uniforms, whether lay ministers are needed, and whether the parish council president is really an idiot. But basically the parish is flourishing, despite their own need for money and limited income.

It was the fact that many parishioners were contributing their time and money beyond what would normally be expected that led the worship commission to the conclusion that maybe the parish was being asked to be a special "sign" of God's caring for the neighborhood. Participation in such groups as the St. Vincent de Paul Society was high; large donations were made to the Society for its work. The social justice committee thought that there might be a large reservoir of human resources in the parish who were also generous and giving people, but who either couldn't contribute financially, or were not the type to feel comfortable doing the sort of work the Society did. The rectory staff and the commissions prayed together regularly during the time preeding Lent, and came to the conclusion that the Lord was asking them to change their whole parish lifestyle so as to concentrate more on ministering to the needy of all kinds. This was not seen as merely a Lenten program; rather Lent was seen as a chance to awaken people to Jesus' total giving of himself for them, and to their need to share that with others.

Step Two: Setting a Limit Geographically

It may sound contradictory to urge people to share the generosity of Jesus, and then immediately to limit the sharing. Actually, it became clear to the staff of St._____'s parish that they were not being asked to solve all of the world's problems, just a few of them. They decided that the first goal was to change their view of parish boundaries. The typical attitude of parishioners was that the parish consisted of all Catholic families in the neighborhood, even those individuals who no longer practiced their religion or believed in it. This narrow attitude had to be widened so that everyone who lived within the geographical boundaries of the parish was a "member" of it, at least in the sense that they were potential members.

The parish decided that before they could enlarge their ministry to the neighborhood, they had to make sure that their brothers and sisters in the worship community were not being neglected. On the first Sunday of Lent they began a campaign to find out not only what needs there were in the worship community, but also what skills and talents were available. Volunteers from the parish societies and the parish at large began contacting every member of the worship community, drawing up long lists of those who were chronically ill or bedridden, or whose houses needed repairs, who were out of work; and lists of those who had nursing skills, who could do house painting, who knew how to cook and sew, etc. As many needs as possible were matched with volunteers with skills. An out-of-work carpenter not only earned some needed money repairing porch steps and houses, but also met some pressing needs, even as his own were being met. A dietician organized classes to teach those living on a fixed income how to buy and cook good food wisely and inexpensively. One of the women in the class, who was a daily house cleaner, volunteered some time to help out an elderly couple no longer able to do heavy housekeeping. Once the program was established, and there was a viable means for people to have their needs met or their skills used, the same program was expanded to the rest of the neighborhood. Advertising was done in local stores, supermarkets, schools, bars, etc.

After this initial advertisement had been completed, volunteers from the worship community began a door-to-door campaign in their own blocks or streets to meet people and find out what kinds of help or talents were available.

Step Three: Bringing Needs to Liturgy

Still, the parish found out that there were people in the worship community who did not feel they had either pressing needs or special skills, but wanted to help. Also, as the community became more aware of the ministry of giving, and prouder that they were beginning to care for others in an active way, the need to bring this concern and ministry to the liturgy became apparent. It was decided that on the last Sunday of the month, a special food offering would be made at the Eucharist, as a symbol of what the parish was trying to achieve. The time during the preparation of gifts, which was usually taken up with a hymn, was extended briefly. Along with the bread and wine, the collection basket, etc., those who had brought donations of food brought them forward and left them at the foot of the altar. The hymn or antiphon at this time often focused on the nature of giving or ministry. It was agreed that ten percent of the parish collection would be given to the St. Vincent de Paul group and the others which were actively meeting needs in the expanded parish. To take this step was a great leap in faith for the parish, since it had barely enough income to meet its own needs. However, the grim financial disaster prophesied by some did not materialize. Some parishioners were moved to increase their contributions to the parish. The school, a large drain on parish resources, found ways to economize; in fact, some local businesses actually donated various services and materials or supplied them at cost. The parish remained fairly stable financially.

The parishes described above did not, of course, accomplish all their goals during the few weeks of Lent. Rather, the program took several years to establish. Clinics, programs for the retarded, half-way houses for battered wives, thrift shops did not spring up overnight, nor did the type of lifestyle characterized by generosity which begets such efforts.

Holy Thursday: The Blessing of Bread

One parish in California decided that as a parish effort, all who could would fast on bread and water on Good Friday, and include the money they would have spent on food in their Easter collection. Each family or individual brought with them to the Holy Thursday Mass a loaf of bread, the bread that they were going to eat the next day. For reasons of good nutrition, parishioners were urged to bake their own rather than use cheap sandwich bread; many baked extra loaves for those who could not bake them, and for their neighbors.

Celebrant: My brothers and sisters, many of you have come to celebrate this evening, bringing loaves of bread to be blessed. Bread such as this is the staff of life. It stands between life and starvation for half the world's population. Like bread, we are but a single loaf, formed of many grains. Many of us have been milled and crushed so that our dead hulls could be blown away. Although the process is painful to us, it makes us a better loaf, better able to feed the hungry who live in our midst, whether they hunger for food, self-respect, jobs, or for the Lord.

This is the food many of us will eat tomorrow. We fast, not to harm ourselves, or worse, turn in on ourselves; rather, we fast so that we may be more open to the hungers of the world, as Jesus ministered to the hungers of the world. By fasting, we hope to become more generous with ourselves and what we have. We hope to become like Jesus, who gave himself completely, offering his life that we might live.

(The celebrant then asks the congregation to hold up the bread in their hands. An unsliced loaf seems to work best.)

Celebrant: Father, we ask you to bless this bread which we will eat tomorrow as a sign of our dying to self. You sent the Israelites manna when they wandered in the desert, showing them that you cared for them and their needs. May this bread nourish our bodies, so that we, too, may care for the needs of others. Increase the ministry of generosity in us, so that we may be sensitive to those around us; in our families, our jobs, and our neighborhoods. We ask this through Christ our Lord, who was obedient to your will, and who gave his life for the life of the world.

All: Amen.

(Because holy water can make some of the bread "soggy," the celebrant uses incense as a sign of blessing, going through the aisles with the thurible. A hymn is sung, during which time a number of loaves of bread, made especially to be distributed to the sick or those who could not attend the Holy Thursday Eucharist, are brought forward along with the bread and wine for the Eucharist itself. The bread for the sick is placed on a table in front of the altar.)

Epilogue

Parishes like the ones described here really do exist; this writer knows of several. They do not trumpet their existence, although sometimes the world does it for them. The New Testament records that Jesus and his apostles had a monetary fund into which donations went, and from which they gave money to the poor. Yet we never hear about these small acts of generosity done by Jesus. Because we cannot yet work miracles so as to feed all the hungry of the world and cure all illness we think we are powerless. Nothing could be further from the truth. The Kingdom of God is built everyday by the small acts of love and self-giving that we all are capable of. Jesus gave us his body and blood, his very life. If we want to be considered his followers, we must in our own ways, do the same.

This Is The Passover Of The Lord

by J. Frank Henderson

The more one understands the Jewish Passover Seder, the better one can understand the Christian Eucharist. More and more, Christians are coming to appreciate that our present Eucharistic celebrations have their roots in the Passover Seder, and are beginning to learn about the Seder through both study and experience.

"Seder" is a word meaning "order", and hence the order or agenda of a service. It refers preeminently to the ritual meal held each year in Jewish homes on the Feast of Passover, and to the fifteen traditional parts of this liturgical celebration. The Passover Seder has been a highlight of the Jewish year for some 3,000 years. Although scholars disagree as to whether the historical Last Supper really was a Seder meal or not, Paul and the four Evangelists interpreted the theological meaning of the Last Supper as if it were a Seder. This article will discuss briefly four points of contact, similarity, and dependence between the Christian Eucharist and the Passover Seder.

Both the Passover Seder and the Christian Eucharist celebrate *exodus.*

Passover commemorates the central mystery of the Hebrew Bible: the exodus from Egypt. In this context exodus must be seen broadly; it includes not only the initial deliverance from Egyptian power and the passing through the Red (Reed) Sea, but also the making of the covenant between God and his people at Sinai, the wandering in the desert for forty years, and finally the entrance of the chosen people into the promised land.

The original exodus from Egypt became the paradigm of the saving love of God for his people, and when in subsequent generations he saved the people from other calamities and captivities (especially the exile in Babylon), each new act of deliverance was seen as a new exodus. Thus, it was natural to look forward to the final and perfect deliverance, that of the Messianic era, as another new exodus. Jews of today still celebrate in the Passover Seder the original exodus from Egypt and all the other acts of deliverance through which God has shown his favor to them. They also look forward to the final exodus which is still to come.

Christians have always seen Jesus as Savior or Messiah (after all, the title "Christ" comes from the Hebrew word for "anointed" which is translated as "Messiah"), and the early Church saw in his great acts of love, especially in his death and resurrection, the final exodus and passover to which all had looked forward. In his death and resurrection Jesus identified fully with the original and subsequent "exodus," and in describing Jesus' action, Paul used the words "Christ, our paschal lamb, has been sacrificed" (I Cor. 5:7). At the same time, of course, the exodus-passover event was transformed and given new meaning by Jesus' experience.

At Easter, which is the Christian Passover festival, we commemorate the death and resurrection of Jesus—our new exodus; at the same time we look forward to his second coming. The connection between new and original exodus is clearly and forcefully expressed in the Exultet of the Easter Vigil:

"This is our Passover Feast, when Christ, the true Lamb, is slain whose blood consecrates the homes of all believers.[1]

"This is the night when first You saved our fathers; You freed the people of Israel from their slavery and led them dry-shod through the sea.

"This is the night in which the pillar of fire destroyed the darkness of sin.

"This is the night when Jesus Christ broke the chains of death and rose triumphant from the grave."

Both the Passover Seder and the Christian Eucharist are ritual meals.

In Biblical times, the special paschal lamb was the main course of the meal of the Passover Seder; this was eaten with wine, unleavened bread, green vegetables, bitter herbs and condiments. Since the destruction of the Temple by the Romans, the paschal lamb can no longer be sacrificed, and its place is symbolized by a lamb bone; lamb is no longer eaten at the Seder meal. Now, in fact, there are two types of food at the Seder: one type constitutes the 'regular' meal of special, festive foods, which do not have to be specifically associated with the exodus. Other foods, however, have a special meaning through their association with the story of the exodus or by their traditional use.

Unleavened bread and the four cups of wine are particularly important among the ritual foods, which also include bitter herbs (usually horseradish), green vegetables (parsley or celery), and haroset (a mixture of ground apples, nuts, cinnamon and wine).

The bread and wine of the Eucharist obviously come from Jesus' use of them at the Last Supper. The use of unleavened bread in the Latin Rite is based on the traditional identification by the Western Church of the Last Supper with the Passover Seder. (The Eastern Churches do not make this identification and hence use leavened bread.) Of the four cups of wine at the Seder, the third is drunk at the conclusion of the lengthy and highly developed blessing after the meal; it is called the "cup of blessing" and this term is used by Paul (I Cor. 10:16) in a Eucharistic context. The "institution narrative" tells what Jesus said and did as he gave the bread and wine to his disciples at the Last Supper.

At the weekly assemblies of the very early Church there were both a dinner meal and the ritual Eucharistic meal. For a variety of reasons, the full meal was soon abandoned, and the Eucharist began to take its present form. The fact that the Eucharist is a ritual meal has been strengthened and emphasized in the new Order of Mass. Thus the blessing prayers at the "preparation of the gifts" are based on Jewish meal blessings. The altar, in addition to the use of candles and tablecloth, is now free standing in order to look more like a table. The bread used remains unleavened and is supposed to look more like bread, and communion from the cup has been restored to the laity. The washing of hands before the meal is also a link with the Seder.

Both the Passover Seder and the Christian Eucharist are memorial celebrations.

In Biblical language and thought, "memorial" (Greek: *anamnesis*; Hebrew: *zikkaron*) refers to liturgical celebrations that celebrate and re-present past mysteries of salvation in forms that can be participated in and appropriated personally by those living in the present. By participating in the prayers, readings, songs, and customs of the Passover Seder, by seeing the symbols of the exodus, hearing their meaning explained, and eating some of them, those present today relive the experience of the original exodus and join with their ancestors who took part in the original event.

This is explictly expressed in one of the great statements of the Seder: "In every generation each Jew should regard himself as though he personally went forth from Egypt. It was not only our forefathers whom the Holy One, blessed be He, redeemed from slavery, but us also did He redeem together with them..."

In the Eucharist, Christians obey Jesus' injunction, "Do this in memory of me." They tell and do what Jesus did at the Last Supper (take, bless, break, eat), and they say what Scripture records that he said on that occasion. In the Eucharistic prayers, we proclaim that we are indeed carrying out this command, that we are celebrating a memorial feast, "the memorial of our redemption", "the memory of Christ". We are recalling his death and his resurrection.

Unfortunately our language really does not convey very well the Biblical meaning of memorial/anamnesis/-zikkaron, and this must be considered a real defect in the new Eucharistic prayers. We might do well to paraphrase the Seder prayer and say, "In every time and place Christians should regard themselves as though they each personally died and risen with Christ. It was not only Jesus whom the Holy One, blessed be He, redeemed from the slavery of death, but us also did He redeem together with him."

Both the Passover Seder and the Christian Eucharist signify and strengthen community.

Although one usually becomes a member of the Jewish people through birth from a Jewish mother and (for males) through circumcision, it is by annual participation in the Passover Seder that Jewish tradition sees one as reaffirming, continuing and strengthening one's bond with the community of Israel.

It was in the event of the exodus from Egypt that the people were constituted as God's own people, and it is in the annual Passover Seder that one participates in the exodus and renews one's identification personally with this central event of salvation. If one deliberately neglects to participate in the Passover Seder, it is as if one turns one's back on the exodus, on the event which constitutes community, and on the God who saved and saves.

Christians become part of the people of God through baptism, in which we identify ourselves with the death and resurrection of Jesus, and hence with his exodus (Romans 6:3ff). To signify this new identity on an ongoing basis, to renew its meaning and strengthen the association with the community of believers, one must annually celebrate Easter, the Christian Passover feast, and come together weekly in the Eucharistic celebration on the Lord's day. If one regularly neglects to celebrate the memorial of Jesus' exodus, the promise of baptism remains unfulfilled and one dissociates one's self from the people of God.

In conclusion, we must remember that Jesus and all of the first Christians were Jews, who had celebrated the Feast of Passover since childhood and for whom it had overwhelming theological significance. If we are to understand what was in the mind of Jesus as he went to his death, and what was in the minds of his first disciples as they reflected on the meaning of his life and death and as they began to celebrate their first Eucharistic meals, we must come to understand the meaning of Passover. This can be done especially by studying, or better, experiencing the Passover Seder. In the Seder, Jews of today still celebrate faithfully and with joy the saving acts of God throughout history.

A Passover Meal For Christians

by Eileen E. Freeman

The traditional Passover meal can be celebrated by a single family, a group of families, or an entire parish. In fact, according to Jewish custom, if a family were too small to eat a whole lamb, it was supposed to join together with other families. In some parishes there are three or four Passover dinners for parishioners. Families generally reserve space for dinner on a sign-up sheet, since participation tends to be on a large scale. Usually a small donation is requested to help pay for expensive items like lamb and wine. Parishes either use paper dishes or ask families to bring their own place settings. When the families arrive they are given a copy of the service; and the dinner begins.

Generally speaking, parish Passover celebrations usually take place on a day other than Holy Thursday. This is to allow the whole community to participate in the liturgy of the day. However, many parishes schedule at least a small celebration after the liturgy, and most family celebrations take place on Holy Thursday. Few places aim for the actual day of Passover as celebrated yearly in the Jewish community. To do this would mean that in some years the Passover meal would be celebrated weeks before Easter.

The early Christians often held what were called "love feasts." These were not necessarily eucharistic services as we think of them, but rather opportunities for them to share their faith, their love and their support for each other in the context of a meal. For the family or parish of today, the Passover meal has many of the qualities of these early Christian gatherings. The ritualized setting helps structure what might be an otherwise amorphous group into a united gathering. The meal itself provides opportunities for relaxation and fellowship to grow. The whole event helps bind together the many diverse elements that make up any parish community.

There are a few items that are traditionally served at the Passover meal. These include unleavened bread, salt water, a bitter vegetable such as cress, endive or parsley, and *haroses*, a mixture of applesauce, cinnamon, nuts and wine. Wine and lamb are also traditonal, but any main dish can be used; and grape juice can substitute for the wine.

If the celebration is a large one, the seating should be divided up into numerous tables. Families should sit together. At each table, the oldest man and woman take the roles of Mother and Father, while the youngest person who can read takes the role of the Child.

In addition there is a leader, a man or woman, who reads the commentaries and encourages participation. If the meal is a large one, a song leader would also be helpful.

The Order Of The Service

Leader: We have come together this night as the people of God, to proclaim the mighty deeds of the Lord, to praise Him and worship Him, and to thank Him for loving us and caring for us. Even though we have often forgotten Him, He has never forgotten us. When we were in bondage to sin, He broke our chains and set us free. When we were wandering in the darkness, lost and alone, he found us, and led us back to His people. When we were hungry, He fed us with water from the rock and with manna. It is fitting, therefore, for us to give to God our Father all praise and glory and honor, and to bless Jesus Christ His Son, who came into our midst to show us how to celebrate this feast.

All: Praised be Jesus Christ, the Lamb of God.

Kindling The Lights

(On each table there should be candles. The mother [at each table] lights the candles as all look on.)

Mother: Blessed are You, O Lord our God, King of the universe, who hast made us a holy nation by Your laws, and hast commanded us to kindle the festival lights.

All: Holy is Your name from the rising of the sun unto its setting.

Mother: Let the light of Your face shine mercifully upon us, O Lord, and let it dispel the darkness of our lives and bring us peace.

All: Blessed are You, who made the sun to light the day and the moon and stars to light the night, and have made us to be lights to one another.

Mother: Amen.

Blessing Of The Festival

Father: Blessed are You, O Lord our God, king of the universe, who have redeemed us from the land of bondage and brought us to this night and this feast in Your honor. May we celebrate this feast and all others until the day we share the great feast in the kingdom of heaven.

All: Holy is our Redeemer who has delivered us from death.

Washing Of Hands

Leader: Let all those who share this meal come with clean hands and hearts washed of every evil. Let no one come who has not been made clean.

All: Jesus, wash our hearts clean, as once You washed the feet of your disciples.

(At this point the account of how Jesus washed the feet of the apostles may be read. If there is a separate table for the leader and others, the actual footwashing may be re-enacted while the account is read [see the Gospel for Holy Thursday for the full text]. In a small family setting, perhaps the Father could wash the feet of the whole family; or members could take turns.)

The First Blessing Of Wine

Leader: To share wine together was a sign of friendship and caring. Those who passed the cup around knew that in some way they were bound by the wine, united in a deep way.

Father: Let us drink together in honor of the Holy One, blessed Be His name. *(He pours either into separate glasses, or into one which is circulated.)*

Father: Blessed are You, O Lord our God, King of the universe, who have created the fruit of the vine.

All: All glory be to You, O King, for giving us life and strength and for bringing us to this happy feast. *(Everyone should drink the wine.)*

Blessing Of The Bread

Father: This is the bread of affliction which our ancestors ate in the land of Egypt. It is the bread which sustained them in the wilderness. It is the bread which Jesus gives his people today to sustain them on the journey. It is our life.

All: Blessed are You, O Lord our God, King of the universe, who have brought forth bread from the earth.

Leader: This bread that we are breaking and eating unites us in friendship. During the Last Supper, it was at this point that Jesus gave the apostles his body to eat. The blessing that he said we have just pronounced. "Do this in remembrance of me," he said. "And know that whenever you do it, you proclaim my death until I come again."

The Questions

Leader: In the account of the first Passover, the Lord commands parents to explain to their children the meaning of the feast.

Child: Why is this night different from all other nights? Why do we eat unleavened bread only tonight?

Mother: Once we were slaves in the land of Egypt. The Pharaoh was cruel to us and oppressed us for many years. Then the Lord our God took pity on us, and in the dead of night, he struck down the Egyptians and led us out to freedom. That is why this night is different; for on this night every year we celebrate the deliverance our God wrought for us.

Father: We eat unleavened bread tonight to remind us of the haste with which we left Egypt. So quickly did we go that there was not enough time for the dough to rise.

Child: Every other night we eat all kinds of vegetables. Why tonight do we eat bitter tasting ones only?

Father: The bitter herbs remind us of the bitterness of life in Egypt when we were slaves, before the Lord freed us from the yoke and brought us into the Promised Land.

Child: Why do we dip our food into the salt water?

Mother: The salt water is the tears we cried in the land of Egypt. For our captors had made life a misery for us. We cried until our tears became a flood of water. Then the Lord heard the sound of our weeping and sent his servant Moses to set us free. *(Everyone takes a piece of bitter herb and dips it in the salt water and eats it.)*

Child: What is the meaning of the haroses?

Father: When we were slaves in Egypt we toiled all day in the blazing sun making bricks. The haroses reminds us of the mortar we used to cement the bricks together.

(Each should scoop some of the haroses between two pieces of unleavened bread and eat it.)

Child: What is the meaning of the lamb?

Father: The lamb is the creature whose blood was put upon the lintel and doorposts of our houses, so that the angel of the Lord would pass over us and spare our first born.

Mother: The lamb is also a symbol of Jesus, who shed his blood on the cross so that we would be redeemed.

The Hallel

Leader: Let us give thanks to the Lord our God who has set us free from all our enemies and has brought us into the kingdom of His Son.

All: Blessed are You, O Lord our God, King of the universe, who have saved us from evil and set our feet on the right way.

Leader: *(Psalm 114)* When Israel went out of Egypt, the house of Jacob from a people of foreign tongue,

All: Judah became their sanctuary; Israel their new land.

Leader: The sea beheld and fled, the Jordan River turned back.

All: The mountains skipped like rams; the hills, like the lambs of the flock.

Child: Sea, why do you run away? Jordan, why stop flowing?

Leader: Why skip like rams, you mountains? why lambs, you hills?

All: Because of the coming of the Lord, the coming of the God of Jacob, who turns rocks into pools and flint into fountains. Hallelujah!

The Meal

(At this point the rest of the meal is served and the company enjoys the food and the fellowship.)

The Thanksgiving

(The wine glasses should be filled once more for the final thanksgiving. Everyone should stand, if possible.)

Leader: It was after the meal that Jesus gave the cup of the new covenant in his blood to the apostles. "Take this, all of you, and drink it," he said. "As often as you do this, do it in remembrance of me."

(If at all possible, a cantor or musician should lead everyone in a musical setting of Psalm 116. Perhaps the best known is "For You Are My God" [John Foley, SJ, NALR]. Another alternative is the familiar doxology, "Praise God From Whom All Blessings Flow.")

Father: Blessed are You, O Lord our God, King of the universe, who have created the fruit of the vine.

(All drink the wine.)

Leader: It was after they had sung the psalm and shared the cup that Jesus and his disciples left the upper room for the garden named Gethsemane. It was there that Jesus knew he must drink another cup...

(The service may end at this point, or with the Lord's Prayer. If musicians are available, a hymn may be sung.)

Renewal Of Commitment Service

by John P. Mossi

The feast of Holy Thursday is a special celebration of unity in the Church year. It is a time when bishop, assistant priests and laity realize their interdependence in Christ and his call to serve.

There are two distinct liturgies on Holy Thursday. In the morning, the Chrism Mass is celebrated at the cathedral. Here the bishop, with as many of the priests of the diocese as possible, blesses the chrism, the oil of the catechumenate and the oil for the sick. The blessed oils become a symbol of the pastoral concern of the Church for the spiritual welfare of its flock. At the end of this Mass, the oils are distributed to the priests in order that they may be taken to the respective parishes of the diocese. The second liturgy of Holy Thursday is the Evening Mass of the Lord's Supper.

A Call To Renewal

During the homily of the Chrism Mass, the bishop invites his priests to renew publicly their priestly promises. This particular ceremony is always moving to experience. The chief shepherd calls upon his assistants to sacrifice their personal ambition for the sake of the people of God. He then asks them to renew their promises to be faithful ministers of the Word and sacraments. The interrogation concludes with the bishop asking the faithful to pray for their priests and for himself.

Adaptation

The Chrism Mass, an important expression of diocesan unity, possesses a few inherent disadvantages. It is celebrated in an already too hectic liturgical period of Holy Week. Because of the morning time and designated cathedral setting, it is inconvenient for the majority of priests and working people to attend. These problems are only magnified in dioceses which cover large geographical areas. Consequently, the significance of the blessing of the oils and the renewal of commitment receive reduced emphasis.

As a means of overcoming some of these problems, some dioceses have moved the Chrism Mass to an evening time on an earlier day of Holy Week. Other dioceses have encouraged the renewal of commitment ceremony be celebrated at the Evening Mass of the Lord's Supper.

The following is an outline for a possible ceremony of commitment renewal designed for local parish use. Its place in the liturgy is either after the homily or the washing of the feet. The last section of this renewal service incorporates some brief intercessory prayers.

The person chosen as commentator should be a recognized leader of the parish, coming from a service group, or an active member of the board of trustees or parish council. The commentator addresses the priest(s) in these or similar words:

The Renewal Service

Commentator: The priests of _____ parish will now renew their commitment as ministers in the service of the Church. Fathers, please stand.

Today we celebrate the memory of the First Eucharist, at which our Lord Jesus Christ shared with his apostles and with us his call to the priestly service of his Church. Now, in the presence of the people of_____ parish are you ready to renew your own dedication to Christ as priests of his new covenant?

Priests: I am.

Commentator: At your ordination you accepted the responsibilities of the priesthood out of love for the Lord Jesus and his Church. Are you resolved to unite yourselves more closely to Christ and to try to become more like him by joyfully sacrificing your own pleasure and ambition to bring his peace and love to your brothers and sisters?

Priests: I am.

Commentator: Are you resolved to be faithful ministers of the mysteries of God, to celebrate the Eucharist and the other liturgical services with sincere devotion? Are you resolved to imitate Jesus Christ, the head and shepherd of the Church, by teaching the Christian faith without thinking of your own profit, solely for the well-being of the people you were sent to serve?

Priests: I am.

Commentator: Dear people, pray for your priests. Ask the Lord to bless them with the fullness of his love, to help them be faithful ministers of Christ the High Priest, so that they will be able to lead you to him, the fountain of your salvation. For this, we pray to the Lord.

People: Lord, hear our prayer.

Commentator: Members of the following parish groups, please stand. Parish Council, Parish Board of Trustees, Liturgy Commission, Music ministers, Altar Society, Ushers, Lectors, Ministers of Communion at Mass, Ministers of Communion to the Sick and Elderly, Altar Servers, etc., *(other parish service groups are added here)*.

To you is entrusted the Christian care of the parish, the proper liturgical celebration of the actions of the Mass and sacraments, and the maintenance of the church and buildings. In imitation of Christ our Servant, are you resolved to fulfill your special tasks in a spirit of love, selflessness, and devotion?

People: I am.

Commentator: Dear people, let us pray for these our servants that they may worthily exercise their ministry. For this, we pray to the Lord.

People: Lord, hear our prayer.

Commentator: Will the members of the following parish groups please stand._____Community of Sisters, _____ School faculty, School or Religion Teachers, Parent Teachers Guild.

To you are entrusted our children, their proper instruction in the Faith and love for the Church. In imitation of Christ our teacher and servant, are you resolved to fulfill your ministry of education in a spirit of love, selflessness, and devotion?

People: I am.

Commentator: Dear people, let us pray for our children, for our parish school and school of religion, for our Sisters and teachers, and all those involved in the communication of the Faith. May this Holy Faith be transmitted in a spirit of loyalty to Christ and his Church and taught with love, selflessness, and devotion. For this, we pray to the Lord.

People: Lord, hear our prayer.

Commentator: Parishioners of_____, please stand.

In Baptism, you were incorporated into the priesthood of Christ. Are you resolved to bind yourself more closely to Christ and his Word?

People: I am.

Commentator: The Eucharist is our food from heaven. Are you resolved to live your life in imitation of the holiness of this bread?

People: I am.

Commentator: The response to our petitions will be "Lord, hear our prayer."

That all Christians may learn the joy of serving one another, we pray to the Lord.

For our Jewish brothers and sisters, who on this day begin their venerable Passover celebration, we pray to the Lord.

For those returning to the sacraments during this holy season, may they experience the consolation of the Father, we pray to the Lord.

For our own private intentions, let us now pause *(pause 15 seconds)*. For these intentions, we pray to the Lord.

Heavenly Father, hear our prayers and answer our needs. We ask this through Christ Our Lord.

People: Amen.

**Part III
Good
Friday**

Sprung From Disaster

by Michael E. Moynahan, SJ

Sprung from disaster
the result of much strife.
Confounding all reason
death produces life.

Perennial confusion
blinds weary eyes
as from burnt ashes
a Phoenix will rise.

A problem perplexing,
a mystery profound:
dead seed's new borning—
life underground.

Irony unparallelled,
a paradox encored:
in sharing bread and wine—
Christ proclaimed Lord!

The Good Friday Passion Narrative

by C. Gibson, C. Finney, J. Klein, and M. Marchal

Preface

The readers' parts are designated as 1, 2, and 3; the parts for the community are marked by XX. The community does *not* have the complete text, but simply a sheet containing their words. They are given sight and text cues for speaking. Reader 1, who has the role of Christ, moves but ideally is never seen. Readers 2 and 3 divide between them the other roles and the narrative. Reader 2 moves and is always visible. Reader 3, who is responsible for the cues, remains at the lectern. No sexual identity was presupposed in the roles given to any reader.

A six-foot high, rough-hewn Cross with no corpus stands at the most prominent place in the sanctuary. The reason for the absence of the corpus and the invisibility of Reader 1 is two-fold: first, as a stimulus to the imagination of the community more powerful than any plastic representation; and second, as a preparation for their own veneration in which they put themselves upon the Cross.

Introduction

After the Epistle reading, the three readers come from their seats, stand before the Cross, and bow. Reader 1 then moves to the rear of the church at stage right; Reader 2 moves outside the sanctuary at far stage left; Reader 3 moves to the lectern at stage right. The congregation remains seated. Since our liturgy was in the evening, all the lights except those in the sanctuary were extinguished, Reader 1 using a pencil flashlight to read by.

THE HOLY WEEK BOOK

The Text

3: The Passion of Our Lord Jesus Christ according to John.

2: At that time Jesus went out with his disciples across the Cedron Valley. There was a garden there, and he and his disciples went into it. This place was also familiar to Judas (the one who was to hand him over), for Jesus had often met there with his disciples. Judas took a cohort of soldiers, together with the police supplied by the Chief Priests and Pharisees, and they came there with lanterns, torches and weapons. Jesus, knowing all that was to happen to him, went out and said to them...

1: Whom do you want?

3: They replied...(saying)

XX: Jesus, the Nazorean!

1: I am he.

3: As he said to them "I am he," they stepped back and fell to the ground. So he asked them again.

1: Whom do you want?

3: They repeated themselves...(saying)

XX: Jesus, the Nazorean!

1: I have told you that I am he; and if I am the one you want, let these other men go.

3: This was to fulfill what he had said: "I have not lost even one of those whom you have given me."

2: Then Simon Peter, who had a sword, drew it and struck the slave of the High Priest, severing his right ear. At that Jesus told Peter:

1: Return your sword to its scabbard. Am I not to drink the cup the Father has given me?

2: So the cohort, their tribune, and the Jewish police arrested Jesus and bound him. They led him first to Annas, for he was the father-in-law of Caiaphas, who was High Priest that year. (Remember, it was Caiaphas who had advised the Jews that it was more advantageous to have one man die for the people.)

Now Simon Peter was following Jesus along with another disciple. This disciple, who was known to the High Priest, accompanied Jesus into the High Priest's courtyard, while Peter was left standing outside at the gate. The first disciple came out and spoke to the woman at the gate and brought Peter in. This servant girl who kept the gate said to Peter:

3: Aren't you also one of this man's disciples?

2: No, I am not.

3: Since it was cold, the servants and police who were standing around had made a fire and were warming themselves; so Peter, too, stood with them and warmed himself. At this time the High Priest was questioning Jesus about his disciples and his teaching. Jesus answered him:

1: I have always spoken publicly to all the world. I have always taught in a synagogue or in the temple precincts where all the Jews come together. There was nothing secret about what I said. Why do you question me? Question instead those who heard me when I spoke. Obviously, they should know what I said.

3: At this reply, one of the nearby policemen slapped Jesus across the face.

2: Is that any way to answer the High Priest?

1: If I've said anything wrong, produce some evidence of it. But if I was right, why do you hit me?

3: Then Annas sent him bound to Caiaphas. In the meantime, Simon Peter had been standing there with the others, warming himself. And again they spoke to him...(saying)

XX: Aren't you too one of his disciples?

2: No. I am not!

3: One of the High Priest's slaves, a relative of the man whose ear Peter had severed, insisted: "Didn't I see you with him in the garden?"

2: NO!

3: And just then a cock began to crow.

Interlude 1: (*A musician at stage right immediately begins a soft, death-march beat on a bass drum. He continues while Reader 1 moves to the exact center of the rear of the church. Reader 2 moves into the sanctuary and stands slightly stage left facing directly towards the community and Reader 1 in the rear. The drumming stops.*)

3: At daybreak, they brought Jesus from Caiaphas to the Praetorium. They did not enter the Praetorium themselves, for they had to avoid ritual impurity so that they could partake of the Passover supper. Pilate came out to them.

2: What accusation do you make against this man?

3: They replied...(saying)

XX: If this fellow were not a criminal, we certainly would not have handed him over to you.

2: Take him yourselves and pass judgement on him according to your own law.

3: The Jews answered him...(saying)

XX: We are not permitted to put anyone to death.

3: (This was to fulfill what Jesus had said, indicating the sort of death he was to die.) Pilate went back into the Praetorium and summoned Jesus.

2: Are you the King of the Jews?

1: Are you saying this on your own, or have others been telling you about me?

2: I am no Jew, am I? It is your own nation and the chief priests who handed you over to me. What have you done?

1: My kingdom does not belong to this world. If my kingdom belonged to this world, my subjects would be fighting to save me from being handed over to the Jews. But, as it is, my kingdom does not belong here.

2: So then, you are a king?

1: You say that I am a king. The reason why I have been born, the reason I have come into this world, is to testify to the truth. Everyone who belongs to the truth listens to my voice.

2: Truth? What does that mean?

3: After that comment, Pilate again went out to the Jews.

2: For my part, I do not find a case against this man. Remember, you have a custom that I release some prisoner for you at Passover. Do you want me, then, to release the King of the Jews?

3: At this, they shouted back...(saying)

XX: No! We want Barabbas, not this man!

3: Barabbas was a bandit, a thief and a murderer. Since the crowd continued shouting "Barabbas! We want Barabbas!" Pilate finally had Jesus taken to be flogged. The soldiers fashioned a crude crown out of thorns and fixed it on his head. Then they threw a purple cape around his shoulders. Time again they slapped his face and mocked him...(saying)

XX: All hail, King of the Jews!

3: Once more Pilate went out to them.

2: Now, I am going to bring him out to you to make you realize that I find no case against him.

3: Jesus came out then, wearing the crown of thorns and the purple cloak.

2: Look at the man.

3: As soon as the Chief Priests and the temple police saw him, they yelled all the louder...(saying)

XX: Crucify him! Crucify him!

2: You crucify him. I find him not guilty.

3: The Jews answered him...(saying)

XX: We have our own law, and according to that law, he has to die because he made himself God's son.

3: When Pilate heard this, he was more frightened than ever. Going back into the Praetorium, he asked Jesus:

2: Where do you come from?

3: But Jesus would not give him an answer.

2: You refuse to talk to me. Don't you realize that I have the power to release you and the power to crucify you?

1: You would have no power over me at all if it weren't given to you from above. For that reason, those who brought me to you are guilty of the greater sin.

3: After hearing this, Pilate was eager to release him, but the Jews argued with him...(saying)

XX: If you free this man you are no friend of Caesar's. Any man who declares himself a king becomes the Emperor's rival.

THE HOLY WEEK BOOK

3: Once he heard what they were saying, Pilate brought Jesus out to them. He then sat down on a judge's bench. It was the Preparation Day for Passover, and the hour was about noon.

2: Look! Here is your king!

3: At this, the crowd cried out...(saying)

XX: Away with him! Away with him! Crucify him!

2: What! Crucify your king?

3: The Chief Priests interrupted...(saying)

XX: We have no king but Caesar!

3: Then, at last, Pilate handed Jesus over to them to be crucified.

Interlude 2: *(The drumming begins again. Reader 1 moves stage left but remains in the rear. Reader 2 moves somewhat stage right and also stands relatively near the Cross. The drumming does not cease during the resumed reading: instead, it increases in tempo until its peak at "It is finished!" when it abruptly stops.)*

3: So they had him at last, and he was taken out of the city, carrying his cross to what is called the 'Skull-Place,' Golgotha. There they crucified Jesus, and with him two others, one on either side and Jesus between them. Pilate had an inscription placed on the cross above him. Written upon it were these words: "Jesus the Nazorean, the King of the Jews." This inscription, in Hebrew, Latin, and Greek, was read by many of the Jews. The chief priests protested to Pilate: "Change it from 'The King of the Jews' to 'He claimed, "I am King of the Jews."'"

2: What I have written, I have written.

3: When the soldiers had crucified Jesus, they took his garments and separated them into four parts, one for each soldier. There was also his tunic; but this tunic was woven in one piece from top to bottom and had no seam. They discussed this, trying to decide what to do. Finally, one said "We shouldn't tear it; let's toss dice to see who gets it." This, then, was what they did, thereby fulfilling the Scripture passage... "They divided up my garments among them, and they rolled dice for my clothing."

2: Near the cross of Jesus stood his mother, Mary, his aunt, the wife of Clopas, and Mary Magdalene. Seeing his mother there with the disciple whom he loved, Jesus said to his mother:

1: Woman, there is your son.

2: In turn he said to the disciple:

1: There is your mother.

3: From that hour on, the disciple took her into his care. After that, Jesus was aware that all was now finished. So to fulfill the Scripture he said:

1: I am thirsty!

2: There was a jar of cheap wine nearby. A sponge was soaked in it, placed on a hyssop branch and raised to his lips. When Jesus had tasted the wine, he said:

1: *It is finished!*

3: ...and bowing his head, he handed over his spirit.

Interlude 3:

(Silence. No one moves. Then the organist begins a light atonal figure on the organ as the background for the concluding narration.)

2: The Jewish leaders did not want the bodies left on the crosses during the Sabbath Day, for that Sabbath was a solemn feast day. So they asked Pilate to have the legs broken and the bodies taken down. Accordingly, the soldiers came and broke the legs of the men crucified with Jesus. But when they came to Jesus and saw that he was already dead, they did not break his legs. However, one of the soldiers jabbed his side with a lance and blood and water flowed out. This testimony was given by an eyewitness. He tells what he knows is true, in order that you may believe. These events fulfilled the Scripture passage, "None of his bones are to be broken"; and still another Scripture passage which says, "They shall look on him whom they have pierced."

When it was growing dark, a wealthy man from Arimathaea, named Joseph, who was a secret disciple of Jesus, went to Pilate requesting permission to take the body of Jesus for burial. With Nicodemus, another disciple, he anointed the body of Jesus with spices and wrapped it in linen cloth, as is the Jewish custom of burial. Not far from the place of crucifixion was a new tomb carved out of rock, where no one had ever been buried. Because of the Jewish Preparation Day, they buried Jesus there, for the tomb was close at hand.

Conclusion:

(After the reading is finished, the readers return to the sanctuary, stand again before the Cross, bow, and return to their seats. The homily is given, and everyone venerates the Cross.)

Celebrating The Glory Of The Cross

by Ed Hurlbutt, SJ

The Good Friday liturgy, like all the Holy Week liturgies, is immensely rich in possibilities for celebration. Unlike celebrations of other aspects of the Paschal Mystery, however, the Good Friday liturgy is peculiarly susceptible to a misrepresentation of its meaning, to a misinterpretation of its symbols, and to a misuse of its possibilities that can render the liturgy anything but a celebration of God's saving love.

When we see only the suffering and death of Good Friday, we fail to celebrate the Lord's death in terms of the whole triumphant Paschal Mystery. To consider how a myopic view of suffering can misrepresent Good Friday, one need only think back to the days of the *3 hour* liturgies that were used to "celebrate" Good Friday. Black copes, constant kneeling, fasting, fatigue, and an agonizingly slow unveiling of the cross all evoked anything but Christian joy. Even the original focus — that we should be with Christ in the three hours of his suffering — became not a joining of Christ on his cross, but a punishment for the death we had inflicted on our God. The liturgy became an exercise in producing horror, shame, and ultimately tremendous guilt.

In the face of all this guilt however, St. Paul tells us that we must *glory* in the cross of our Lord Jesus Christ. Instead of viewing the cross as a defeat, we must view it as a triumph. We are Christian people living in the power of the resurrection and we must celebrate Christ's death accordingly. Our Good Friday liturgies must become not a mourning but a celebration of the Lord's death. Or more specifically, our liturgies must become a celebration of the meaning of that death. And that meaning can only be found in the *whole* Paschal Mystery: We remember the death but celebrate the victory.

What, then, is the meaning of the cross that the Christian community glorifies on Good Friday? Among innumerable possibilities the following four viewpoints provide sound bases for liturgical celebration.

Our Salvation in Christ. The fact of our salvation through the cross is good cause for Christian celebration. As St. Paul tells us, God was pleased to reconcile everything in Christ, both in heaven and on earth, "making peace through the blood of his cross". This viewpoint is nearest the traditional explanation of Good Friday, but an important distinction must be made. The peace of the cross is not peace by paying the price of sin (as the cross is so often misinterpreted), but peace by providing the grounds — the sacrifice of union — where God and man can meet.

The Sanctification of our Humanity. Through his incarnation Christ lived, touched and made holy every aspect of our human existence. On Good Friday we celebrate the wondrous way in which Christ has touched, and thus sanctified and given meaning to our death. By his cross, Christ brings light to our darkest

moment; he brings his own life to the very experience that most denies our lives.

The Compassion of the Lord. Through his death Christ lovingly invites us to join him in his saving act, to pick up our crosses and follow him. And so on Good Friday we celebrate the love of God, a love so great it allows us, even urges us to be co-workers in his great act of love — our own salvation.

Christ's Victory. As Christians, we know that Christ's whole life was a triumph of light over darkness, and on Good Friday we celebrate the final crowning of that triumph. Christ's triumph comes in his very dying because he acts in loving obedience to his Father's will. His death is the glorious completion of his work on earth.

These are but four aspects of the real meaning of the cross and thus the real cause of our Good Friday celebration. If our liturgies are to be Christian celebrations, they must celebrate salvation, peace, compassion, love, and triumph; Good Friday must be a celebration of life that calls forth great joy and gratitude from God's people. Moreover, once we have determined that the reason we celebrate is life and love, then we can also focus on the suffering, confusion, and shame that so envelop the cross. For these painful experiences are part of our human existence, and if the cross is to have meaning for us, it must touch the darkness of our lives, too. But it must touch the darkness with light, the suffering with joy, the shame with triumph.

In short, as the Christian community celebrating the death of Christ, we must touch the incredible mystery that our greatest shame is our greatest glory, that our final despair is actually our final triumph. Indeed, the sense of confusion that may (hopefully *should*) result from this juxtaposition of such diametric opposites is the best experiential means of placing Good Friday in the context of Holy Week. Like an unresolved chord, it is beautiful in itself, but it demands resolution. Good Friday demands Easter.

To express it in another way, Friday is Christ's real triumph, and Easter is our liturgical means of expressing the results of that triumph: ours is, to be sure, an Easter faith. But true faith demands that we experience Good Friday as Christ's victory.

True faith demands that we glory in the cross of Our Lord Jesus Christ.

Planning the Good Friday Liturgy

To decide that the Good Friday liturgy must celebrate the glory of the cross is only the first step towards a meaningful liturgy. The liturgy must also be carefully planned, rehearsed wherever necessary, and celebrated by ministers and assistants who have a full understanding of its meaning. The following suggestions are designed to aid in the incarnating of a Good Friday liturgy that truly celebrates the glory of the cross.

Celebrating a living event. Before any planning can begin, the planners must bring to mind the fact that we celebrate a living event on Good Friday. The Paschal Mystery is not just something that happened to Jesus some 2,000 years ago; it is a mystery that we live with Christ today. If our focus is only on specific crucifixion twenty centuries ago, we will end up planning memorial ceremonies for the dead, instead of Christian celebrations for the living.

Simplicity does not mean that music, incense, mime, dramatization, slides and the bring to mind the fact that we celebrate a living event on Good Friday. The Paschal Mystery is not just something that happened to Jesus some 2,000 years ago; it is a mystery that we live with Christ today. If our focus is only on specific crucifixion twenty centuries ago, we will end up planning memorial ceremonies for the dead, instead of Christian celebrations for the living.

Choosing a theme. The Good Friday liturgy is so rich in celebratory possibilities that the first essential task in planning the liturgy is to select a theme; that is, to select that aspect of the cross' meaning that the community will celebrate. Once established, the theme unites the various parts of the liturgy — the readings, the intercessory prayers, the adoration of the cross, the communion service, and the sign of hope — into a meaningful whole. It also provides a standard for judging the bewildering array of liturgical possibilities: does this song, or that reading, or this prayer fit into the perspective we are using to celebrate the cross? And most importantly, the use of a central Christian theme is a constant reminder that what we celebrate is life and love, not death.

Simplicity. More than any other liturgical celebration, the Good Friday liturgy both *demands* and *benefits from* profound simplicity. First, the nature of the event we commemorate is so powerful, so potentially overwhelming that our approach to it should be solemn and simple, a fitting reminder of our total poverty in the face of such tremendous love. Second, an unbridled attempt to capitalize on all the potential meanings of the cross can cause confusion and ultimately dissipate the power of the liturgy; a simple, direct focus on a single theme, however, can so powerfully involve the community that all the fullness of meaning, while not expressly stated, is still felt. Third, simplicity encourages congregation participation in a liturgy that can be confusingly unfamiliar because it comes only once a year.

Simplicity does not mean that music, incense, mime, dramatization, slides and the full range of liturgical aids must be eliminated. On the contrary, it means that they must be used with more care than ever. Moreover, the whole purpose of liturgical simplicity on Good Friday should be to free us: to free us from attempts to do the impossible, and to free us to do a few things surpassingly well.

Starkness. The counterpart of liturgical simplicity on this day is liturgical starkness. Christianity abounds in stark paradoxes — life through death, love in the face of hate — and nowhere are these paradoxes more powerfully portrayed than in the cross. Indeed, the very idea of remembering a death with a celebration of life seems an irreconcilable conflict. And so Good Friday becomes our best opportunity to express and experience those paradoxes. A liturgy that truthfully presents the stark contrasts between good and evil, light and dark, and triumph and tragedy that so fill the cross can become a tremendously powerful experience in the meaning of a Christian life.

Once the theme has been selected and the commitment made to simplicity and starkness in the liturgy, then planning can begin on the specific parts of the liturgy.

Liturgy of the Word. The liturgy of the word is both a calling to mind of the first, individual Paschal Mystery (Christ's own dying and rising) and a proclamation that the same Paschal Mystery still transforms the world today. Because it recalls the death of Christ and proclaims the present power of his resurrection the liturgy of the word provides the best opportunity for the celebrant to present the particular meaning of the cross that the community will celebrate that day. The official Liturgy of the Word is quite long, and in spite of its dramatic content can become stiflingly boring, so that steps must be taken to make its proclamation effective. The Passion, of course, should always be proclaimed, but one or both of the other readings can sometimes be profitably changed or eliminated. And all the readings, including the Passion, can gain greatly in effectiveness by the use of mime, dramatization, music, and slides.

Prayers of the Faithful. The general intercessory prayers are the first part of our response to the cross. These prayers indicate how we come to the cross: as humble sinners, impoverished in the face of such love, and unable to fulfill our deepest needs and desires. In these prayers we ask the Father to remember us in the moment of his Son's triumph. In many places, then, the usual general intercessory prayers are being replaced with prayers that focus on such current realities as war, racism, starvation, and damaged natural resources. As part of our response to the Liturgy of the Word these prayers gain greatly in effectiveness if one or more of them specifically responds to the theme presented in the word liturgy. The prayers can also benefit from the use of such aids as slides, enlarged photos, and music.

Veneration of the Cross. The veneration of the cross is the climax of our response to the Passion. We behold Christ in his great act of love and we respond with loving veneration. For Christians, however, veneration does not mean slavish bowing to some idol; it means loving service. And so the veneration of the cross means service to the cross: it means taking up one's cross and following Christ crucified. The method of veneration used on Good Friday, then, should emphasize the taking up of one's own cross. For these reasons, the traditional kissing of the cross seems of doubtful symbolic value because it connotes slavish bowing more than it symbolizes the taking up of one's cross with Christ. Other methods — actually holding aloft a good sized cross; or coming to the altar, turning to face the entire community and deliberately making the sign of the cross; or actually putting on a small cross attached to a piece of yarn or string — can bring a richer Christian meaning to the veneration of the cross.

Communion Service. The focus of the entire liturgy is on the meaning of the cross, a meaning which comes to immediate and real existence in the communion service: in the breaking of the bread and the sharing of the Eucharistic meal. By the time the liturgy reaches the communion service, the breaking and sharing should have such enormous signficance by themselves that any more words, music, or slides can easily become distractions rather than aids. The communion service, then, should almost always be kept very simple. The Our Father and a simple Fraction Rite should be sufficient. During the distribution of communion appropriate songs can be sung. On this day more than any other day of the year, an attempt should be made to use real bread for the entire congregation. The breaking of a whole loaf of bread so that the Christian community can be nourished is central to the meaning of the cross, and a Fraction Rite that includes the actual breaking of bread is an enormously powerful symbol of that meaning.

Sign of Hope. As the Good Friday liturgy commemorates the death of our Lord, it should come to an end with a sense of completion, a real sense of the death of Jesus. This feeling can be achieved in a variety of ways: by a signficant period of post-communion silence, for example, or by a post-communion slide meditation on the deposition from the cross.

In any event, this sense of completion should always end on a note of hope: a sign that even though we have celebrated the death of the Lord, as Christians we live in joyful hope of the resurrection. The sign of hope can be a song, a candle left burning in front of the cross, a silent exchange of the greeting of peace, or any number of Christian symbols of life.

Rhythm of the Liturgy. In planning the liturgy, it is good to bear in mind the power of the events we celebrate on Good Friday: a celebration of the passion of Christ, of man's reconciliation with God, and of our own dying and rising. The meaning of these events can be so moving that it is essential to build a sense of rhythm into the liturgy; that is, the congregation must be given time to rest. If, for example, a particularly

powerful word liturgy and cross adoration are planned, the intercessory prayers that come between them should be much more relaxed, much quieter. A constant demand for a high level of emotional involvement will simply force people to tune out the liturgy.

This sense of rhythm can also be applied to the means used to celebrate the liturgy. It can be most effective to alternate verbal and nonverbal sections, music and silence, or light and dark. For example, a silent, kneeling adoration of the cross can be effective when it comes between a highly verbal word liturgy and the highly verbal intercessory prayers.

Music. Like all the aspects of the Good Friday liturgy, the music benefits from simplicity. With voices, for example, a solo voice, *a cappella* choirs, and community repetition of a simple refrain can be very effective. The number of instruments used at any one time should be kept to a minimum, with solo instruments like a harmonica, a guitar, a muffled trumpet, and a piano being particularly effective. In general the organ is too rich and too powerful an instrument to be an appropriate expression of Good Friday simplicity.

Congregation Participation. Because the liturgy can be unfamiliar, the readings can be so long, and activities like the cross adoration and reception of communion can leave long unfilled periods of time, it is essential that methods be found to actively involve the congregation in the celebration. During the proclamation of the passion, for example, individuals seated in the congregation can be assigned certain lines, or the entire congregation can be assigned certain lines to read. During the intercessory prayers, time can be provided for members of the congregation to express their own particular concerns.

The veneration of the cross provides the best opportunity to actively involve the congregation. Both the veneration and the reception of communion provide excellent opportunities for the congregation to sing a simple refrain in response to verses sung by a choir or solo voice. The songs should effectively communicate the meaning of what is happening so that they bring a sense of community participation, and do not become meaningless fillers.

Actual physical activity can be an effective means of involving the congregation. In addition, the various positions of the people during the liturgy — standing, kneeling, sitting — should not be haphazardly assigned, but carefully planned to enhance the liturgy's meaning.

Practice. While the practice of songs or group responses is appropriate before many liturgies, on this day such practice should be kept to a minimum and eliminated where possible. The nature of the occasion — solemn, simple, and stark — is more appropriately set before the liturgy begins. And during the liturgy itself, the congregation should not be distracted from direct participation by worry over its next response or the words to an unfamiliar song. The need for minimal practice again reinforces the need for simplicity in the ceremony.

The Cross. Some churches have a large crucifix that can serve as the focal point for the Good Friday liturgy. Where there is no such crucifix, however, or where it is placed (either off to the side or high on the back wall) so that it is impossible to see both the cross and the celebrant at the same time, the construction of a large cross can significantly enhance the liturgy. It can be constructed beforehand, or put together during the reading of the passion, and should be placed directly in front of the altar. A strong spotlight can greatly increase its effect.

Time. While the Roman Missal suggests an afternoon hour for the Good Friday liturgy, it also allows a later time for pastoral reasons. For our society an evening hour seems a better time for the liturgy. A time of 8:00 p.m. gives people an opportunity to relax after work and eat dinner so that they can fully participate in the liturgy.

In addition to this prime advantage, a night time liturgy gives the planners a more complete control over the liturgical environment through the effective use of lighting. Mimes and dramatizations can benefit from the use of good lighting effects. The symbolic importance of the cross is also powerfully emphasized when all light seems to emanate from it. This effect can easily be achieved when the area around the cross is fully illuminated and the rest of the church is as dark as safety and community participation will allow.

The Song Of Good Friday

by Eileen E. Freeman

Friday of the Passion and Death of our Lord Jesus Christ is one of the most dramatic liturgical events of the Church Year. It is a solemn celebration, stark and plain. It has none of the warmth of Holy Thursday, none of the splendor of the Vigil. It is as though Good Friday were a wire stretched taut, almost to the breaking point between Holy Thursday and the empty tomb.

People who enter the church on Good Friday have a strange look on their faces. They are forcibly confronted with darkness and the effects of sin in the world. The church is bare, the altar stripped, the tabernacle empty. Worshippers find pews quickly, wondering uncertainly whether or not to genuflect. Good friends hardly take notice of each other, passing by with bowed head, as though in a world of their own. It is as though each person had withdrawn into his or her inner self. Everybody seems to be occupied with private devotions recalling the sufferings of Christ on the cross.

This tendency of people to turn deeply inwards on Good Friday is not surprising. It is hard for any Christian to contemplate the Passion of Christ without asking "What does it mean for me?." We are not so inured to violence in our lives that we can ignore that done to Christ (but how ironic that we can weep for a now glorified Christ and ignore those all around us who still suffer!).

When it comes time to celebrate the Good Friday service, this tendency to focus on "me and Jesus on Calvary" is unfortunately often over-emphasized, especially in the music used for the service. If the actual service is examined, it is clear that it does not focus on vividly recalling the sufferings of Christ at all. Rather, what is emphasized is the communal nature of our redemption in Jesus. Christ's death is proclaimed, not with wild joy, but with solemn thankfulness, communal thankfulness. The emphasis is not on, "Thank you, Jesus, for saving me," but, "Thank you, Father, for saving us."

The Intercessions emphasize even more the communal nature of redemption, for they extend the saving action of Jesus to all people, both Christians and non-Christians. And of course in the communion service, the Body of Christ shares a common Bread.

Good Friday is a day of peace, not agonized grief. The Lord has already been raised from the dead and sits at the Father's right hand. It is senseless to make the day a funeral service for Jesus — no human could be less in need of one! Naturally we are solemn and subdued; but as St. Paul says, "We are not like those who have no hope."

There are two approaches to the music of Good Friday which seem to work best. The first approach is the liturgically rich one, with choir, organ, cantor, etc.. The second approach is the very simple one, using only a cantor and an instrumentalist.

The first approach has certain advantages. It lends a note of pageantry and festivity to the Good Friday service. In recent years the use of musical instruments *ad libitum* on Good Friday has resulted in not only new compositions for the celebration, but also the added note of grandeur. However, when using this approach, it is important not to take away from the people their part in the service. If the choir does anthem after anthem, it will deaden the service and keep it from flowing smoothly. Choir directors should be careful to avoid the syrupy and sentimental type of hymn which causes the individual who sings it to turn inward, instead of outward towards the rest of the Christian community. The skilled organist will exercise restraint and skill in not choosing registrations which accentuate the sentimental, such as the heavy use of tremolo and vibrato seem to do; and will use instead registrations that are clean and crisp.

The simple approach is slightly harder to accomplish, because so much depends on the cantor, but it can work extremely well. Instead of a hymn during the solemn procession, the procession may be accompanied by a drum roll. A tenor drum with felted mallets played from the choir loft or sacristy works well. The cantor leads the psalm. If a guitarist is available, John Foley's setting of Psalm 16, "You are My God." (NAL) is ideal. It expresses the hope and trustful confidence of the suffering Christ in his Father. Also suitable are "To You I Lift Up My Soul," (NAL), "Blest Be The Lord," (NAL), and "I Will Sing," (NAL). The cantor also leads in the Gospel acclamation before the solemn Passion. Although there are many Lenten acclamations, one that this writer knows from experience is that of David Isele, from his "Notre Dame Mass" (GIA); it contains several verses especially appropriate and is easy to sing, while having a very interesting organ part.

THE HOLY WEEK BOOK

The solemn reading or singing of the Passion is an essential part of the Good Friday service. Although Gospels are not often sung anymore, the Passion Narrative is important enough to warrant its being chanted. Normally this requires three singers, and some preparation as well. GIA has a setting of the various Passion Narratives which uses the traditional chant. This is about the only one available commercially, and is adequate, although its phrasing is often quite awkward, with unimportant words receiving two or three notes. It does not take any longer to sing the Passion in the traditional or similar chant than it does to read it. During the chanting, slides may be projected, slides of the way of the cross, the Holy Land, a Passion Play, or artwork depicting the Passion. People should be invited to sit.

During the veneration of the cross, the Reproaches are traditionally sung. The Reproaches from the old liturgy can be used with great effectiveness. Two cantors can alternate singing the Latin from the *Liber Usualis*. There are four basic sets of Reproaches. The first, the "Popule meus," alternates verses with the Trisagion in Greek and Latin. The second set alternates the "Popule meus" verse with very short Reproaches set to a psalm tone. The third set, the "Crucem tuam," is the shortest and consists of a verse, "We adore your cross, Lord, and we celebrate your holy resurrection..." plus a psalm verse. The last set consists of the hymn "Pange Lingua" (the Passiontide Pange, not the one used at Eucharistic devotions). There is a more solemn tune for the "Pange Lingua" in the *Liber*, which ought to be tried, rather than the usual "Tantum Ergo" melody.

Recently, the use of the Reproaches has been questioned. In some circles they have been viewed as anti-Semitic. However, most Christians seem to internalize the verses, seeing themselves as the sinful and rebellious people, rather than impute Christ's crucifixion to the Jewish nation.

As with the choosing of any music, pastoral considerations are primary.

During communion, the cantor should lead a hymn and/or a responsorial piece such as Deiss' "Keep in Mind," (WLP). The same considerations in choosing hymns that apply to the choir apply also to the cantor. Hymns which turn people inwards to ignore the rest of their brothers and sisters should be avoided. If they have been used in the past in a particular church, it may be hard to break with tradition, but it is better in the long run to do so.

If "O Sacred Head" is sung, as it so often is, one should be aware that most of the translations of the original German are really quite hideous. They concentrate on blood and gore with a delight that would have pleased the Marquis de Sade. If such is the case with the version one has in a parish hymnal, do not hesitate to find other words and print them up as part of a Holy Week supplement, taking care to obtain copyright permission first, if the words are not in public domain.

The cantor's work ends after communion, since the ministers leave the sanctuary in silence. However, if the above principles have been followed, what will have happened will be that instead of being overwhelmed with richness and pageantry, people will be "underwhelmed" with subtlety. The judicious use of music will cover the bare skeleton which is the Good Friday service with just enough flesh to tie it together. We need a day when our celebration can be less lush, but not less rich than we hope our typical celebrations are. By emphasizing the psalm and other responses of the people, by letting the solemnity of a sung Passion touch people's hearts, we can open up a side of Good Friday that is so seldom seen; that of Jesus' hope and trust in the Father, even as He gave Himself up to that strange and terrible will.

Good Friday Symbolism And The Liturgy

by Eileen E. Freeman

For the past decade the Good Friday liturgy has been struggling to emerge from its centuries' old cocoon. Long cloaked in the purple and black of sorrow, the public worship of the Church is gradually yielding to an ancient tradition, long obscured.

Until recently the major problem inherent in the Good Friday liturgy was its sense of gloom and grief. The experience of Good Friday worship was not unlike that of attending a funeral and wake service. Some of the symbols of this liturgy were not unlike those found at the ordinary Requiem Mass. Black was the prevailing color for vesture, followed by purple. Instead of a pall-draped casket, the statues were draped. The absence of liturgical doxologies was also typical of both, and the absence of the blessing, too. Many people dressed in mourning on Good Friday, as though they had just lost a loved one.

This emphasis on symbols of death was not limited to the formal liturgy for Good Friday. Devotional services even further emphasized that the Church was in mourning. The recitation of the rosary, a common devotion for wakes, was also used on Good Friday, as well as the Stations of the Cross.

Even the social customs attendant among various ethnic groups seem to relate Good Friday to the funeral liturgy. In many places in Europe, for instance, children carry a small coffin from the church and bury it near a stream, to be unearthened on Easter Sunday. Such is the custom particularly in the Balkans, where homes are also draped in mourning crepe from Holy Thursday until after the Mass of the Resurrection.

Even for those of us who have no particular ethnic traditions, there remains the discipline of fasting on Good Friday. Psychologically and in terms of the history of religions, such fasting is an attempt on the part of the one who fasts to identify with the person who has died. Some cultures go even further; out of devotion people have themselves crucified or whipped or crowned with thorns.

Why have the symbols of Good Friday been so heavily laden with death motifs? The study of religions gives us some clues. Most of the agricultural societies prior to the coming of Christ believed that there was one chief god who ruled the world. But because he did not choose to involve himself too deeply in human affairs, he sent his son to watch over the earth. The son was the god of fertility and growth. Without his rain the crops would not grow. Unfortunately, every year the son was challenged to do battle with the god of the underworld, who brought drought on the earth. The myth goes on to tell how the god of drought fought with the high god's son and killed him, threatening the world's survival. However, the son is raised from the dead and puts down the underworld rebellion, thus saving the earth. During this period when the son was believed to have died, all the people were mourning; they fasted; and they lamented for the dead, with the same laments they used when humans died.

THE HOLY WEEK BOOK

Members of these communities believed that their rain god physically died and was raised again each year. When the first missionaries came to them with the Gospel, they had little trouble explaining Jesus to them, using many of the terms the people had always known. Jesus was, after all, the Son of God, and he did die and was raised. But as St. Paul tried to make clear to them, "...Christ, having died once, will never die again. Death has no dominion over him." In many cases, this message was lost on the new converts, who still kept traces of the yearly mourning for the dead weather god in their christianized worship.

We are far removed from the rain god of the ancients, but the cycle of the seasons still affect us. In half the world, Easter comes at the end of a cold winter, when the world of nature seems dead. In the other half, Easter comes at a time when the torrid and scorching summer is near. Something in us seems to need to die and be reborn with the seasons.

However, we must remind ourselves that Good Friday is not a funeral service for Jesus. It is a commemoration of a historical event that happened many centuries ago. It is also a celebration of a transcendant moment in human history and in the salvation history of each one of us. It is a celebration of our redemption. It is a time of thanksgiving and fervent hope.

Cognizant of this fact, the revised liturgy for Good Friday focuses on different symbols than in the past. Gone are the purple drapes which draped the statues and illogically, the very cross which the season honored. Vanished are the black and purple vesture which so vividly brought the funeral liturgy to mind. Gone are references to the killing of Christ and the cursing of the Jews. Instead of homilies, prayer and music that concentrated people's attention on their sins and the awful consequences, an attempt is being made to help people see even Good Friday as a time when we worship as a community, not just as isolated individuals.

The liturgy of Good Friday is almost totally devoid of the symbols we see during the year. The sheer absence of flowers, elaborate musical instruments, colors, incense, processions, and familiar ritual is itself a powerful symbol. This can be viewed as another attempt to identify with the "dead" Christ, or it can remind us that our faith in Christ's resurrection is not dependent on the physical images and symbols of belief. The empty tabernacle can allow us either to see that, as Mary Magdalene put it, "they have taken the Lord away," or that "He is no longer here. He has risen, as he said he would."

There are four main symbols in the Good Friday liturgy: the long prayers, the proclamation of the Passion, the veneration of the cross, and the communion service. Of these the veneration of the cross is the most ancient.

The veneration service began following the discovery of what has been believed to be the cross on which Christ was crucified. This discovery was made by Helena, the mother of Constantine, and by 380 A.D. had become the object of Christians' veneration. Egeria, a nun who undertook a pilgrimage at this time, described the veneration of the wood of the cross. In time, innumerable slivers of this cross were sent to dioceses all over the known world, and the practice spread.

The difference between the ancient practice and today's is one of emphasis. The use of crucifixes for veneration places the emphasis on Jesus dying in agony, rather than on the redemption wrought by Jesus through his death. Further, the use of a number of crucifixes, while it may "speed up" the "line", destroys the symbolism of the one, true cross. For this reason, an increasing number of places are reverting to the use of one large cross without a corpus for veneration. This is a step in the right direction.

The proclamation of the Passion is perhaps the most important event of the Good Friday liturgy. The major symbol of this part is the procession with the Gospel book. The book represents God's word to us; and as the Passion is narrated, we are put into contact with this living Word, Jesus, who is in our midst — not dead, but vibrantly, immortally alive. That is why a certain amount of solemnity must surround the Passion, whether we chant it formally, or use mime or a slide program or whatever. Proclaiming the Passion is more than reading an account of the historical crucifixion; it is personal contact with the living Lord.

The long prayers of the faithful and the communion service are later developments in the Good Friday liturgy. The prayers stem from the natural desire of the community to beg God's mercy on all sorts of people. These prayers are only intelligible in a context in which people are aware of themselves as a redeemed community, not merely individual sinners.

The communion service has had a somewhat erratic history as part of the Good Friday liturgy. It is difficult to know precisely where it is heading. Whether it will be a symbol of the redeemed community or whether it will degenerate into a private act of individuals is not yet sure. Hopefully, it will be the former, as people come to see Jesus as the every-risen Lord who dies no more.

The true symbols of Good Friday are meant to give us hope in the face of our hard struggles with sin and untruth. They are designed to encourage us and to help us realize that no one is alone trying to live the Christian life. They are not designed to lay burdens of guilt on our shoulders for the death of Christ. Our Good Friday seriousness should be one, not of grief, but of reflection.

As the Easter Vigil will remind us, "O felix culpa...!"

Making A Cross

by Eileen E. Freeman

The veneration of the cross on Good Friday has always been one of the more dramatic moments in the liturgical year. Coming forward to reverence the cross has been for countless Christians their affirmation of Jesus' death for their sakes. With the revised liturgy for Holy Week, we have a chance to make this rite even more effective.

The liturgical guidelines offer two possibilities for the veneration of the cross. The first one is the traditional approach: the gradual uncovering of a veiled crucifix. The second approach, one which is being increasingly used, is similar in many respects to the Vigil procession with the Paschal candle. An unveiled cross is brought down the aisle in procession. At each of three stages, the same stages used for the Paschal candle, the announcement, "This is the wood of the cross..." is made and the people reply.

The only difficulty with this second, more logical approach to the veneration is that few parishes have crosses suitable to such a procession. For the procession to work, the cross must be quite large, almost life-size. An ordinary processional cross or a wall cross is too small to be seen in all but the tiniest of chapels. Moreover, there is something un-aesthetic about a "life-size" person holding a small cross. A life-size cross needs to be made.

Two kinds of crosses can be made, depending on whether one wants to be historically accurate or traditional. It is quite likely that Jesus did not carry an entire cross to Calvary. Instead he carried only the crosspiece on or over his shoulders. When he arrived at Golgotha his wrists were nailed to the crosspiece which was then lifted onto the upright, permanently fixed into the ground, and secured to it by nails. Then Jesus' feet were nailed to the upright. An entire cross would have weighed several hundred pounds; even with Simon the Cyrenian's help, Jesus could hardly have lifted the whole thing.

The traditional idea of the cross shows it as shaped like a small "t," while the more historical cross is shaped like a capital "T." When deciding which to use, one must take the congregation into consideration. Will the historical cross have the same sign value for the congregation as the more traditional cross already does? Although in recent years artists have designed more and more crucifixes in a better historical perspective, most congregations would probably need a little catechesis in order to understand better how the crucifixion took place. An older book, but with several succinct descriptions of the crucifixion of Jesus, is that of Pierre Barbet, M.D., *A Doctor at Calvary,* published by Doubleday Image Books.

Making the traditional cross is not too difficult, and can be done by a group of parishioners in many ways. However, it is often best not to use freshly cut wood or tree limbs for the project. From past experience many parishes have learned that tree sap causes unnecessary grief; it drips on the floor, gets into people's hair, and requires a time-consuming clean-up. Also, in many areas, trees are a valuable ecological resource and should not be wasted. However, if a suitable tree is cut at the beginning of Lent and later replanted by a seedling (perhaps an acorn grown by school children to remind them of the grain that falls into the ground and dies), then the situation is improved. A dead tree can be cut down more easily. The upright should be about six feet, the crossbeam three feet. The crossbeam should be fastened one and one-half feet from the top of the upright; this yields the classic Latin cross. Round beams are not recommended, but if planks are too hard to saw, the beams should be notched at the place where they join and fixed with heavy nails or pegs. The Romans would have probably used bronze nails, since iron was rather precious to waste on execution of criminals.

Pine boards from a lumberyard can also be used, or roughly sawn cedar. The latter has fragrance which is very pleasant. The cedars of Lebanon were always biblical symbols of indestructability, since they are rarely bothered by insects. These boards will not need to be notched. Whether the wood is sanded, varnished, stained or left in its natural form will depend on the individual's feelings. Another possibility for wood is the use of old fence rails. Often they are a little thin, but their weathered appearance is visually attractive.

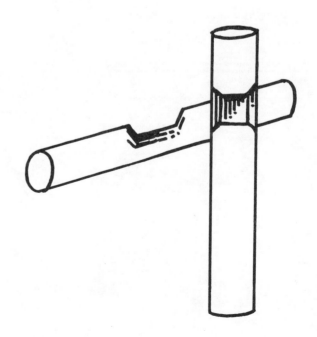

If the "T" cross is chosen, the most convenient type of wood to work with is the squared-off log; railroad ties are ideal, provided they have not been treated with creosote. It is difficult to secure a round log to the top of the upright and have it remain firm, especially if both pieces are heavy. Lumber yards, too, sell pieces of wood that are from six to ten inches on a side.

When the cross is carried in procession it will have already been nailed together, in most cases. However it is possible for the crucifer to carry only the crossbeam, while two others hold the upright from the sanctuary. When the crucifer reaches the sanctuary, the crosspiece is nailed to the upright in full view of the congregation. This, incidently, is an excellent way of demonstrating graphically how Jesus was crucified. If this approach is chosen, the wood should be prepared beforehand, since driving nails through several inches of wood requires some skill. With a power drill, make three holes completely through the crosspiece and into the top inch of the upright. The drill bit should be large enough to accommodate the circumference of the nails used. The nails or pegs will then be inserted into the holes and hammered only another couple of inches, depending on the type and thickness of the wood used. It would be helpful to have a parishioner who is a carpenter to do this.

If the cross is fully assembled when carried up, it may be necessary to have several people carry it, as they do in Jerusalem during Holy Week. Adults should carry the cross; it will be too heavy for servers or school children. It ought to be carried upright, so that everyone in the church can easily see it. A stand for the cross will not be necessary, even after it reaches the sanctuary. The symbolic value of Christians taking hold of the cross themselves and keeping it raised up is greater than if the cross is merely placed in a stand.

When the cross is held up for veneration, we are invited to "Behold the wood of the cross." The most important word here is *wood*. In an age of plastic and plaster "wood" we still need to be reminded that Jesus died on a "tree," not on a modern substitute. Symbols from nature speak louder than those of modern technology. However, in several places an outdoor procession with the cross has become the custom. In addition to the main cross, each family or parish organization makes its own to carry in procession. These crosses represent an individual or family's life, and could well be made of something other than wood, if the material means something to the family. One family of skiers made a cross of crossed ski poles. A pipefitter's family used copper tubing. A housewife made a cross from her mop handle. A garage mechanic used the type of tire iron that is shaped in a cross with socket wrenches at the four ends. The possibilities are enormous.

The home-made cross for the parish Good Friday procession does not have a corpus on it, unlike the majority of commercial crucifixes used in the liturgy today. This can be an advantage, since it stimulates the individual's imagination and identification with Jesus. A home-made crown of thorns could be fixed to the cross for emphasis.

If at all possible, only this one cross should be used during the veneration. Of course this will slow down the veneration somewhat. But the sign value of the one cross is obscured by having several, and aesthetic sensibilities are blunted where the extra crosses are of different sizes, colors and artistic styles. The object at liturgy is not to hurry. If the flow of "traffic" is well coordinated so that no one gets trampled or confused, and if suitable responsorial music is used with cantor and congregation, people rarely become impatient, except for the people in the sanctuary who have already venerated the cross and are back in their seats! If one cross is really impractical, then cut smaller crosses from the same material used for the processional cross and use them rather than others dug out from boxes for the occasion.

Faithful cross, among all others
One and only noble tree!
None in green'ry, none in flower
None in fruit your peer may be,
Sweet the wood and sweet the nails,
Sweet the burden hung on thee!
(from the *Pange Lingua*)

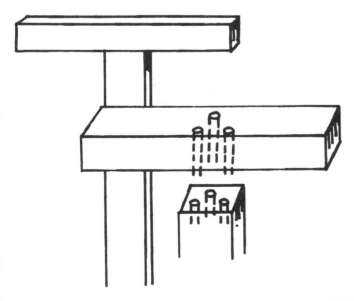

Christ's Broken Body Makes Us Whole

by J. Mossi and A. Miller, SJ

This liturgy takes its theme from the fourth and greatest of Isaiah's "Servant of the Lord" oracles: "Upon him was the chastisement that made us whole, and with his stripes we are healed." The focus of the liturgy is on the cross as Christ's saving act, a focus that illuminates our wholeness in our Lord's broken body. There is no attempt to incite guilt or shame, but simply to evoke a loving response to the great mystery of the Lamb who makes peace through his blood.

Although this theme is not explicitly stated anywhere in the service, several notable means are used to draw it out of the liturgy: the use of music in order to emphasize the first reading, the oracle of Isaiah, the use of a communal method of adoring the cross, the refrain sung by the congregation during the intercessory prayers, and the Fraction Rite all present the cross as a breaking of Christ that makes us whole.

The liturgy is planned for evening celebration, and extensive use is made of lighting effects. The visual center of attention is the crucifix. The larger the crucifix, the greater will be its impact. Also consider new media in which liturgical items can be constructed; e.g. a ten foot cross can be economically built from driftwood, a life-size body mold corpus can be shaped with heavy aluminum foil, and large nails can be added where needed. The use of red drapes as a backdrop will further serve to communicate the message of Good Friday.

Entrance

The deacons, or priest and deacon, wearing red vestments, go to the altar. There the crucifix is reverenced with a profound and prolonged bow. All pray for awhile, during which time a solo baritone voice, unaccompanied, sings two verses of *O Sacred Head Surrounded*[1]. When the song is completed, a nail is driven into the wood of the cross.

Opening Prayer

Deacon: Let us pray in silence, calling to mind the Passion of Our Savior, Christ Jesus.

The ministers extend their arms in cruciform.

Liturgy of the Word

In addition to the use of recorded music in the first reading, the following proclamation of the Word is enhanced by the elimination of the second reading, and the use of slides, mime, dramatic reading, soliloquy, and congregational participation in the Passion.

First Reading: *Isaiah 52:13-53:5*

As the lector begins the verse of Isaiah 53:4, the instrumental prelude to Handel's "Surely He Has Borne Our Griefs"[2] commences softly in the background. The volume increases as the lector finishes the reading. The music continues, becoming the meditational response to the first reading. A period of silence follows. Then the ministers move to their respective podiums, which are draped in red cloth.

The Passion of Our Lord Jesus Christ

The dramatic reading of the Passion according to John is arranged for the following ministers: two deacons, one of whom is the Narrator and the other *Jesus*; two mimes, one of whom plays *Jesus* and the other *Judas*; *Pilate*, a member of the congregation dressed like a well-to-do business man; *Peter*, dressed in an alb; a bass-baritone soloist with guitar accompanist; *Congregation*, including a group of about half a dozen rabble-rousers in óne corner of the room.

18:1-4a The *Narrator* commences;

18:2 mime *Judas* enters;

18:4 mime *Jesus* enters;

18:4b-9 *Narrator* silent; mimes act out the betrayal, seizing, binding of Jesus, at the end of which they freeze;

18:10 *Narrator;*

18:11 *Jesus;*

18:12-17a *Narrator*, interrupting at 13a to allow for the mimes to move a few steps, *Jesus* pausing briefly to look at the crucifix and then be led away by *Judas;* in another room the mimes put white albs over their black tights;

18:17b is not read, but rather *Peter* in his alb enters with a large cardboard sign which he shows to the *congregation;* on the sign is written in large black letters: "I know not the man;"

18:18-19 *Narrator;*

18:20-21 *Jesus;*

18:22 *Narrator;*

18:23 *Jesus;*

18:24-27 *Narrator;* a screen (a sheet attached to two poles) is brought from one corner of the room and unfurled in front of the crucifix; this is done by the two mimes who stand there holding the screen up; during the following sequence, a series of 2X2 slides is projected onto this screen by two syncronized slide projectors at the opposite wall; the slides are, first, a series taken of the previously shown cardboard sign, and secondly a series of various color patterns;

18:25a screen moved into position,

18:25b lights dimmed,

18:25c Slide #1: "I know not the man!"
    Slide #2: same, closeup.

18:26 screen removed so that future slides are projected onto the crucifix itself.

18:27a Slide #1: "I know not the man!"
    Slide #3: I
    Slide #4: know
    Slide #5: not
    Slide #6: the
    Slide #7: man

18:27b lights slowly rise;

18:28-29a *Narrator:* "So Pilate...." (At this cue, *Pilate* comes forward from the *congregation*);

18:29b-38a *Pilate* delivers the following soliloquy, after which he returns to his place:

"The temple crowd is out there again howling for some poor man's blood. God! How I detest those petty vultures and their power games. Those hypocrites want to use me as their hatchet man so that they can keep their grasping hands ritually pure. As if I couldn't see through their pitiful 'charade of concern for the welfare of the empire'. The charges against this man out there are sheer nonsense. The truth is that this is purely a power play; nothing more. They know that I can't afford trouble now, especially with half the Empire in the city for the holidays. I haven't the vaguest idea why they want this man killed. I could never fathom Jewish politics, and frankly, apart of course from my concern to keep the province running smoothly, I couldn't care less.

"But the man they brought in this morning, I have to admire him. He's got a haunting sort of presence. He's got character—very self possessed. The King of the Jews. God, I wish he *were* King of the Jews!

"He told me his destiny was to witness to the Truth. You know, I have a great deal of sympathy for his position. I guess I was that way when I was his age. But while his Kingdom, as he puts it, 'may not be of this world', my kingdom definitely *is*. Moral crusaders simply don't understand the complex realities of public administration. You have to develop a certain flexibility in dealing with situations as they arise.

"I'll try to do what I can for the man—he's obviously innocent. But you have to realize that I have a responsibility for the whole province and sometimes duty demands that we do things we don't particularly enjoy, things that run against the grain. It's not easy. But for a person in my position, what is Truth?"

18:38b-39 *Narrator;*

18:40 *Congregation*, here and at the subsequent crowd responses, the rabble-rouser group adds imprecations to the liturgical text to increase the dramatic effect of simulating an actual crowd scene;

19:1-5 *Narrator;*

19:6a *Congregation;*

19:6b-9a *Narrator*, at 19:9b the *Narrator* turns with a questioning look to the mime *Jesus*, who is still standing off to the side;

19:10 *Narrator;*

19:11 *Jesus;*

19:12-14 *Narrator;*

19:15a *Congregation;*

19:15b *Narrator;*

19:16a *Congregation;*

19:16b *Narrator*, lights are lowered; *Congregation* stands;

19:17-30 *Narrator* and *Jesus* as appropriate;

19:30 lights out; silence

Veneration of the Cross

The veneration of the cross is very simple in contrast to the complex proclamation of the passion. The adoration of the whole community at one time is symbolic of our wholeness in Christ's broken body. This type of adoration may be particularly suited to very large congregations where individual adoration may be so time consuming as to lose its impact. The adoration of the cross and the intercessory prayers have been switched from their usual positions so that a symbolic physical activity comes between two highly verbal sections of the liturgy.

During the silence following the passion, the mimes leave the room and return immediately with several lighted candles, which they hold in reverence before the crucifix; they and the deacons face the crucifix along with the congregation. The lights are raised slowly. A single base-baritone, accompanied by one guitar, sings "Now In Joy We Sing Thy Praises"[4] while all remain silent and motionless. During the second verse, the deacons incense the crucifix. A long profound bow replaces the kissing of the crucifix; this begins as the soloist reaches the climactic final repetition of the refrain. A period of silence follows.

Intercessory Prayers

The lights are brought all the way up and the deacons turn to the congregation, standing again at their podium. For this liturgy, the deacons alternate reading the Intercessory Prayers for Good Friday from Huub Oosterhuis' book *Your Word Is Near*[5]. During these prayers, the congregation is only asked to sing the following repeated refrain in response to each prayer:

Defend me, O God and plead my cause against a godless nation; from deceitful and cunning men rescue me, O God![6]

Communion Service

The consecrated bread is brought in silence from its place of reservation and is placed on the altar.

Deacon 1: Let us sing in confidence to the Father in the words our Savior gave us.

All: Our Father in heaven, holy be your Name, your kingdom come, your will be done, on earth as in heaven. Give us today our daily bread. Forgive us our sins as we forgive those who sin against us. Do not bring us to the test, but deliver us from evil. For the kingdom, the power, and the glory are yours now and forever.[7]

During the Fraction Rite, simple recorder music is played in the background.

Deacon 2: Abba, Father, you have sown in us your word, given us your Son ... he, who was broken and died for us, is bread and life for the world.

Deacon 1: We break bread for one another as a sign of our unity and receive the Son of your love delivered into the hands of men and put to death. We ask you that, strengthened by him, we may live in love and peace so that he may be present wherever we speak words and we may become his body in this world, for ever.

Deacon 2: This is the Servant who washes away the sins of the world. Happy are those who are called to his supper.

All: Lord, I am not worthy to receive you, but only say the word and I shall be healed.

During the distribution of the bread, *In the Midst of Death*[8] is sung by the whole congregation, to guitar accompaniment. At the end of communion there is a period of silence before the concluding prayer.

Concluding Prayer

Deacon 2: All loving Father, You awoke in your Son, Jesus of Nazareth, the desire to be a man without power or prestige in the world. And he experienced in his person what that meant, dying, as he did, like a slave on the cross. Let us, we beseech You, recognize in him your power and wisdom, and give us faith in your power to bring even the dead to life again, faith in You, the living God, today and every day forever and ever.[9]

All: Amen

Sign of Hope

A choir sings three verses of "Wood Hath Hope"[10] (or another appropriate hymn which reflects a sign of hope). During the first verse an Easter lily is brought in and placed in plain view before the crucifix. The deacons process out as the second verse begins. At the end of the third verse, the finger snapping of the singers provides a stark symbolic incompletion.

1. "O Sacred Head Surrounded," by J. S. Bach.
2. The chorus "Surely he has born our griefs and carried our sorrows", from *The Messiah*, by G. F. Handel.
3. Gospel according to John, New American Bible
4. "Now in Joy We Sing Thy Praises", *People's Mass Book*, World Library of Sacred Music, Cincinnati, Ohio, 45214, p. 51.
5. Adapted from "Prayers of Petition for Good Friday", *Your Word is Near*, by Huub Oosterhuis, Newman Press, 1968, pp. 68-71.
6. "Defend Me, O God", Psalm 42-43, *Twenty-Four Psalms and a Canticle*, by Joseph Galineau, The Grail, London, 1955, p. 20.
7. International Consultation on English Text "Lord's Prayer" from *Prayers We Have In Common*, Philadelphia: Fortress Press, 1970, p. 92.
8. "In the Midst of Death", by Rik Veelenturf, *Celebration* (album by the St. Gabriel Singers), Burns and Oates Ltd., London, 1969.
9. Adapted from a prayer of Huub Oosterhuis, *Your Word is Near*, Newman Press, New York, 1968, p. 63.
10. "Wood Hath Hope," by John Foley, SJ (NAL).

The Stranger

by Jack Miffleton

Every nation and culture has a story. In a sense a nation's story gives it a life of its own. As Americans we share the central story of our formation into a nation, and as Christians we share an even larger, more mythical and longer lasting story of our identity in Christ. The following tale is an example of one way to share with children some of the images and symbols of our formation and identity as Christian Americans.

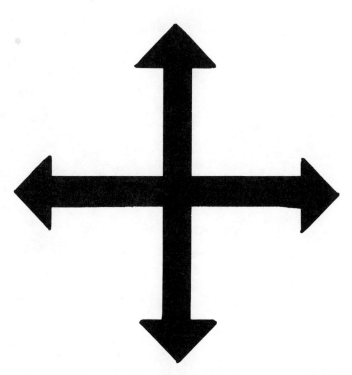

Once in a land not far from here, there grew a garden of many delicious vegetables: Sweet Native American Corn, Virginia Red Beets, California Artichokes, Peoria Pumpkins, New York Italian Tomatoes, Boston Irish Potatoes and Wonderful Kentucky Green Beans!

The vegetables were filled with nutritious colors, and they lived and grew in harmony. Gentle raindrops and warming sunrays left a sign of peace in a rainbow which hung high over the land.

The town people loved the garden and cared for it. They willingly shared its produce with one another. It was a time of great accord, love and justice.

One day, however, a stranger appeared in the colorful garden. The stranger was not a vegetable like the others. The stranger was a prickly Cactus plant.

"What an odd looking creature!" remarked the Native American Corn.

"Looks like he needs a shave to me!" said the New York Italian Tomatoes, trying to ease their discomfort with a nervous laugh.

The vegetables had never seen anything like this Cactus before, and they were afraid but hid their fright behind a lot of bold talk.

Then the stranger cleared his throat and spoke out in an unusual language never before heard in this land.

"Buenos dias," said this Cactus cordially.

"Listen to that noise he makes," said the Virginia Red Beets, "Surely, this is an enemy, a spy, who has come to steal the secret of our good health and plentiful yield." They were all suspicious but did not venture too close for fear of the sharp Cactus needles.

Just then the Cactus began to move a little. "Look Out!!" cried the Kentucky Green Beans, "He's going to attack!" They huddled together, losing their brave composure. But the Cactus stopped and said slowly and cheerfully, "Paz, mis amigos."

"We can't have this kind of thing around our children," protested the Peoria Pumpkins. The Boston Irish Potatoes joined in saying, "Just think what will happen to our neighborhood." "And remember," added the New York Italian Tomatoes, "We have our freedom and reputations to protect."

They continued to protest, saying how dangerous it was to be different. Once in a while when they paused to take a breath, they could hear the same strange sounds coming from the Cactus: "Paz, mis amigos."

THE HOLY WEEK BOOK

They all spent many days and nights arguing and gossiping and trying to make a case against the Cactus. In fact, they spent so much time quarreling and wrangling that none of the vegetables noticed that it had not rained for months and that the lovely rainbow had long since disappeared. Nor did they realize that their own rich colors were fast fading away. The once beautiful garden became a dry and dreary sight.

The town people, however, were well aware of the sad state of the garden for their food supply was very poor and tasteless. Many of the people had begun to hoard and to steal. The town people blamed the vegetables and the vegetables blamed the Cactus, and the Cactus stood quietly and said sadly, "Paz, mis amigos."

"We've gotta get rid of this thing," insisted the American Corn, "It's making me nervous." They all agreed. But what to do?

So the vegetables began to conspire with the town people against the Cactus, looking for a way to destroy it and to restore peace once again.

Together they decided to come at night, catch the Cactus off guard and cut it down.

At midnight they came sneaking into the garden, armed with clubs, shovels and axes. When the signal was given, they all broke into a fierce battle cry, and with one mighty whack someone sliced into the side of the Cactus.

At that something very unusual happened. Water, sweet water, began to flow from the side of the Cactus, soaking the garden and refreshing the parched vegetables. No one could understand it. Everyone was stunned and silent. A sense of shame came over the group for what they had done. And the vegetables began saying to one another, "Surely, this was a friend."

Morning came and the sun shone brightly on the garden. The vegetables were filled with their old color for the sweet water of the Cactus had wonderfully restored them to life. The rainbow again hung high over the land and the simple words of the Cactus burned in their hearts and on their lips. And to this day the language of the stranger is remembered as a common sign of welcome for all who come to this land. "Buenos dias." "Paz, mis amigos." Good day. Peace, my friends!

Resounding Scripture:

Genesis 9: 13-15 (adapted)
A rainbow hung in the sky, a perfect arch all the way from the earth to heaven. And Noah said, "It is God's special sign. When we see the rainbow, we will remember the agreement that God has made with us and with all creatures."

John 19: 16ff; 20: 1 & 2 (adapted)
In the end Pilate handed Jesus over to be crucified. They led him away, carrying his cross by himself. When they came to the "Skull Place," they crucified him between two thieves. Jesus, realizing his work was finished, bowed his head and died.

Later the soldiers came back, and when they saw he was dead, one of them thrust a lance into his side and water and blood flowed out. His friends then took the body of Jesus and laid it in a new tomb and sealed it with a heavy stone . . .

Early in the morning on the first day of the week, Mary Magdalene came to the tomb. To her surprise, the heavy stone had been rolled away! She ran to Peter and the others saying, "They have taken the Lord from the tomb and I do not know where they have put him!"

The Compassion Of The Lord

by Michael E. Moynahan, SJ

The Good Friday liturgy is not simply a commemoration of a 2,000 year old event, it is a celebration of the living reality of the Pascal Mystery. This liturgy celebrates that living reality by calling the Christian community to "compassion", to a loving response to Christ's call to "love one another as I have loved you". This call to compassion is not a mere call to suffering, however, but a call to join lovingly Christ on his cross, so that we can also join him in his infinite love, join him in his great work of salvation, and finally join him in his triumph over death.

Again and again the liturgy presents Christ's passion and death as a present event, and invites us to celebrate that passion by living it in our own lives. Dominated by the powerful "Come Passion" mime that proclaims the passion, the liturgy maintains a very tight thematic unity. The intercessory prayers, cross adoration, communion service and sign of hope all draw their meaning from the mime, and all are designed to evoke a compassionate response to Christ's suffering. Notice, too, the extreme simplicity of the liturgy: there are no elaborate ceremonies, nor any action or prayer that is extraneous to the celebration of compassion.

The liturgy is planned for evening celebration, due especially to the extensive use of lighting effects during the mime.

Entrance.

The liturgy begins with the lights dimming in the church. After a few moments of silence, a spot light goes on the big crucifix on the back wall. Then the song *Were You There When They Crucified My Lord?* is sung without accompaniment. After a few moments of silence, the light over the altar goes on and the celebrant and deacon proceed up the main aisle. They make a profound bow to the altar, then kneel for a few moments in silent prayer, and then rise and bow profoundly again. The celebrant then prays the opening prayer.

Prayer

Father of our Lord, Jesus Christ, and Our Father, we are the harvest yielded by the death of your Son. We see in our world an even richer harvest which is yet to be reaped. As we recall this evening the passion and death of Jesus Christ, teach us, and help us to understand, that in our lives we too must die if your kingdom is to grow on our earth, and your love to be made known to men. We ask this in the name of Jesus Christ, who is today and everyday of our lives your precious gift to us. May your name be blessed on earth, now and forever.

The celebrant and deacon then go to their seats which are placed directly in front of the first row of pews.

Liturgy of the Word

Both of the preliminary readings are eliminated and the passion is proclaimed through a mime entitled "Come Passion". The mime echoes Christ's prophetic words: "Greater love no man has than to lay down his life for his friends." When the mime was first performed the clown was costumed and made up as a hobo; the guard and three members of the crowd had clown-white make-up and were dressed in black pants and dark blue sweat shirts; Christ was also in clown-white make-up and wore black pants and a red sweat shirt.

When the celebrant and deacon are seated, the lights go out and the mimes assume their positions for the mime (see diagram #1).

Crowd = X, Y, Z
Guard = B
Christ = C
Clown = D
Performing
Areas = 1, 2, 3, 4, 5

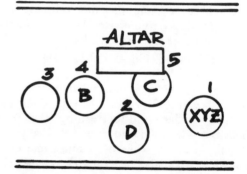

Diagram 1

1) Lights come up and "X" (one of the crowd) raises a placard revealing the name "CROWD".

2) Next, "X" moves to area 4 and raises a new card with "GUARD" on it.

3) Next, "X" moves to area 5 and raises a new card with "CHRIST" on it.

4) Next, "X" moves to area 2 and raises a new card with "CLOWN" on it.

5) Finally, "X" goes back up to the top step of the altar area (area 5) and shows the title card for the mime: "COME PASSION".

6) All the characters are frozen and the lights go out.

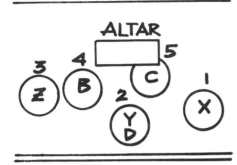

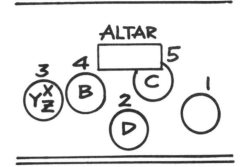

Diagram 2

7) When the lights come up, the members of the crowd have each moved to their new positions (see diagram #2).

8) The music begins (instrumental of Paul McCartney's *Junk*).

9) The clown turns over (exaggerated), sits up, yawns, and generally wakes up. He stands and prepares to greet another day. Things weigh heavy on him. He gathers his tricks, and sets off, through his door, to meet the day.

10) The clown walks from "area 2" to "area 1" where he approaches the first man (character "X"). The man is obviously angry about something. Somewhat downcast. The clown tries to cheer him up, but to no avail. Finally, the clown tries his "buzzer ring" trick on the man. The clown tips the audience as to what will happen. They shake hands and when the man releases, he raises an angry fist at the clown who leaves, sadder.

11) The clown proceeds to "area 2" where he encounters a selfish little boy ("Y") with an all day sucker. The kid is a brat. The clown asks for a lick and gets an emphatic "no!". In the process of this, the selfish kid sticks the sucker to his shirt and begins to cry. To cheer the child up, the clown tries to juggle, but continually drops all the balls. In disgust, the little kid kicks the clown in the arse as the clown tries to pick up the juggling balls.

12) Next, an even more dejected clown moves off to "area 3". He spies a sad man there. Again the clown's life has purpose and meaning. He decides to try and cheer this man up. But the man is bored. The clown then tries his "squirting flower" trick on the man. Only it doesn't work. It winds up squirting the clown. And so the clown leaves dejected and confused.

Diagram 3

13) He cannot understand why everything continues to go wrong for him when he is only trying to help. He is ready to go home when a crowd catches his attention. He has already moved to "area 2", and notices the crowd in "area 3" (where "X", "Y", and "Z" have now moved. See diagram #3). Curious, the clown decides to find out what is happening.

14) When the clown approaches the crowd, they block his view of the altar area (areas 4 and 5). Finally he tries to go around them, but is blocked by the Guard in "area 4". The clown pleads with the guard, but the guard says "no". When his pleading appears to be getting him nowhere, the clown turns to go. But the guard relents and lets the clown go ahead. Here the guard and crowd freeze.

15) At this moment, when the clown makes his way to "area 5", the music changes to the instrumental of Borodin's *Nocturne*.

16) The clown approaches the steps, first curious, then perplexed, then shocked. He sees a man in anguish on the cross. Horror is written on the clown's face as he frantically looks to the man on the cross and the audience. He doesn't know what to do. The clown's heart goes out to the suffering man. The clown clutches his heart and begins to cry.

17) Then an idea strikes the clown. Maybe he can cheer this man up. The clown goes to the middle step near the foot of the cross and takes his juggling balls out. He begins to juggle. And this time the balls do not fall. The man on the cross looks up and smiles. The clown drops the balls (then makes effort to put them down). The clown is frantic. He must help the man.

18) The clown stands up and takes the man down from the cross. The clown gently puts the man on his lap near the middle step. The pose is that of the "Pieta". There the clown comforts the man. The crowd comes alive and protests this action.

THE HOLY WEEK BOOK

19) After a while the guard comes up and tells the clown to put the man back up on the cross. The clown refuses. The guard insists. Finally, the clown offers to replace the man on the cross. The guard hesitates, but then accepts. It's all the same to him.

20) The clown props the man up and goes to the cross. There the guard nails him on. The clown is in terrible pain. The guard returns to the crowd and they all freeze.

21) After a while the man gets up, picks up the balls, and juggles for the clown. The clown smiles, and the man takes the clown down from the cross and assumes the "Pieta" position (middle step) to comfort the clown.

22) The music ends and the lights go down as the man rocks the clown back and forth in his lap comforting the clown.

Intercessory Prayers

The use of slides in these prayers call to mind our current needs, and thus further the liturgy's call to make the passion a living event.

At the end of the mime, the mimes leave in darkness, the lights come on, and the celebrant goes to the altar to begin the Intercessory Prayers. The celebrant reads the invitation to prayer, there is a short slide meditation, and the congregation responds.

1) *For Creation.* Pray, brothers and sisters, that as we see the tragic ways that nature is spent all around us, we may be reawakened to a new sense of care for all creation.

(Picture meditation of five slides: earth, mountains, water, field of flowers, flower superimposed on trash can.)

Response: O God, your love for us is seen in all your gifts to us. But we in our selfishness often misuse many of the gifts around us. Teach us to take only what we need and to use all creatures only in as much as they help us be what you created us to be — your children. This we ask you, Father, through Christ Our Lord.

2) *For the church.* Let us pray, friends, for the church of God throughout the world, that God may continue to guide it and gather it together from the four corners of the earth to praise him in peace.

(Picture meditation of three slides: church steeple, people, hands joined.)

Response: God, Our Father, you have revealed yourself and your great love for us in Jesus Christ. By the power of your Spirit bless the work of your church on earth. Help us all proclaim the Good News by all we say and do. Teach us to bring to our world the healing and hope you have first given us. This we ask through Christ our Lord.

3) *For Life.* Let us pray that God may heal us of the ways we are blind to the value of life in all its forms.

(Picture meditation of four slides: pregnant mother, mother and child, lonely man, Mother Theresa)

Response: Father, we pray for the unborn child, for those who have grown old, for all the poor and suffering in the world. Help us to see in them ourselves. Teach us to see the light and life of Christ revealed in all the gifts of life around us. This we ask through Christ our Lord.

4) *For the Pope.* Let us pray for _____ our Pope, and_____ our bishop, for all the shepherds of Christ: bishops, priests, sisters, deacons, and the entire family of your people — that God may teach them to lead, to tend with care.

(Picture meditation of three slides: bishop, nun, people of various races)

Response: Father, You give us the light of your Spirit. Because You love us, You perfect us and make us whole. Help each of us listen and respond to your call to build up your kingdom. This we ask through Christ our Lord.

5) *For the quality of life in our cities.* Let us pray that we can remake and rebuild our cities so that they reflect the beauty and image of God.

(Picture meditation of three slides: antennae, building in shadow, two children against wall)

Response: Father, You have made us in your image. and do something of the Spirit You first breathed on us. Teach us to break out of the caves and prisons we dwell in, and let us experience the freedom You call us to. This we ask through Christ our Lord.

6) *For unity of Christians.* Let us pray for all those who share faith in Jesus Christ, that God may make us always one in him.

(Picture meditation of two slides: two people, hands reaching out.)

Response: Father, You call us together. You alone can make us one. Bless all who struggle to follow Jesus your Son. As we share one baptism, strengthen our faith and unite us in love. This we ask through Christ our Lord.

7) *For Human Solidarity.* Let us pray that all people may learn to live as one family and that our mutual care can help us look on essential similarity instead of accidental differences.

(Picture meditation of three slides: black being kicked, farm workers, child and policeman)

Response: God, Our Father, Jesus has taught us that we are all one in your eyes. Heal us of our blindness that lets the color of our skin and the shape of our face push us hopelessly apart. Help us look on all men and women as our brothers and sisters. This we ask through Christ Our Lord.

8) *For peace among nations and peoples.* Let us pray that we, as Christians, may always seek peaceful means of dealing with conflict. That we may no longer kill ourselves in others and others in ourselves by our deafness to cries of loneliness, isolation, and injustice.

Response: God of all nations and people, forgive us our sins of violence. Renew in us your understanding and love. Help us never to destroy, even in anger, what you have made. Teach us always to act justly, love tenderly, and walk humbly before You. This we ask through Christ our Lord.

9) *For Public Officials.* Let us pray for those who serve us in public office, that God may guide the minds and hearts, so that all may live in true peace and freedom.

(Picture meditation of one slide: Jimmy Carter)

Response: Father, You know the longings of the hearts of men and women and You protect their rights. In your goodness give us wisdom to elect leaders who will be truthful as your Son was truthful, who will serve as Jesus served: not selfish interests, but the good of all. This we ask through Christ our Lord.

10) *For those in special need.* Brothers and sisters, let us pray that God may allow his healing powers to flow to and through the sickness, the suffering, and dying in the lives of all. That we may always strive to recognize his presence in the very heat of human struggle. And that we may transcend the falsehood and illusion which breed all hatred,. distrust, and despair.

(Picture meditation of five slides: old man in purple, lonely man in corner, aged hands, curled up person, clown)

Response: Father, You give strength to the weary, and new courage to those who have lost heart. Hear the prayers of all who call on You in any trouble, that they may have the joy of receiving your deep embrace in their needs. All this we ask through Christ our Lord. Amen.

Veneration of the Cross

There is strong symbolic value in actually picking up a cross, then turning to face the community and making the sign of the cross. Both actions emphasize the Christian response of taking up one's cross to follow Christ.

At the conclusion of the intercessions, the deacon goes to the back of the chapel where he gets the cross (the stand should be on the cruet table). He brings it slowly up the center aisle, stopping three times to sing: "Behold the cross on which our Lord hung, the sign of our salvation. Let us rejoice and be glad in it." The congregation responds each time by singing: "Lord, by your cross and resurrection, you have set us free. You are the Savior of the world."

When he reaches the sanctuary, the deacon holds the cross up high so the celebrant can revere it. Next, the celebrant takes the cross, elevates it, lowers it, then returns it to the deacon, and slowly makes the sign of the cross. His action sets the pattern for the people who are now invited to adore the cross in the same manner. During the adoration, an instrumental version of *Sometimes I Feel Like a Motherless Child* is played on the harmonica.

Communion Service

Notice the extreme simplicity of the communion service, and also the way in which the Fraction Rite continues the theme of the compassionate suffering with Christ: "There we are on the table, and there we are in the cup," to be broken and poured out.

When the veneration is completed, the celebrant takes the cross to the altar while the deacon gets the stand from the cruet table. They place the cross on the altar, then the deacon spreads a corporal. Immediately two special assistants bring in the Eucharist from its place of reservation. Then the celebrant invites the people to pray the "Our Father."

Then, while the deacon and two assistants break the bread, the celebrant prays the fraction rite:

Because the Lord suffered for us, he left us in this meal his body and blood. Now we are called to become his body, and through his mercy we are what we receive. Therefore, just as we see that the bread which was made is one loaf, so may we be one body by loving one another, by having one faith, one hope, and an undivided charity. Thus too, the wine existed in many clusters of grapes, and now it is one. And now we, in the name of Christ, have come to drink of the cup of the Lord. There we are on the table, and there we are in the cup. We receive together, and we drink together because Christ died that we might live together.

During the distribution of communion, the song *I Am the Bread of Life (GIA)* is sung.

After communion all the remaining food is consumed. Then the celebrant says the concluding prayer:

Let us pray: Father, our hearts are heavy as we focus our gaze on the death of your Son. Yet sadness has given way to joy, and death has yielded the promise of new life. In this lies our hope: that Jesus Christ who has died, has risen from the dead and summons all who would follow him to a land of peace and joy where life will never end. May we who have walked with him in his hour of sorrow share in his glory and his victory now and forever. This we ask through Christ our Lord.
All: Amen.

Sign of Hope.

After communion, the ministers turn to face the crucifix. All lights go out except the spotlight on the large crucifix. Recorded music of the *Godspell* song *Where Are You Going?* is played. During the song, a child places a lily under the cross and the ministers depart in silence.

After the song is ended, a few moments of silence follow and then the lights come on in the church.

Stations Of The Cross: A Mime

by Donald Dilg, CSC

The Way of the Cross presented here combines traditional prayer with contemporary mime. Originally it was done in a typical parish situation, with seventh and eighth grade students doing the mimes.

Each station follows this pattern:
a) The title of the station is read.
b) There is an opening invocation:
Celebrant: We adore You, O Christ, and we bless You;
All: Because by your holy cross You have redeemed the world.
c) A short scripture reading follows.
d) During the reading the appropriate mime is acted out.
e) The celebrant reads a short meditation.
f) The congregation responds with a prayer.

During the stations a server carrying a processional candle moves from one station to the next, while the rest of the ministers remain in the sanctuary.

Because of the congregation part, all those present will need a program with their portions printed in it. Many of those who come to the stations are older people, some of whom have failing eyesight. This consideration necessitates that the congregation's card be printed clearly, in a readable pica type. Glossy ditto paper is hard to read even by those with no sight problems and should be avoided, as should cramped layout.

Ministers needed for this service will be:
a) Celebrant
b) Cantor
c) Server
d) Musician
e) Seven young people who are interested in taking part in the mime.
f) Reader or readers (Adult)

Before the service begins, it is a good thing for all the ministers to pray briefly together. It helps the young people to "settle down" and become more aware of what they are going to do and why. The church should be lit in a subdued way if the service takes place in the evening, with lights especially on the mimers.

As the service begins the celebrant makes a short entrance from the sacristy, if possible, preceded by the candlebearers and reader with the Lectionary, to which have been clipped the readings. An opening hymn or psalm of praise is led by the cantor: *You Are My God* or *Seek the Lord* (NAL) are especially suitable. The celebrant then greets the people and explains briefly in his own words what is going to happen. The young people remain in the sacristy until after the opening hymn and the greeting are finished. Then, as the celebrant begins the first station, the server with candle goes into the sanctuary and leads them out. They take their places; the server goes to the first station, and so forth.

The Stations

Station One
Celebrant: The first station: Jesus is condemned to death. We adore You, O Christ, and we bless You;
All: Because by your holy cross You have redeemed the world.
Reader: Matthew 27:24-26
Celebrant: Pilate was a very busy man. He had many responsibilities as governor, and during the Jewish festivals there were always those who would cause trouble and make more work and worry for him. Obviously he could not waste much time on a petty grievance against a peasant carpenter. He had to dispose of him and get on with things.
All: Jesus, we too, are busy about many things in our daily lives. We pray for the grace never to let things that need to be done become more important than people who need to be loved; or else we may miss You when You stand before us in need.

Station Two
Celebrant: The second station: Jesus carries his cross. We adore You, O Christ, and we bless You;
All: Because by your holy cross You have redeemed the world.
Reader: Matthew 27:27-31
Celebrant: So it has all come to this. The people find it too hard to deal with a Savior who is all loving, always pouring his life out in service to others. This threatens them. It forces them to see how unloving they themselves are. So Jesus must be eliminated. It hurts him deeply; but he loves them even in that.
All: Jesus, we often reject You and fail to live up to the demands of love. But we also find our own efforts to love being rejected by other people; and it hurts us very much. Give us the grace to take up the cross with You, Lord, and go on loving.

Station Three
Celebrant: The third station: Jesus falls. We adore You, O Christ, and we bless You;
All: Because by your holy cross You have redeemed the world.
Reader: John 12:25-27
Celebrant: Not even Jesus can bear the tremendous weight of sin without a great deal of pain and struggle. He was driven to the ground, and must have wondered himself if he could really do what he had to do. Only in calling on the strength of his relationship to the Father can he fulfill what he knows is his mission.
All: Jesus, we find our sinfulness too much to bear. We hate it; we want to get rid of it. Yet it is always with us, even driving us to the ground. Save us from the pride of trying to carry our crosses strictly on our own. In You alone we find the strength to live fully.

Station Four

Celebrant: The fourth station: Jesus meets his mother. We adore You, O Christ, and we bless You;

All: Because by your holy cross You have redeemed the world.

Reader: John 19:25-26

Celebrant: What is she doing here? Hasn't she suffered enough? But yet she knows she ought to be here, even if she cannot fully understand what is happening, and no words can express her feelings. She loves, and stands in silent support.

All: Jesus, we are willing to do anything for those we love very much — for our family, for our friends. And we feel so inadequate when we cannot help them, when we cannot find the right words in times of sorrow. Lord Jesus, help us realize that we are not their savior, You are. Help us stand in silent support when we need to.

Station Five

Celebrant: Simon helps Jesus. We adore, You, O Christ, and we bless You.

All: Because by your holy cross, You have redeemed the world.

Reader: John 23:26.

Celebrant: What thoughts must have gone through Simon's mind: I don't have time for this: My family is waiting for me — they'll be worried: What will my friends think if they see me: I don't mind helping people, but...

All: Lord Jesus, there are always many good reasons for not getting involved with others, especially when this involves an interruption in whatever we are doing. Give us the grace to see when You are calling us to bear one another's burdens, and so fulfill your law of love.

Station Six

Celebrant: The sixth station: Veronica wipes Jesus' face. We adore You, O Christ, and we bless You.

All: Because by your holy cross You have redeemed the world.

Reader: Isaiah 53:1-3.

Celebrant: This seems a bit foolish. What did this woman hope to accomplish anyway? Here Jesus is dying, and she offers him a simple towel to wipe his face. But that was all she had — and she gave it, she gave herself, completely.

All: Jesus, so often we look only for the big things, the heroic things we can do for our brothers and sisters. Help us to be aware of the little things, the day to day things that we can do to communicate your image of love to others.

Station Seven

Celebrant: The seventh station: Jesus falls again. We adore You, O Christ, and we bless You.

All: Because by your holy cross You have redeemed the world.

Reader: Isaiah 53:6-7.

Celebrant: Just when things seem to be easing up, oppression returns with a vengeance. The momentary relief given by Simon, the simple loving gesture of Veronica are wiped out by a crushing return to the cruelty of the Passion.

All: Jesus, why do things have to fall apart just at the time they seemed to be coming together? We work hard to conquer a particular failing; and just when we think it is overcome, we fall again. May we never forget our constant need of your grace.

Station Eight

Celebrant: The eigth station: Jesus comforts the women. We adore You, O Christ, and we bless You;

All: Because by your holy cross You have redeemed the world.

Reader: Luke 23:27-31.

Celebrant: At first these words of Jesus don't seem comforting at all, but very sharp. Yet Jesus was trying to say to them that tears can be a way of hiding from responsibility; at times we need to be confronted by the reality of a situation.

All: Lord Jesus, what You said was not, perhaps, what the women wanted to hear. But it certainly was what they needed to hear. Your word of love to us in our lives is not always easy to hear; but help us be open to that word, so we may follow You and live.

Station Nine

Celebrant: The ninth station: Jesus falls a third time. We adore You, O Christ, and we bless You;

All: Because by your holy cross You have redeemed the world.

Reader: Isaiah 53:10.

Celebrant: This has to be the end. There is no way Jesus is going to make it up the hill. He has been beaten all night, whipped and prodded through the streets of the city, and now he lies exhausted on the ground. Yet somehow he gets to the top of Calvary.

All: Jesus, there are times in our lives when the situation seems absolutely hopeless. There is no way to turn; and all that is ahead is darkness. These times are terrifying, Lord. Give us the grace to hope. The Father will get us to Calvary — and to the Resurrection.

Station Ten

Celebrant: The tenth station: Jesus is stripped of his clothes. We adore You, O Christ, and we bless You;

All: Because by your holy cross You have redeemed the world.

Reader: John 19:23-24.

Celebrant: Even though beaten and exhausted, Jesus proves to be aggravating to the soldiers; he does not cower at their callousness. They realize they can't manipulate him, and so they take out their frustrations by stripping him of his clothes and gambling for them.

All: Lord Jesus, You are not ashamed to stand naked before the crowds; for You have stood before them in absolute openness and honesty all your life. Such openness frightens us, Lord. We have so many little ways of hiding our true feelings, of keeping up phony fronts and false appearances. Strip us of these things, Lord, that we may be free to mount the cross with You.

Station Eleven

Celebrant: The eleventh station: Jesus is nailed to the cross. We adore You, O Christ, and we bless You;

All: Because by your holy cross you have redeemed the world.

Reader: Mark 15:25-26.

Celebrant: No one can be so inhuman as to nail someone to a tree. This is something done to animal hides, not to a person. Yet it is done; and no one seems to raise a cry.

All: Jesus, we are shocked at the amount of inhuman cruelty people daily inflict on one another. We are terrified of the evil which lurks in our own hearts. May we never ignore this evil, but work actively against it in what ever ways we can.

Station Twelve

Celebrant: The twelfth station: Jesus dies on the cross. We adore You, O Christ, and we bless You;

All: Because by your holy cross You have redeemed the world.

Reader: Luke 23:43-47

Celebrant: This is the greatest, yet most horrible moment in all history. In this one death, all death is forever destroyed. In this absolute failure is found ultimate victory. In this depth of despair is found the source of all hope.

All: Lord Jesus, there is no way we can understand your death without participating in it. But we are afraid, Lord. We don't know what it will mean for our lives if we were really to die with You. Give us the peace to say Yes to the cross, and by that Yes to find true freedom and life.

Station Thirteen

Celebrant: The thirteenth station: Jesus is taken down from the cross. We adore You, O Christ, and we bless You;

All: Because by your holy cross You have redeemed the world.

Reader: Luke 23:50-53

Celebrant: Could anyone possibly enter into Mary's desolation at this moment? The promise of the angel was that she would give birth to a King who would rule forever. What had gone wrong? How could this have happened? Could she have been cruelly deceived? All these thoughts must have gone through her heart; yet she remained faithful.

All: Mary, pray for us at the times when we are tempted to give up in our journey of faith, those times of emptiness when Jesus seems to lie lifeless in our arms. Pray that at that point we may go on and discover the true power of hope.

Station Fourteen

Celebrant: The fourteenth station: Jesus is buried. We adore You, O Christ, and we bless You;

All: Because by your holy cross You have redeemed the world.

Reader: Isaiah 53:9-10.

Celebrant: Most people must have stood at the tomb in shocked silence. But for some, undoubtedly, it was a relief when the stone was finally rolled into place. For now they knew that Jesus would no longer be confronting them in their daily lives.

All: Jesus, so often our faith becomes a faith of the tomb. We feel we know You well enough; we have figured you out; we know what You want; we know what we have to do. Lord, neither the tomb nor our own conceptions are big enough to hold you. Help us ever to await the Resurrection, and grow in following your way.

When the stations are finished, the candlebearer returns to the center edge of the sanctuary, and stands holding his or her candle facing the congregation. Those doing the mimes turn to face the altar in a line, bow and then exit into the sacristy. The cantor announces the final hymn, *Keep in Mind* (WLP). During the last verse of the hymn the celebrant and reader follow the server to the main exit, so as to greet the people; or they may return to the sacristy.

The Mimes

One mime accompanies each station; it is performed while the scripture reading is going on. The diagrams represent the final positions of the actors. Since some of them change roles during the mimes, it is better if they are not costumed, but wear ordinary clothes coordinated so the combined colors, styles, etc., are pleasant and relaxing. Because of the movements, girls will probably feel more comfortable in long leotard skirts or slacks.

Abbreviations: D Down, U Up, R Right, L Left and C Center.

Station One

Players 1 (Pilate) and 5 (Jesus) cross directly D four steps and face each other. Other players circle 5, extend their inside hands, take two steps toward 1, turn and point at 1. 1 raises hands, palms toward players, then points straight at 5. Players slowly turn and also point at 5. Players then circle clockwise around 5, and 5 turns with them until he is facing upstage. Players drop to one knee, and their pointing fingers turn into fists. Meanwhile 1 turns and walks two steps upstage.

Station Two

5 reaches out his hands slightly, palms upward, and turns slowly clockwise. As he faces each of the players, they bring up their other fists and place their arms in a cross. 5 continues to turn until he is facing player six. Players 2 and 3 rise, come up behind 5 take his elbows and wrists, and turn them down, facing him DR. 4, 6, and 7 rise and form an angled line, facing UR.

Station Three

Player 7 raises fist in the air, pivots L behind 5, brings fist down on 5's L shoulder. 4 pivots R in front of 2 and brings left fist down on 5's R shoulder. 5 falls to his knees, stretches his arms and looks up. 2 and 3 keep hands on 5's shoulders.

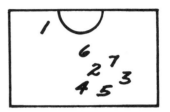

Station Four

Player 6 (Mary) turns to her L and crosses slowly DR as if searching for someone. She then turns and faces 5. 5 looks at 6, rises and turns to her. He tries to cross to her DR, but 3 quickly crosses in front of him, and stands facing him and blocking his path. 5 then tries to cross UR, but 4 moves in front of him to block his path. 6 stretches upstage hand to him and 5 also reaches upstage hand toward her. But 2 reaches out to grab the wrist of 5.

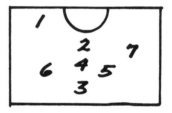

Station Five

Player 1 (Simon) turns to his R and crosses straight C, brushing through 6's outstretched hand. 1 then looks at R and starts to cross L. 3, who has turned to face him, blocks his path with arm. 1 tries to continue to cross by circling U between 3 and 4; but they both raise their hands to block him, then turn him around to face straight R; and 3 points R with downstage arm. 4 takes upstage arm of 5 and places it on the R shoulder of 1. 6 crosses UC.

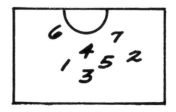

Station Six

Player 7 (Veronica) crosses DL, turns, and stretches both hands toward 5. 5 turns toward 7; then 3 turns and 1 and 4 slowly cross UC, face front and look at 7. 5 crosses to 7, 7 drops to one knee. 5 reaches down to 7 and takes both her hands in his. Then he slowly raises her up.

Station Seven

Player 3 crosses slowly L until between 5 and 7; looks at 5 and 7 for a second, then breaks their clasp with an upward motion of both arms. 7 is turned completely L and stands with arms folded. 5 is turned DC and falls as 1 and 4 reach out and mime pushing him along.

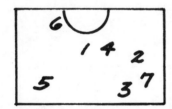

Station Eight

Player 6 crosses slowly to UR of 5: meanwhile 2 and 7 cross to directly U and DR of 5 respectively, then 2 assumes a weeping posture and 7 drops to one knee and bows her head. 5 notices women, rises, motions 7 to rise, then very subtly motions the women to form a triangle facing each other.

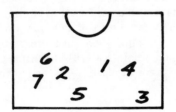

Station Nine

3 deliberately crosses to DC of 5 and takes his downstage arm and turns 5 to D. 1 then crosses to UR of 5 and mimes pushing him forward. 5 stumbles D and falls.

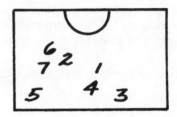

Station Ten

All players beginning with 4, then following in order 1, 3, 6, 2, 7, circle 5, who kneels U. Players have their hands over head of 5 as they circle, and make a complete rotation, continuing until 1 and 3 are directly behind 5 toward C. All players then kneel keeping their hands above 5. 5 then rises to his feet, through the hands of the players. When he is standing, players lower their hands together to the feet of 5.

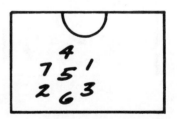

Station Eleven

1 and 3 slowly reach up, take 5 by his shoulders and lower him backwards to the floor. Then they stretch out his arms on the floor. Slowly, all players raise their fists.

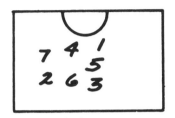

Station Twelve

1 and 3 raise 5 up to a standing position, (with 5's help of course). When 5 is standing in position of crucifixion, remaining players are still on their knees in a circle around him, and with their hands upraised to three separate gestures moving their hands in a waving motion towards and away from Jesus; first with palms away from 5; second with palms toward 5; third with clenched fists. Then players separate hands in a sunburst motion, and continue a sweep with their hands until their hands are on the floor and their heads are looking D over their R shoulders.

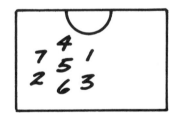

Station Thirteen

4, 2, and 7 sequentially rise, pivot and cross to triangle position UL. 1 and 3 rise and cross four steps URC facing upstage. 6 slowly raises her outstretched arms to 5. Pause for a second. Then 1 and 3 return, cross to either side of 5, lower his arms while he lowers his head. 6 bows to the ground.

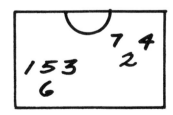

Station Fourteen

6 returns to upright kneeling position. 5 faces L; 1 and 3 raise their hands in a wrapping motion around 5, then also turn and face L. 1, 5 and 3 then cross UL until 5 is directly U of the triangle, after first placing 5 in a sitting position facing D with his arms crossed on his knees and his head on his arms. 1 and 3 crisscross in front of the triangle and continue their cross for about five steps until 1 arrives from DL and 3 arrives DLC.

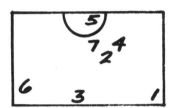

The Enthronement Of Our Lord Jesus Christ

by Ed Hurlbutt, SJ

The Passion is the enthronement of our exalted Lord, Jesus Christ. It cannot be told as a horrible inexplicable event, for it is the glorious conclusion of our King's victory over darkness. This liturgy celebrates the whole Good Friday Liturgy in terms of the coronation of a King; the Passion becomes "The Enthronement"; the Intercessory Prayers are "The People Greeting Their King"; the Adoration of the Cross becomes "The King Sharing his Throne"; the Communion Service is "The Royal Banquet"; and the Sign of Hope is "The King's Repose".

The liturgy draws its meaning from St. John's account of the Passion. In John's account, it is Christ who freely decides to take up his passion. He is not the sufferer of these events, but the one who takes the initiative: "Father," he prays, "the hour is come! Glorify your Son!" But Christ is not just a king of power; he is the perfect King because he is also the perfect servant: even as he is enthroned he lays down his life for his friends.

Despite what we see — the execution of a criminal, the call to be executed with that criminal, an absurd "banquet" of broken bread, and the death and burial of a man — we know that what we celebrate is the crowning of a King; our glorification with that King; the most lavish banquet ever given, the banquet of eternal life; and the explosion of a new and everlasting life into the lives of all men.

The paradox is incredible, but repeatedly the liturgy demands that the Christian community celebrate the devastating irony: this "execution" is really the enthronement of the King of the Universe.

This liturgy is planned for evening celebrations because it relies heavily on the contrast between light and dark to symbolize its meaning.

Entrance
Only the baldacchino light is on. The celebrant, wearing only an alb and cincture, enters alone and goes to the top step in front of the altar. He begins the worship with the sign of the cross. Next he begins the Opening Prayer.

Opening Prayer
God our Father, we gather this evening to remember the life, death and resurrection of your Son, our brother Jesus.

Transform us, through your fidelity and love, into your paschal people: a people who can see in the cross not defeat, but ultimate victory.

Help us, by remembering these events, to pass, with Jesus our King, from cross to crown, through ignominy to glory.

We ask this in the name of Jesus, now and forever.

Amen.

The Enthronement
In this word liturgy, the first two readings have been eliminated, and John's Passion has been edited to exclude everything that does not touch directly on the theme: the enthronement of a king. Dramatization, lighting effects, candles, slides, music and physical participation by the congregation are used to proclaim the Passion.

I.
After the opening prayer the lights go out. The celebrant moves to the tabernacle area (see diagram).

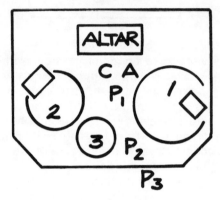

1 = Area for "The King's Prayer"
2 = Area for "The Royal Escort"
3 = Crowd position during Pilate's inquiry.

   A = Stand for Candelabra
   C = Position of Christ during Pilate's inquiry; then, position of cross
P1, P2, P3 = Position of Pilate during 1) inquiry of Christ, 2) inquiry of crowd, 3) confrontation with entire congregation.

The dramatization is written for 4 major characters, 2 mimes, a "crowd" of 3 persons, and 5 people scattered in the congregation. All the characters except the celebrant, who is Christ, are seated in various places in the congregation at the beginning of the dramatization. Each time new characters are needed, the mimes go down to the congregation to lead them up. The 5 people scattered in the congregation never go up to the sanctuary, but are assigned certain lines to shout from their seats, and also join the "crowd" in shouting "crucify him" at the appropriate times.

After the celebrant has moved from the altar, a slide comes on reading "The Enthronement of Jesus According to John". All slides are projected on the wall behind the altar. Next, two mimes come down the center aisle with a seven candle benediction candelabra, unlit. The mimes are dressed in black pants and blue sweat shirts; they have white mime make-up on. They place the candelabra on its stand (see diagram), and light one candle. Candles should be lit alternately on either side of the candelabra so that the top, center candle is the last one lit at the end of the passion.

II.

The slide then changes to "The King's Prayer". The mimes go to the congregation, find the Narrator, and lead him to the tabernacle area (area #1). The mimes then go and sit on the top step of the altar, next to the candelabra stand. (Note: before each scene begins, the mimes return to their seats next to the candelabra.) The Narrator then steps in front of Christ — the celebrant, the lights go on area #1, and the Narrator begins:

Narrator: After Jesus had shared himself with his apostles in his final meal, he sought to prepare them for the coming events.

Narrator moves into the darkness towards the altar and Christ moves forward and says:

An hour is coming — indeed has already come—when you will be scattered and each will go his own way, leaving me quite alone. Yet I can never be alone; the Father is with me. I tell you all this that you may find peace in me. You will suffer in the world. But take courage! I have overcome the world.

Christ then picks up the red stole that rests on the tabernacle stand and continues with this prayer:

Father, the hour has come! Give glory to your son that your son may give glory to you, in as much as you have given him authority over all mankind, that he may bestow eternal life on those you gave him. I have given you glory on earth by finishing the work you gave me to do. Do you now, Father, give me glory at your side, a glory I had with you before the world began.

Lights down. Mimes light two candles. Celebrant and narrator move up center and over right to the organ area, area #2.

III.

The slide changes to "The Royal Escort." (Note: with each of the title slides, they are flashed on, left on a few moments, and then turned off.) Mimes go down to the congregation and get four people, one for Peter and three for the Jewish crowd. They move them to the organ area. The mimes return to their place by the candelabra. The light comes up on the organ area.

Narrator: After this prayer, Jesus went out with his disciples across the Kidron Valley. There was a garden there, and he and his disciples entered it. The place was familiar to Judas as well (the one who was to hand him over) because Jesus had often met there with his disciples. Judas took the cohort as well as the guards supplied by the chief priests and pharisees and came there with lanterns, torches and weapons. Jesus, aware of all that would happen to him, stepped forward to meet them.

Narrator then moves back towards center left into the darkness. Christ moves forward towards the crowd:

Christ: Who is it you want?
Crowd: Jesus the Nazarean!
Christ: I am he.
The crowd retreats slightly and falls back. Jesus again says to them:
Christ: Who is it you want?
Crowd: Jesus the Nazarean!
Christ: I have told you I am he, if I am the one you want, let these men go.
Peter jumps up and makes violent rush toward crowd ruffli-g some of them. Jesus responds by saying:
Christ: Enough of your violence! Am I not to drink the cup my Father has given me?
The lights go out. Mimes light two more candles and Peter returns to his seat.

IV.

Slide changes to "Liturgy of coronation." Mimes go to congregation and get Pilate and lead him to his position on second step of altar (postion P1 in diagram). Mimes return to candelabra. Meanwhile, Narrator makes his way to the floor area left of Pilate. Light (altar spot) comes on and Narrator says:

Narrator: At daybreak they led Jesus to the Praetorium. They did not enter the Praetorium themselves, for they had to avoid ritual impurity if they were to eat the Passover Supper.

Narrator then moves left of altar into darkness. Christ moves to the top step, position "C". Pilate looks at Christ, then walks down the steps to position P2. He then says to the crowd:

Pilate: What accusation do you bring against this man?
Crowd: If he were not a criminal, we would certainly not have handed him over to you.
Pilate: Why do you not take him, then, and pass judgement on him according to your law?
Crowd: Because we may not put anyone to death.
Pilate goes up to position P1 and says to Christ:
Pilate: Are you the King of the Jews?
Christ: Are you saying this on your own, or have others been telling you about me?
Pilate: Am I a Jew? It is your own people and the chief priests who have handed you over to me. What have you done?
Christ: My kingdom does not belong to this world. If my kingdom were of this world, my subjects would be fighting to save me from being handed over to the Jews. As it is, my kingdom is not here.
Pilate: So, then, you are a king?
Christ: It is you who say I am a king. The reason I was born, the reason why I came into the world, is to testify to the truth. Anyone committed to the truth hears my voice.

Pilate: Truth! What does that mean?

Then, Pilate walks down to the crowd, position P2 and says:

Pilate: Speaking for myself, I find no case against this man. According to a custom of yours, I should release one prisoner at the Passover; would you like me, then, to release to you the King of the Jews?

Crowd: Not this man, but Barrabas.

Pilate: I tell you I find no case against him, but to satisfy your blood thirst, I will have him flogged.

Narrator moves down sanctuary and says:

Narrator: So Pilate handed Jesus over to the cohort to have him scourged. The soldiers then wove a crown of thorns and fixed it on his head, throwing around his shoulders a cloak of royal purple. Repeatedly they came up to him and said, "All hail King of the Jews!", slapping his face as they did so.

Narrator then moves up sanctuary into darkness and Pilate comes down to congregation. (Note: During Pilate's next lines, slides of Christ being scourged, crowned with thorns, and mocked will be alternating with certain words or lines. This will be indicated in the text by the appearance of the word "slide" or "slides" in parenthesis after the proper word or words.)

Christ turns his back to the congregation. Pilate comes down center to the congregation, position P3, and says:

Pilate: Observe what I do. I'm going to bring him out to you to make you realize that I find no case against him.

Pilate points to Jesus who has his back to the congregation and announces as the first slide comes on:

Pilate: Behold the man!

(second slide in silence)

(third slide goes on) and crowd says:

Crowd: Crucify him!

(fourth slide goes on) as the crowd repeats:

Crowd: Crucify him!

(fifth slide goes on) as Pilate replies:

Pilate: Take him and crucify him yourselves.

(sixth slide)

I find no case against him.

(seventh slide) as crowd retorts:

Crowd: We have a law, and according to that law *(eigth slide)* he must die, *(ninth slide)* because he made himself God's son.

Pilate: *(in confusion)* He what?

Christ turns back around as Pilate goes up to altar, position P1, and Pilate says:

Pilate: Where do you come from? *(silence)* Do you refuse to speak to me? Don't you know that I have the power to release you and the power to crucify you?

Christ: You would have no power over me at all unless it were given you from above. That is why he who handed me over to you is guilty of the greater sin.

Pilate goes down to the front pew (position P3), says to the congregation:

Pilate: I must release this man.

Then someone in the congregation stands up and shouts:

Person: If you free this man, you are no friend of Caesar. Anyone who makes himself a King becomes Caesar's rival.

Pilate: *(pointing at Jesus)* Look at your King!

Congregation (certain people seated in the congregation) and crowd begin scattered and building shouts of:

Crowd: Away with him! Away with him! Crucify him! Crucify him!

After several seconds Pilate screams:

Pilate: What? *(total silence, short pause)* Shall I crucify your King?

One person in congregation *(stands up and shouts):* We have no King but Caesar!

All characters freeze as the mimes light two more candles. Pilate moves back into the darkness behind the altar.

V.

Slide changes to "Enthronement." Mimes go and get the long upright beam for the cross, hammers, bolts and nails. They give them to the crowd. Meanwhile, Christ walks to the back of the chapel and picks up cross beam for the cross and stands in back. Narrator comes forward and says:

Narrator: So finally, Pilate handed Jesus over to be crucified. Jesus was led away and, carrying his cross by himself, he went out to what is called "the place of the skull."

Narrator returns to darkness as Christ walks up the center aisle. When Christ reaches the crowd he hands them the cross bar and goes up to position "C." The crowd assembles the cross, lays it on the floor, and the mimes go down to congregation and bring members up so that they can each drive a nail into the cross. The action of hammering a nail into the cross has such a great connotation of guilt that it can become a very negative symbol unless it is later "redeemed." Therefore, it is strongly suggested that this action never be used unless it is accompanied by the precise method of cross adoration used in the liturgy. When a person takes a small cross from the very nail he has hammered into the cross, he takes a symbol of life from what had been a very negative symbol.

The crowd will help the congregation in this. When all are done, they return to their seats and the mimes bring the stand for the cross up to position "C." They then start to lift the cross into place. Pilate stops them with the cry:

Pilate: Wait!

Pilate then attaches the sign "Jesus of Nazareth, King of the Jews" on the top of the cross. Pilate returns to his seat and the mimes put the cross in the stand. Celebrant comes down to floor. Mimes light one candle.

Then the lights go out, and a series of slides come on, accompanied by a solo piano playing the musical accompaniment to "Movin' On" (by Raymond R. Hannisian. Shawnee Press Inc., Delaware Water Gap, PA #B-336).

The words are not sung. The slides include artistic representations of the Way of the Cross, including Jesus' meeting of his Mother, his falls, the nailing to the cross and his death on the cross. Slides of the deposition from the cross should not be used in this section.

When music and slides are finished, pause; then the celebrant goes up and lights last candle. He then turns to the congregation and says:

Christ: It is accomplished. *(pause for a few moments of silent prayer).*

The People Greet Their King

These intercessory prayers are the people greeting their new king by praying to his Father. The prayers are all very quiet in contrast to the very powerful and demanding proclamation of the Passion. For most of the congregation, the prayers are even more relaxed because only one individual reads the response for each prayer; they need not struggle to read anything.

After a few moments of silent prayer following the Passion, the altar spot comes on again. From now until the end of the liturgy, this is the only light used. All light comes from the cross. The celebrant comes down and faces the congregation and begins the first prayer. The respondents for each prayer are scattered in various places throughout the congregation. For the last prayer, the celebrant faces the cross and all kneel.

1) **Celebrant:** Pray brothers and sisters, that all the gifts of creation may awaken in us a deeper sense of care and responsibility.

Responder: All the gifts of the earth, Father, reveal your great love for us. Forgive us our thoughtless and wasteful use of them. By the power of your Spirit, teach us to begin again to reclaim and reverence all the resources of our earth. And this we ask through our enthroned King, Jesus Christ our Lord. Amen

2) **Celebrant:** Let us pray that God may open our eyes and our hearts so we can recognize his presence in all forms of life.

Responder: Father, your love is present in the young, the old, the unborn, the dying. You are present in the orphan and the widow, in the poor, the hungry, the naked, the lonely, in prisoners and the dispossessed. Give us eyes to see Christ's light shine clearly through all your gifts of life around us. Give us also generous hearts and hands to reach out, protect and serve you in all of them. This we ask through Christ our Lord. Amen.

3) **Celebrant:** Let us pray, friends, for the church throughout the world, that God, the Father who established it through Jesus Christ, may continue to guide it through the power and ever-renewing breath of his Spirit.

Responder: God our Father, continue to gather us from the ends of the earth to proclaim your glory, to celebrate your love as revealed to us through Jesus Christ your son. Help us continue to walk in freedom as your sons and daughters. Increase our faith, strengthen our hope, make visible our love. Teach us to proclaim your name and bring your good news to people everywhere. This we ask through Christ our Lord. Amen.

4) **Celebrant:** Let us pray for_____our Pope, _____ our bishop, and for all bishops, priests, nuns, deacons, and for all people everywhere.

Responder: Father, through your Spirit you make us holy. By the power of the Spirit you breathe into each one of us, help us build up your kingdom on that little piece of earth on which we stand. And this we ask through Christ our Lord. Amen

5) **Celebrant:** Brothers and sisters, we are the buildings in which God's spirit dwells. Let us pray with all our hearts that we can make of our cities and communities dwellings that serve and respect the human spirit.

Responder: Father, call us out of our loneliness and isolation into community. Help us stand together and share with each other the healing we have first received from You. Teach us to use all our strength and love to make of our cities, communities that build up your kingdom here on earth. This we ask through our King, Christ the Lord. Amen.

6) **Celebrant:** Let us pray for all who share God's gift of faith in Jesus Christ, that we who are fragmented may become whole, that we who are many may someday be one.

Responder: Father, Jesus' prayer for us was that we might be one even as You and He are one. Out of love you created us. We share in baptism a common call to witness to your love revealed to us in Jesus Christ. Heal us of our divisions. Bring all Christians closer to the day when we can witness to all the world that we worship one Lord in spirit and in truth. And this we ask through Christ our Lord. Amen.

7) **Celebrant:** Let us pray, brothers and sisters, that God can help us look beyond the grand illusions of prejudice to the common dignity we all share as his children.

Responder: Father, forgive us our insensitivity to one another. Help us believe again in the goodness of each person. Bind us into one people through our care. Let us experience an injustice to one member of our human family as a blow to all. This we ask through Christ our Lord. Amen.

8) **Celebrant:** Let us pray that there may be an end to all violence once and for all.

Responder: God, our Father, You have made us and you know what is in our hearts. Heal us of our violence. Teach us to throw down our arms, to open the clenched fist, to melt our hardened hearts. Help us imitate Jesus' suffering, dying and rising. In this way, heal us of our violence so peace can once again have a home in our hearts, our homes and our world. And this we ask through Christ our Lord. Amen.

9) **Celebrant:** Let us pray for all those in positions of public trust as well as those who put them there.

Responder: Father, your Son has told us "no servant is greater than his master. As I have done for you, so you must go and do for one another." Teach us to serve one another out of love. Help us never to expect from our leaders what we are unwilling to give ourselves. And raise up among us, Father, other teachers like your Son who can drive the lesson deeper into our dull hearts. May we all follow the life and example of Jesus: pouring ourselves out to the last in loving service of our fellow men and women. All this we ask through Christ our Lord. Amen.

10) **Celebrant:** Let us pray that God's healing may flow to and through the sickness, the suffering, the dying of ourselves and all his people.

Responder: God our Father, You strengthen the faint-hearted, you renew the weary and fill with courage those who have lost heart. Help all who call upon You in their need to experience your presence and know You are near. We ask this through Christ our Lord. Amen.

11) **Celebrant:** And finally, brothers and sisters, let us kneel and ask God to help us follow Christ our King through ignominy to glory, through suffering and death to the fullness of new life in resurrection. *(all kneel).*

Everyone: God our Father, here we are kneeling before our King. We place ourselves entirely at his service. We want to be part of his kingdom. In this spirit, Father, we place before our King all we have and are. Do with us what You will. It is our intention and desire to follow Jesus' life and example to the limit of our powers. We wish to imitate him in putting up with every situation which brings unfairness, indignity and hardship upon us personally. All we ask, Father, is that this loyalty spring from the deep desire of our hearts to praise You, love You and serve You more. We make this prayer to You through Christ our Lord and King, now and forever. Amen.

(Stand at this point)

The King Shares His Throne

For this liturgy, a large number of plain wooden crosses are made and attached to a loop of yarn large enough to fit easily over someone's head. The veneration of the cross thus becomes a putting on of the cross: the Christian symbol of life and loving service.

When the intercessory prayers are finished, the celebrant stands, faces the congregation, and the slide "The King Shares His Throne" comes on. Mimes go to back of chapel, down center aisle, and meet deacon who is holding a platter of crosses. Deacon sings: "Behold, behold the wood of the cross, on which has hung our salvation. O come let us adore." People repeat this antiphon. During this the mimes hold up two small crosses.

Deacon and mimes next move to the edge of the sanctuary and turn toward the congregation. Deacon then repeats singing of the antiphon. Congregation then responds again with antiphon. Deacon and mimes then turn and approach the celebrant. All four hang crucifixes from nails on large cross. When they are through they all turn and deacon and celebrant sing antiphon. Then celebrant and deacon go with mimes to bottom step. Celebrant and deacon then step up to the cross. Each takes a cross off the large cross. They turn to congregation, put it on, make a sign of the cross deliberately, and step to the side of the cross. Next the mimes step forward and do the same. They then step down and go to the congregation, sending them up to adore two at a time. During the veneration of the cross, the *Good Friday Hymn* is sung by a solo *a capella* voice. The tempo should be mournful. If there is a large number of people to venerate the cross, the soloist should be given time to rest by having a solo instrument play a verse in between those verses sung by the soloist. When all have completed veneration, celebrant, deacon and mimes come to the bottom step.

Good Friday Hymn (tune: *Battle Hymn of the Republic*)
Revised for Good Friday, Adoration of Cross Liturgy

1. Mine eyes have seen the glory of the coming of the Lord;
He is trampling out the vintage where the grapes of life are stored;
He has come to greet his people as our all-triumphant Lord;
His truth is marching on.

2. Upon a tree they nailed him, the Lamb upon his throne;
And from his broken body the blood of life did flow;
O faithful tree of beauty, O noble tree of life;
O Saviour crucified.

3. With a wreath of bloody thorns Christ was crowned for you and me;
On a barren wooden throne, he was raised up for all to see;
As he died to make us holy, let us live to make us free;
Our God is marching on.

4. He has sounded forth the trumpet that shall never call retreat;
He is sifting out the hearts of men before his judgement seat;
O be swift my soul to answer him, be jubilant my feet;
Our King is marching on.

5. O sing the Saviour's glory, sing his triumph far and wide;

And tell the wond'rous story of his body crucified;
O let our song proclaim it, that Christ Jesus is the Lord;
The King of all the world!
Refrain: Glory, Glory, hallelujah!
Glory, Glory, hallelujah!
Glory, Glory, hallelujah!
His truth is marching on.

The Royal Banquet

The communion service is very simple and plain, an ironic contrast to the idea of a "royal banquet."

The next slide goes up: "The Royal Banquet." Deacon goes down center aisle to back of chapel and greets two ministers who have the Eucharist reserved from Thursday. He leads them in with a candle. They all go to the altar; candle and Eucharist are placed on the altar. Celebrant leads congregation in the *Our Father*. Then the ministers and deacon break the bread, while the celebrant prays as follows:

Good Friday Fraction Rite
by Robert Walsh
Must not the lonely grain of wheat be thrashed to make the bread we eat?
Must not the grapes grown ripe in time be crushed before they yield their wine?
Yet, hard to grasp this simple thing, that life is born through suffering.
Now from the cross our King is come to share the life his death has won.
with each of us. In this bread blessed and sacred wine our King expressed
His victory for all to see:
Christ crowned in death is Christ set free!
And though his cross is bittersweet
(a coronation through defeat)
here, now the Living Christ we eat!

When all is readied, the ministers communicate. For distribution, celebrant then takes bread and positions himself in front of the cross. The other two ministers take the wine to either side of the celebrant. Mimes come to communion first and demonstrate the procedure. They then go and lead congregation to communion. During communion, the song *This is My Body* (NAL) by John Foley, SJ, is sung.

When all have partaken, the ministers return to the altar, consume the rest of the Eucharist, and remove the baskets and chalices to the cruet table. They blow out the small candle and take their places in chairs placed in front of the pews, sanctuary right. Mimes sit on floor.

The King's Repose

A slide comes on reading "The King's Repose." Slides begin to the music *Sometimes I Feel Like a Motherless Child*. The song is sung by a soloist, unaccompanied. The first verse is "Sometimes I feel like a motherless child..."; the second verse is "Sometimes I feel like a bird with no wings..."; the third verse is "Sometimes I feel like a fire with no flame...". The fourth verse is played by a single muffled trumpet. And for the fifth verse the solo unaccompanied voice returns to sing "Sometimes I Feel Like a Motherless Child."

Slides consist of a picture meditation beginning with slides of Madonna and Child, continuing with slides of the deposition from the cross, and ending with slides of the Pieta. When picture meditation is finished, mimes go to candelabra and begin extinguishing candles. When one of the mimes goes to put out the last candle, top center candle, the other mime restrains his or her hand. They leave it lit. They put down their extinguishers and go to the floor. There they make a profound bow to the cross. Then the mimes turn and go get the ministers. The ministers rise and lead the mimes out the center aisle.

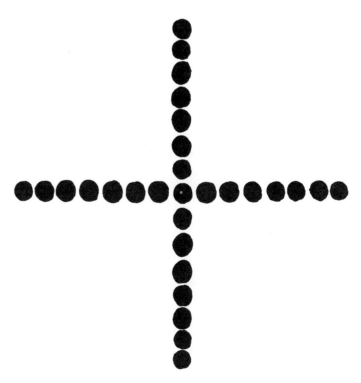

My Dancing Day: A Carol Service For Holy

by Eileen E. Freeman

We are quite accustomed to Christmas carols during the holiday season; we can even think of a few New Year's carols. But when someone asks us about Easter carols, we are usually puzzled. We name some well-known Easter hymns like "Jesus Christ is Risen Today." But the fact is, carols are quite different from hymns. Carols are songs that were originally meant to be danced to. They have a quality of movement about them that differentiates them from the hymn. Carols also stem from the folk-stratum of life, while most hymns come from a more erudite stratum. Finally, carols differ from hymns in that their subjects are often legendary rather than historical. The stories that carols tell are paradigmatic rather than didactic.

In many places choirs present services of carols for Christmastime. This article presents a carol service for Passiontide. It is designed as a para-liturgical service with a choir or small singing group, a troupe of mummers in the old English tradition, and a few other ministers. Three of the carols used are late medieval or an imitation of the medieval style. The fourth, "Friday Morning," is a modern carol by Sidney Carter.

Ministers and performers:
Leader of prayer
1-4 Readers
Small choir for unison or two-part singing
Soloist
Guitarist
Flautist or recorder player
A group of mummers, about seven.

All the ministers; the leader, readers and soloist (cantor) should be vested in alb and cincture. The choir and instrumentalists should also be vested or costumed in a medieval fashion, if possible. The mummers should be costumed in black leotards or the like, with white make-up. Or medieval costumes could be used, if available, for a different effect.

Position of players: As the service begins, the choir is already in place in the front of the church, on the right side of the sanctuary. The instrumentalists are similarly placed. On the left side of the sanctuary is an elevated podium or pulpit for the reader. The celebrant or leader of prayer sits just behind and to the right of the lectern. The reader(s) sit(s) against the left wall of the sanctuary. The mummers perform from the center front of the sanctuary.

Entrance procession: The crossbearer leads, followed by the reader(s) holding aloft the book of readings. (The readings should never be proclaimed from single sheets of paper; this creates a bad visual effect.) The mummers follow two by two. The celebrant comes last.

The entrance procession is a quiet, but solemn thing. The congregation remains seated. Just before the entrance procession begins, the soloist goes to a microphone on the right side of the sanctuary and announces:

Good evening (morning, etc.). We have come together this evening to commemorate the Passion of our Lord Jesus Christ. During this season of Lent, and in particular, during this Holy Week many of us have been asking ourselves the question, "What would I have done if I had been on Golgotha when Jesus was crucified?" We have tried to place ourselves in the shoes of the Apostles, of Mary, of Magdalen, and imagine how they felt, how they reacted to the death of Jesus.

We are not the first to ask such questions. In the Middle Ages and later centuries, anonymous poets and balladeers turned these questions into popular songs or carols. Often they would invent people or events surrounding the Passion, so as to give their listeners more familiar models of how the good Christian should act in the face of Jesus' death.

We would like to present a short service based on some of these carols, both old and modern. As in former times the singing of the carols will be accompanied by miming and dancing to represent more vividly the events of the first Good Friday. We invite you to relax and to participate with us in our service of Passiontide carols.

Celebrant: May the grace of the Lord Jesus, who laid down his life for us, be with you always.
All: And also with you.
Celebrant: Let us pray.
All loving and all merciful Father, You reveal yourself to your people in many ways. But it is through Jesus your Son that You have most clearly revealed yourself. Open up the eyes of our hearts and minds this night, so that we may better understand what Christ suffered for our sake, and in understanding, believe more deeply. We ask this in Jesus' name.
All: Amen.

Reader: Our first reading is from the Gospel according to Luke (Luke 19:28-44). (Alternate readings are Mark 11:1-10 or Matthew 21:1-11.)
Soloist: How did the bystanders feel the day Jesus rode into Jerusalem? What did the foreigners think: the Greeks, the Africans, the Orientals? What went through the minds of those who had come to Jerusalem for business rather than prayer: the buyers, the sellers, the merchants?

The Merchants' Carol

1. As we rode down the steep hillside,
Twelve merchants with our fairing,
A shout across the hollow land
Came loud upon our hearing,
A shout, a song, a thousand strong,
A thousand lusty voices:
'Make haste,' said I, I knew not why,
'Jerusalem rejoices!'

2. Beneath the olives fast we rode,
And louder came the shouting:
'So great a noise must mean,' said we,
'A king, beyond all doubting!'
Spurred on, did we, this king to see,
And left the mules to follow;
And nearer, clearer rang the noise
Along the Kidron hollow.

3. Behold, a many-coloured crowd
About the gate we found there;
But one among them all, we marked,
One man who made no sound there;
Still louder ever rose the crowd's
'Hosanna in the highest!'
'O King,' thought I, 'I know not why
In all this joy thou sighest.'

4. *A Merchant:*
'Then he looked up, he looked at me;
But whether he spoke I doubted:
How could I hear so calm a speech
While all the rabble shouted?
And yet these words, it seems, I heard:
"I shall be crowned tomorrow."
They struck my heart with sudden smart,
And filled my bones with sorrow.'

5. We followed far, we traded not,
But long we could not find him.
The very folk that called him king
Let robbers go and bind him.
We found him then, the sport of men.
Still calm among their crying;
And well we knew his words were true—
He was most kingly dying.

During the introduction the mummers come out to the sanctuary floor. Player 1, who is the narrator of the carol, stands front and stage left, facing the congregation. The others stand in a straight line behind him, facing front. From left to right they are players 2-7.

During verse 1: *Player 7, Jesus, turns right and starts to climb the altar steps. Players 2-6 turn to face him, waving their arms enthusiastically in rhythm. Player 1 turns as if startled by their silent noise, then slowly turns back to the congregation. Meanwhile 7 crosses the altar and moves down the other side to stand in front of 2-6, who once again face the congregation.*

During verse 2: *Player 7 leads 2-6 who are still waving hands, around toward stage right, away from 1. Players 3 and 4 break the line to move ahead of Jesus. They kneel on either side, as if spreading their cloaks before him. 1 crosses right, across the sanctuary floor, moving here and there as if trying to get a better view.*

During verse 3: *Player 7 leads 2-6 left across the stage in front of 1; in effect, 7 and 1 change positions. 2-6 this time are behind 7 in a semicircle. All face front. This leaves 7 and 1 standing a few feet apart, looking intently at each other. The crowd, 2-6, continue their waving, but Jesus pays no heed to them.*

During verse 4: *Player 1 moves a pace or two closer to 7. 7 holds up his hand as if in greeting. Player 1 puts his right hand to his chest as if in pain, then sinks to one knee, looking at the floor, while 7 holds both his hands over his own head as though placing a crown there. 2-6 hold 7 back as he attempts to take a step towards 1.*

During verse 5: *The crowd changes its tune now. The waving hands become fists, beating at 7. They push him across the stage right and up one or two altar steps. There they turn him around to face the congregation and stretch out his hands. 7 stands in the position of crucifixion. As 2-6 move 7, 1 gets up and slowly follows. After 7 is crucified, 2-6 stand on either side of 7, a little toward the front of the sanctuary, facing Jesus. They do the same waving motion that they did in verse 1, but their hands are made into fists. Player 1 moves to within a few steps of 7, approaching from stage left, so he is half-facing the congregation, and makes a deep bow or genuflection. 2-6 freeze their jeering motions.*

End of carol: *Players rise turn, etc., so they are in a straight line facing the congregation. They bow to them and go back to the sidelines.*

Celebrant: Let us (stand and) pray.

Soloist: Our response is "Lord, help us to follow You." When we feel the same joy that your followers felt the day You came so triumphantly to Jerusalem, we pray...
When a crowd of confusing or distracting events hides You from our sight, we pray...
As we minister to those who are suffering and in need, we pray ...
When we are called fools for believing in You, and it seems wiser to disown You temporarily, we pray ...

Celebrant: Father, you look into our hearts, and You see how many things make us too worried to hear you. Our businesses, our families, our health all concern us. Help us to be like the merchants in the carol, who refused to let anything stand in the way of their learning the truth which your son Jesus taught. We ask this in his name.

All: Amen.

"My Dancing Day"

Reader: The second reading is taken from the book of Wisdom (2:12-20).

(The reading follows)

This is the Word of the Lord.

All: Thanks be to God.

(During the reading the mummers come out to the front of the sanctuary. Six form a straight line across the sanctuary; the seventh, who represents Jesus, stands in the middle in front of them.)

Soloist: "My Dancing Day" is a carol from the time of Shakespeare. In it Jesus speaks about his redemption of humanity, a redemption which He calls his "Dance." His great desire is to lead his true love, that is, the Church, in the steps of the dance.

My Dancing Day

1. Tomorrow shall be my dancing day:
I would my true love did so chance
To see the legend of my play,
To call my true love to my dance:

Refrain

Sing O my love,
O my love, my love my love;
This have I done for my true love.

2. Then was I born of a virgin pure,
Of her I took fleshly substance;
Thus was I knit to man's nature,
To call my true love to my dance:

Refrain

3. In a manger laid and wrapped I was,
So very poor, this was my chance,
Betwixt an ox and a silly poor ass,
To call my true love to my dance:

Refrain

4. Then afterwards baptized I was;
The Holy Ghost on me did glance,
My Father's voice heard from above,
To call my true love to my dance:

Refrain

5. Into the desert I was led,
Where I fasted without substance;
The devil bade me make stones my bread,
To have me break my true love's dance:

Refrain

6. For thirty pence Judas me sold,
And with me made great variance,
Because they loved darkness rather than light,
To call my true love to my dance:

Refrain

7. Then on the cross hanged I was,
His covetousness for to advance;
Mark whom I kiss, the same do hold,
The same is he shall lead the dance:

Refrain

8. Then down to hell I took my way,
Where Barabbas had deliverance;
They scourged me and set me at nought,
Judged me to die to lead the dance:

Refrain

9. Then up to heaven I did ascend,
Where a spear to my heart did glance;
There issued forth both water and blood,
To call my true love to my dance:

Refrain

10. Then down to hell I took my way,
For my ture love's deliverance,
And rose again on the third day,
Up to my true love and the dance:

Refrain

11. Then up to heaven I did ascend,
Where now I dwell in sure substance
On the right hand of God, that man
May come unto the general dance:

Refrain

During verse 1: *Players 1-5 make a circle around 7, a wide circle with spaces in between the players. Player 6 moves outside the sanctuary towards the congregation. Those in the circle move counterclockwise slowly, using some type of stylized dance step. 7 stands still.*

During verse 2: *The circle stops, then begins a similar movement in the opposite direction. Jesus, player 7, weaves through the circle in the other direction, grasping the hands of 1-5 in square-dance fashion. During the chorus he steps out of the circle towards the congregation and looks towards 6 (a woman); 6 looks away towards the congregation.*

During verse 3: *The circle breaks into a semi-circle open towards the congregation. Player 1 on stage right end steps out. Jesus turns to face him, moves toward him, kneels before him with arms outstretched in a relaxed fashion. Player 1 scoops "water" with both hands cupped and then opens them over Jesus' head. Meanwhile player 5 moves to stand on the top altar step, stretches arms out over the group. Jesus rises, turns towards 6 and stretches out right arm toward her. She backs away a step.*

During verse 4: *All players 1-5 stand aside, leaving 7 alone. He sits down, clasping hands around knees and bending head forward. Player 2 (Satan) moves forward, touches him on the shoulder. 7 looks up. 2 cups hands, offers them to Jesus. 7 rolls away from 2 on the ground, then leaps up and begins to run toward 6, who turns away from 7 and also runs a few steps. 7 stops as if in mid-stride, then slowly bends shoulders as if in deep discouragement.*

During verse 5: *Players 3 and 4 meet in the center of the stage, join hands, and engage in some stylized dance steps, perhaps moving towards each other and back several times. Players 1, 2, and 5 clap silently in time. During the chorus 7 looks up again at 6, who slowly, as if unwillingly, turns to him, but with bent head.*

During verse 6: *Players 1-5 come up behind 7. 1-2 take his arms and bring them around his back, as if tying him. Jesus drops to right knee. The others circle him raising and lowering their right arms, hands in fists, as if striking him. Jesus topples forward, looking toward 6. 6 takes a few quick, hesitant steps towards him, as far as the edge of the sanctuary, then stops, turns halfways, hands covering face.*

During verse 7: *1-5 raise Jesus up, lead him to altar steps. He mounts them, at least one or two of them, and stands facing the congregation, arms stretched out. 6, overcoming hesitation, re-enters sanctuary, kneels before Jesus in classic Magdalen pose, embracing his feet. 1-5 stretch out arms, pointing at her.*

During verse 8: *1-5 leave, and stand on the sidelines for the moment. 7 leaves, and dances through the sanctuary. 6 remains as she was for the last verse. 7 comes up behind her, touches her, raises her up. He joins his left hand to her right, leads her in a dance around the sanctuary.*

During verse 9: *7 and 6 continue their dance. As they do so, one by one, players 1-5 join in the chain. During the chorus they form a circle on the sanctuary floor and step counter-clockwise. As the chorus is repeated they stop, raise hands and then bow simultaneously towards the center of the circle. During the final chorus, 7 has left the circle and entered the center of it, so they are all bowing towards him.*

End: *The circle opens, so that all are as they were in the beginning; all bow to the congregation, go back to their places on the side.*

Celebrant: Let us (stand and) pray.

Soloist: We respond with, "Lead us, Lord, along your way."

For the grace to follow You, even when there is no light ahead to see, we pray...

For the faith to believe that You lead us along the right paths, we pray...

For the strength not to dance to the tune of everyone who plays a pleasant melody, we pray...

That we may never be afraid to take each other's hands and dance together before the Lord, we pray...

That we may always seek out our neighbors' hands so as to bring them into the Lord's dance, too, we pray...

Celebrant: Father of our Lord Jesus Christ, give us the strength to follow Christ wherever He may lead us, so that one day we may join in the great Dance which all creation dances around your throne. We ask this in Christ's name.

All: Amen.

"Friday Morning"

Reader: Our third reading is from the Gospel of Luke (23:39-43).

Solist: What occupied the thought of the two men who were crucified with Jesus? Did they spend their last day beset by hate, or fear, or remorse? Did they wonder what was going to happen to them? Did they speak to Jesus as the three of them struggled to carry their cross-beams? Did they wonder who He was at all? Did they, too, have friends in the crowd, crying for them?

During the introduction the players come forward. Player 7, Jesus, and 2, Dismas, stand together on the left of stage center, Jesus closer to the congregation. Players 1 and 3 face 7 and 2 respectively. 4-6 stand together right of center, about six feet away.

Friday Morning

1. It was on a Friday morning
That they took me from the cell,
And I saw they had a carpenter
To crucify as well.
You can blame it on to Pilate,
You can blame it on the Jews,
You can blame it on the Devil,
It's God I accuse.

Refrain

It's God they ought to crucify
Instead of you and me,
I said to the carpenter
A- hanging on the tree.

2. You can blame it on to Adam,
You can blame it on to Eve,
You can blame it on the apple,
But that I can't believe.
It was God that made the Devil,
And the Woman and the Man,
And there wouldn't be an Apple
If it wasn't in the plan.

Refrain

3. Now Barabbas was a Killer
And they let Barabbas go.
But you are being crucified
For nothing, here below.
But God is up in heaven
And he doesn't do a thing:
With a million angels watching,
And they never move a wing.

Refrain

4. To hell with Jehovah,
To the carpenter I said,
I wish that a carpenter
had made the world instead.
Good-bye and good luck to you,
Our ways will soon divide.
Remember me in heaven,
The man you hung beside.

Refrain

During verse 1: *1 and 3 cross the wrists of seven and two as if tying them. They take them by the wrists and lead them toward the others. Player 2 pulls back, resisting, then moves forward. Players 4-6 break apart to let them pass, then follow them. 1 leads 7 up the altar steps and arranges his arms as though crucifying him. 3 leads 2 to the step below and to stage left of Jesus and does the same.*

During verse 2: *All players but 7 and 2 form a semi-circle on the sanctuary floor facing the congregation. 6 is on the stage left end; 3 on stage right end; the others may take any intermediate position. 3 points to 6, who turns around away from 3, with forearm across forehead; then 6 turns back, kneels, lowers arm as if to strike his breast; then rises, stands with arms outstretched, as if pushing 3 away. As soon as 3 has pointed to 6, initiating 6's movements, 3 does the same to the other players in the semi-circle. At the end of the verse, when the chorus begins, all but 3 point to 7; 3 points at the crowd.*

During verse 3: *Players 1, 4-6 make a circle around 3, moving in a counter-clockwise direction with clasped hands, as 3 tries to break the circle. 3 breaks the circle, runs to the sidelines. The others sit facing the congregation at stage right, off to the side, with hands over eyes, ears or mouth in the classic "See no evil..." pose.*

During verse 4: *Player 2 leaps down the step, as if to run away, then whirls around, stretching out a hand toward Jesus 7. 2 hesitates, withdraws hand, then as 7 lowers his hands and reaches out to him, 2 grasps both his hands and lets 7 pull him up beside him. The two turn to face each other, and stretch out their hands, still clasped, back into the crucifixion pose. Jesus bows his head to stage front, player 2 to stage rear.*

End: *As the song is ending, all the players numbered 1, 3-6 come to the front of the stage and bow to the congregation. 2 and 7 also face the congregation from the altar step and bow. All go back to their places.*

Celebrant: Let us (stand and) pray.

Soloist: Our response is "Lord help us to understand."
In times of trial, when we do not know where to turn, we pray...

When we have been hurt and wonder if we can ever trust others again, we pray...

When the mystery of your death and resurrection seem too much for us to comprehend, we pray...

THE HOLY WEEK BOOK

Celebrant: Father, perhaps the thief who hung on the cross beside your Son knew he didn't have anything to lose by asking Jesus for help. But again, maybe something about Jesus, something He said to him on the way to Calvary, opened his eyes, so that he could trust Jesus and lay his crime, his sin on Jesus for Him to bear. Help us always to come to Jesus with our weaknesses, our failings, our sins, to lay them before the cross, and leave them there. We ask this through Jesus our Lord.

All: Amen.

Mary's Wandering

1. Once Mary would go wandering,
To all the lands would run,
That she might find her son, that she might find her son.

2. Whom met she as she journeyed forth?
Saint Peter, that good man,
Who sadly did her scan,
who sadly did her scan.

3. 'O tell me have you seen him yet—
The one I love the most—
The son whom I have lost?'

4. 'Too well, too well, I've seen thy son:
'Twas by a palace-gate,
Most grievous was his state.'

5. 'O say, what wore he on his head?'
'A crown of thorns he wore;
A cross he also bore.'

6. 'Ah me! and he must bear that cross,
Till he's brought to the hill,
For cruel men to kill.'

7. 'Nay, Mary, cease thy weeping, dear:
The wounds they are but small;
But heaven is won for all!'

"Mary's Wandering"

Reader: Our final reading is taken from the Gospel of John (29:25-30)

Soloist: What of Mary, the mother of Jesus? When did she hear the news that her Son had been arrested and condemned to death? Was she in the middle of her housecleaning? Was she at the well with the other women drawing water? How much did she understand about what was to happen?

(*During the introduction the players come out, except for 6. They form a widespread semicircle opening towards the congregation. Player 4, Peter, sits, clasping arms around knees and hiding face.*

During verse 1: *Player 6, Mary comes out, dancing and whirling around the sanctuary, and stops in front of Peter.*

During verse 2: *Player 6 stretches out her hands to 4, touching his shoulders. He looks up at her, slowly rises, and takes her hands.*

During verse 3: *Player 6 dances around 4, then stops stage left of him, holds out her hands to him.*

During verse 4: *Player 4 turns away, shuddering, hands in front of face; raises left arm in the air, as if saying "Leave me alone." 6 goes to him, puts hands on his shoulders.*

During verse 5: *4 turns to face her. 6 makes a motion as if setting a crown on her head. 4 nods, then holds up his arms in the crucifixion pose.*

During verse 6: *Mary turns away in anguish, her arms making movements as if she could push it all away. She does this while making a circle of the sanctuary, moving in front of the other players, who stretch out their arms to her.*

During verse 7: *4 catches 6, touches her face to wipe away tears; then half kneels, hands cupped together on the floor; then draws hands up and outward as he stands, ending with them nearly together over his head. 6 and all other players follow suit. Their expressions should be joyous.*

End: *All bow from their stations to the congregation, then return to the sidelines.*

Celebrant: Let us (stand and) pray.

Soloist: Our response is, "Lord, teach us to care." For For those around us who are neglected, and in need, we pray...
For the physically and mentally handicapped, for the emotionally ill, we pray...
For all of our brothers and sisters in the Christian community, we pray...
That we might be more generous in sharing our talents and ministries with others, we pray...

Celebrant: Father, we can only guess at the thoughts that must have gone through Mary's heart, when she saw her Son dying in agony. Yet at a time when most of Jesus' followers deserted Him, she cared enough to remain faithful. When the rooster crows, and we feel ourselves too much like Peter, may her example bring us back up the hill of Calvary, and through Calvary, to the empty tomb on our Easter morning. We ask this through Jesus Christ our Lord, who lives and reigns with You in the unity of the Holy Spirit, one God, forever and ever.

All: Amen.

This concludes the service of carols. The participants all leave, crucifer, mummers, reader, celebrant. The singers and musicians bring up the rear. It would be appropriate for them to sing, either in Latin or English, the Easter Sequence, "Victimae Paschali Laudes." The Latin will be found in any *Liber Usualis*; an English translation with the Gregorian melody can be found in the Episcopalian *1940 Hymnal*. It would be pleasant if a small social hour with coffee and cookies could be held afterwards.

Biblical Stations Of The Cross

by Eileen E. Freeman

At some point in any Christian's first visit to a Catholic church he or she is likely to question his guide about the fourteen pictures or crosses lining the walls of that church. The artwork depicting the traditional stations on the Way of the Cross have decorated churches and chapels for quite a while: the Way of the Cross is a venerable devotion. Most Catholics remember "making" the "Stations" at least during Lent, or when they were in Catholic grade school.

Today, the Way of the Cross is struggling back uphill from the decade of the sixties, when it was eclipsed along with other Catholic devotional practices such as the rosary and the parish mission. The last decade has been a rough testing ground of the durability of pietistic forms of worship; some devotions, perhaps less relevant to the Church today, have largely faded away, while others have remained. The Way of the Cross is one that has remained.

That this should be so is not really that surprising. The Way of the Cross fills a definite need in many people's spiritual and emotional lives. Catholicism has always been an emotional Church (in a very good sense). It recognizes that we need to bring our emotions and deepest feelings to prayer, just as much as we need to bring our attention and will. There have always been processions to allow us to dance and shout; and ashes, reproaches and prostrations to allow us to cry. But for a while in the sixties, even the best of our Catholic emotionalism was often considered unwise. It was felt that with the Mass in English, people would automatically be able to participate with more of their body. But such was not the case. We became acclimated to the English as we had to the Latin. Moreover, many of the powerful symbols that stirred our hearts and our faith had been practically eliminated. Banks of candles, the smell of incense, the sprinkling of holy water, Gregorian chant seemed to vanish.

Many people became resigned to this, to a Catholicism that nourished their minds but rarely their heart. However, by the end of the sixties, even most of these people had to admit they were at least a little "thirsty." The phenomenal growth of the Charismatic Renewal, the Cursillo, teenage weekends for Christ, Marriage Encounters and the like, all testify to the people's need to have their deepest feelings fed.

What does all of this have to do with the Stations of the Cross?

Actually, it has a great deal to do with it. The Stations were one devotion that many Catholics could always count on to confront them forcibly with the grim, but ultimately triumphant, mysteries of our salvation. Our lives were always being assimilated to the Cross of Christ. Sister would say to the child who had fallen on the playground, "Think of Jesus on the way to Calvary." A woman's job becomes unbearable, so she thinks of Jesus carrying his cross, and decides to keep trying "just for a day or two more", to see if some good will come out of it. We look at what Jesus bore for love of us and find new strength to carry our burdens. We can weep the bitterness and self-pity out of our lives if we let the Way of the Cross lead us to the Father.

The devotion which we call the Stations of the Cross combines both biblical and legendary material. It is a blend of history and fiction. This has bothered some Catholics, particularly now that the scriptures have come (Thank God!) to be read by an increasing number of them. This concern is justified. It is quite soul-stirring to read of how Jesus met his mother on the Via Dolorosa, but the fact is that there is no scriptural evidence for it, nor is there a real *tradition* of such a thing in the Church. To concentrate on this mythical meeting and to forget that Mary was at the place called Golgotha with the apostle John, is to do a disservice to the whole account of the Passion, a narrative so important that it was committed to writing before almost anything else in the New Testament. The fact is that Veronica never existed, despite various churches' claims to possess her "veil." Nor are we told that Jesus fell three times; we are not even told that He fell once. Jesus' sufferings are enough even without the added ones.

Then, too, consider that in the traditional stations, Jesus is usually viewed as passively submitting to whatever was dealt out to Him. This is quite at variance with the scriptures. In the Passion Narrative, Jesus is always in control of the situation, whatever it is. In Gethsemane, *He* alone has the presence of mind not to fight the mob or run; *He* persuades the soldiers to leave his disciples alone and take Him instead. *He* decides which of his accusers He will answer and when. Faced with a man who can condemn Him to death, *He* asserts that Pilate is a powerless puppet. Even while slowly asphyxiating on the cross, *He* has the presence of mind to give thought to his mother's future.

A biblical Way of the Cross has in it the qualities of both the traditional stations and the old Three Hour's Devotion which was used in many places before the reform of the Holy Week Services. Since we no longer are Crusaders making a Jerusalem pilgrimage, or Romans visiting the various basilicas, the more physical aspects of walking around a church may be downplayed, as in the following sample service.

Ministers needed:
Celebrant
Cantor
Servers
Reader(s)
Equipment:
Fifteen candle-holders
Bible or Lectionary to which is clipped the sheet of readings: the Word of God ought not to be proclaimed from a sheet of paper which has no symbolic value.
Programs for the people
A slide projector and screen
Slides of the Passion: in Art or Drama; or scenes from Jerusalem

As people enter, a sign should invite them to pick up a program. The lighting should be subdued, but not gloomy. The screen is set up behind the altar if possible. If the back sanctuary wall is flat enough not to require a screen, so much the better. The candles are placed in a well spaced row in the front of the sanctuary. The fifteenth candle, however, is placed in the center of the altar. All are lit. Mass candles are removed. When all things are ready, the cantor, wearing alb (and cincture,) comes out, reverences the altar, and announces an opening hymn that acclaims Christ's Passion in a triumphant fashion.

THE SERVICE
Celebrant: (*The celebrant makes an appropriate greeting to the people, inviting them to join in the worship. Then he says:*) The Lord be with you.
All: And also with you.
Celebrant: Let us pray. Father, we thank You and praise You for your mercy to us. When we were still far away from You, You sent Jesus your Son to bring us near. He died for us on the cross, giving himself completely. But You raised Him from the dead, to be the life of all who seek You. As we celebrate together this mystery of our salvation, we ask You to fill us with love for each other, to unite our hearts in your Holy Spirit, and to give us a deeper understanding of the Passion and death of our Redeemer. We ask this through the same Jesus Christ our Lord, who lives and reigns with You in the unity of the Holy Spirit, now and forever.
All: Amen.

Station One
Reader: The first station: Jesus is condemned to death. "Pilate...brought Jesus outside and took a seat on a judge's bench...He said to the Jews: Here is your king! But they shouted: Crucify him! ...and in the end, Pilate handed Jesus over to be crucified."
(*The reader should pause after every reading, to allow time for reflection. The following response is said at every station.*)

Celebrant: We adore You, O Christ and we bless You.
All: Because by your holy cross you have redeemed the world.
Reader: What went through Pilate's mind when he gave in to the demands of the mob and ordered Jesus' execution? Was he a man caught between two extremes? Or was he the sort who was ready to compromise at a moment's notice in order to serve his own advantage? Jesus stands before this weak-willed man in absolute control of the situation, for he has never compromised his integrity.
Celebrant: Father, we wish we were all as morally upright and firm in our convictions as Jesus. But we are not; we have let unjust situations go uncorrected because we didn't want to get involved; we have compromised Jesus' death. May your Spirit, dwelling in us, help us to grow in strength, until we, like Jesus, can face any situation unafraid.
All: Amen.
(*After each station is completed, a server extinguishes one of the candles. By the end of the service, only the candle on the altar is to remain lit.*)

Station Two
Reader: The second station: Jesus carries the crossbeam. "Jesus was led away, and carrying the cross by himself, went out to what is called the Place of the Skull (in Hebrew, Golgotha)."
Celebrant: We adore You, O Christ and we bless You.
All: Because by your holy cross You have redeemed the world.
Reader: In the time of Jesus, crucifixion meant a death by slow strangulation. It was one of the most horrible forms of torture available. Normally, the upright part of the cross, which weighed over a hundred pounds, was permanently fixed in the ground. The person who was to be crucified carried the crossbeam, which was only slightly less heavy. When the party came to the place of crucifixion, his hands were nailed to the crossbeam, and the crossbeam nailed on top of the upright.
Celebrant: Father, we believe that at any time Jesus could have crushed his foes and saved himself from death. Yet He chose not to. He *chose*; two possibilities were open to him, and He made a conscious, free decision. Free us from our needless burdens so that we, too, may be free to make responsible decisions in our lives — even when the best choice is to accept a cross.
All: Amen.

Station Three
Reader: The third station: Simon helps Jesus. "As they led Jesus away, they laid hold of one Simon the Cyrenean who was coming in from the fields. They put a crossbeam on Simon's shoulder for him to carry along behind Jesus."
Celebrant: We adore You, O Christ and we bless You.

All: Because by your holy cross You have redeemed the world.

Reader: How odd that the man who helped Jesus carry the cross had the same name as the disciple who denied he even knew Jesus! The fact is, Simon had no choice about whether he wanted to help. It was the law, imposed by the Romans on a conquered people. However, a tradition which makes his sons bishops in the African church suggests that Simon may have helped willingly. At least there was something about Jesus which gave Simon food for thought.

Celebrant: Father, our responsibilities and obligations become so much heavier when we do them unwillingly. May your Spirit stir us up and give us renewed energy to help carry our share of each day's duties.

All: Amen.

Station Four

Reader: The fourth station: Jesus meets the women of Jerusalem. "A great crowd of people followed Jesus, including women who beat their breasts and lamented over him. Jesus turned to them and said, "Women of Jerusalem do not weep for me. Weep for yourselves and for your children. The days are coming when it will be said, "Happy are the sterile, the wombs that never bore and the breasts that never nursed."

Celebrant: We adore You, O Christ and we bless You.

All: Because by your holy cross You have redeemed the world.

Reader: Very few people, when faced with something as immediate as their own deaths, have the presence of mind to care about others, or to give them words of advice. Jesus is not comforting the women of Jerusalem. They come out to Him, lamenting as was customary for the dead and dying. Jesus tells them to sing the dirges for themselves, because of the great sufferings they will know. It is to the women that Jesus gives his last prophecy before his death; not to the disciples who deserted Him, not to the leaders of the people who ordered his crucifixion, but to the women, guardians of home and heart.

Celebrant: Father, we would like to be comforted when we are in sorrow. But sometimes, like the women, we need to hear the truth, even when it is a hard truth to accept. May we be strengthened by the Spirit to face up to the truth that we are a sinful people, and that if we do not change our lives we must die. We pray in hope, through Jesus your Son, our Lord.

All: Amen.

Station Five

Reader: The fifth station: Jesus is stripped of his clothes. "Who is this that comes from Edom, in crimsoned garments, from Bozrah— This one clothed in majesty, marching in the greatness of his strength? "It is I, I who announce vindication,

I who am mighty to save!"
Why is your apparel red,
and your garments like those of the wine presser?
"The wine press I have trodden alone,
of all my people, no one stayed with me" (Is 63:1-3)

Celebrant: We adore You, O Christ and we bless You.

All: Because by your holy cross You have redeemed the world.

Reader: The prophet's words have been taken as a prophecy of the Passion for many centuries. The connection of blood and wine, which we know from the Eucharist, is here repeated. Jesus arrives at Golgotha, and is stripped of his clothes; perhaps he was stripped completely, crucified completely naked. Yet we never hear of His being ashamed; the shame is that of those around Him.

Celebrant: Father, we use clothing in so many of our human games. We use it to impress people, or to show them we are better in some obscure way. We use it in a spiritual sense to cloak ourselves and our real feelings, to hide from the truth. Help us grow responsibly in grace and truth, so that we may be able to withstand your all-penetrating gaze.

All: Amen.

Station Six

Reader: The sixth station: Jesus is nailed to the cross. "When they came to Skull Place, they crucified him there, and the criminals as well, one on his right and the other on his left."

Celebrant: We adore You, O Christ and we bless You.

All: Because by your holy cross You have redeemed the world.

Reader: The usual procedure for crucifying someone was this: the person's arms were stretched out on the crossbeam. With a few quick blows, a half-inch thick nail was driven into the wrist, where the bones are the strongest. The nerve ends there are also the most sensitive. After the crossbeam was nailed to the upright, the feet were crossed over each other, and nailed with one nail, flat to the upright. Jesus was crucified in this way. There was relatively little loss of blood, but unless He could push himself up by pressing against the nail in his feet, He would suffocate at once. And Jesus still had a few things He wanted very much to say.

Celebrant: Father, it is so hard for us to put ourselves out for others, even when they really need our help. Jesus' example is so heroic, it's hard for us to believe we could do the same. We depend on your showing us how and giving us the strength, so we can break free from the protective cocoons we have so neatly wrapped ourselves in.

All: Amen.

Station Seven

Reader: The seventh station: The cross is raised on high. "Just as Moses lifted up the bronze serpent in the wilderness, so must the Son of Man be lifted up. And when I am lifted up, I will draw all things to myself."

Celebrant: We adore You, O Christ and we bless You.

All: Because by your holy cross You have redeemed the world.

Reader: Jesus' perfect wholeness acts as a magnet to draw people to Himself. Even as the crossbeam is nailed to the upright, and the struggle for breath begins in earnest, Jesus does not turn wholly inwards. He is aware of those around Him, tries to speak to them, and to speak to the Father about them. Even the centurion who supervised the crucifixion will be drawn into Jesus' sphere of influence.

Celebrant: Father, most of us do not lead heroic lives. We do not make flocks of friends, nor do we make crowds of enemies. Our personal magnetism is severely limited by crying children, an unsympathetic boss, a bad examination. May your Spirit teach us that love cannot be manufactured or pulled out of a hat; it comes from a heart in which You live. Help us to love without seeking to be loved in return.

Station Eight

Reader: The eighth station: The soldiers dice for Jesus' clothing. "After the soldiers had crucified Jesus, they took his garments and divided them four ways, one for each soldier. There was also his tunic, but this tunic was woven in one piece from top to bottom and had no seam. They said to each other, "We should not tear it. Let us throw dice to see who gets it..." And that is what the soldiers did."

Celebrant: We adore You, O Christ and we bless You.

All: Because by your holy cross You have redeemed the world.

Reader: Gambling is a strange vice. In small amounts or for trivial things, it is not the worst of vices. But there are always two extremes; those who cannot control the urge to gamble, and those who take life so cautiously that they never do anything that would be against the odds or against tradition. The disciples knew that the odds were against Jesus rising from the dead; Peter played it safe, and went back to his boats and nets. Mary Magdalene gambled everything that made her life worth while that Jesus would rise from the dead. Even the good thief played the odds, hoping against hope for salvation.

Celebrant: Father, whenever we sin we are really gambling with crooked dice that we can have both our disregard for your law and our salvation, too. Help us to always cast our lot with You, for You see all the angles of our lives.

All: Amen.

Station Nine

Reader: The ninth station: Jesus addresses the thief. "One of the criminals hanging in crucifixion blasphemed Jesus: "Aren't you the Messiah? Then save yourself and us!" But the other one rebuked him: "Have you no fear of God, seeing you are under the same sentence? We deserve it, after all. We are only paying the price for what we've done, but this man has done nothing wrong." He then said, "Jesus, remember me when you enter upon your reign." And Jesus replied, "I assure you: this day you will be with me in Paradise.""

Celebrant: We adore You, O Christ and we bless You.

All: Because by your holy cross You have redeemed the world.

Reader: From gambling to thievery! Even in his death Jesus refuses to be respectable. He knows that the respectable folk have no use for Him. Only those who have been in need, in pain, in trouble, realize what it can mean to be saved.

Celebrant: Father, save us from complacency. Deliver us from mediocrity. Keep us from becoming luke-warm, lest we grow deaf to your Word. Help us not to be afraid to need, whether it is a friend's hand to steady a ladder for us, or the grace to choose the way Jesus shows us.

All: Amen.

Station Ten

Reader: The tenth Station: Jesus speaks to his mother. "Seeing his mother there with the disciple whom he loved, Jesus said to his mother, 'Woman, there is your son.' In turn he said to the disciple, 'There is your mother.' From that hour onward, the disciple took her into his care."

Celebrant: We adore You, O Christ and we bless You.

All: Because by your holy cross You have redeemed the world.

Reader: In Jesus' day, a woman without a family to rely on was often reduced to begging in the streets or to starvation. Jesus saw her near his cross, and took thought for her future, so special was his love for her. The effort to focus his eyes clearly enough to see her, not to mention speak to her must have been enormous. But then, Jesus was never one to take halfway measures in anything He did.

Celebrant: Father, unlike the disciples, Mary never asked Jesus what her reward would be if she remained faithful to Him always. Her love for Him seems to have been reward enough. Help us to follow Jesus and serve each other not because of the reward we hope for, but because we love Jesus and know He loves us.

Station Eleven

Reader: The eleventh station: Jesus prays from the cross. "From noon onward there was darkness over the whole land until mid-afternoon. Then toward mid-afternoon, Jesus cried out in a loud voice, "Eli, Eli, lema sabachthani?", that is, "My God, my God, why have you forsaken me?.""

Celebrant: We adore You, O Christ and we bless You.

All: Because by your holy cross you have redeemed the world.

Reader: We know that Jesus spent much time in prayer, even whole days and nights. Now He prays from the psalms. Psalm 21 is deeply emotional prayer. Although it begins in deepest sorrow, it ends on a note of sure hope and complete trust. How did Jesus feel, looking down at his mother, while praying the verse that runs: "You, Lord, have been my hope since before my birth; from my mother's womb You have been my helper"? or while praying, "They have pierced my hands and feet; I can count all my bones"?.

Celebrant: Father, help us to pray with the same intensity, the same hope and trust as Jesus did. Even when our feelings say that we feel lost or abandoned, may your Spirit prompt our hearts to remember that You never cast off or leave us alone.

All: Amen.

Station Twelve

Reader: The twelfth station: Jesus dies on the cross. "Suddenly the curtain in the sanctuary was torn in two. Jesus uttered a loud cry and said: "Father, into your hands I commend my spirit." After he said this, he breathed his last."

Celebrant: We adore You, O Christ and we bless You.

All: Because by your holy cross You have redeemed the world.

Reader: The curtain in the Temple screened off the Holy of Holies from the sight of all but the High Priest. The death of Jesus ripped that curtain permanently in half. Through his dying on the cross, Jesus reveals to us the real Holy of Holies — the face of God the Father.

Celebrant: Father, we rejoice and praise You for sending your Son among us as a human being, capable of showing to us your great love and mercy. While we are pained that He suffered so deeply to redeem us, we are still filled with joy, because He is seated at your right hand, and will one day be acclaimed by all who have ever lived. May your Spirit reveal Jesus more and more to us, so that Jesus may lead us to You.

All: Amen.

THE HOLY WEEK BOOK

Station Thirteen

Reader: The thirteenth station: Jesus is taken down from the cross. "Afterward, Joseph of Arimathea, a disciple of Jesus (although a secret one for fear of the Jews), asked Pilate's permission to remove Jesus' body. Pilate granted it, so they came and took the body away."

Celebrant: We adore You, O Christ and we bless You.

All: Because by your holy cross You have redeemed the world.

Reader: What a contrast this scene paints for us! On the one hand is Joseph, a member of the Sanhedrin — one of the few who opposed their plan — performing an act of kindness for the Lord, taking the responsibility of seeing to his burial. On the other hand is Pilate, clearly relieved that Jesus is dead, and can trouble him no more. But it would seem that Pilate's conscience is much more dead than Jesus is. What was Mary's reaction, how did John feel when Jesus' body was slipped off the nails? We can only guess.

Celebrant: Father, save us from the effects of a deadened conscience, which no longer can feel the difference between good and evil. Even if our faith is weak and we are afraid to shout it to the world, like Joseph of Arimathea, save us from the false security of Pilate. Stir us up, move us to indignation and protest at injustice. We ask this through Christ our Lord.

All: Amen.

Station Fourteen

Reader: The fourteenth station: Jesus' body is laid in the tomb. "Taking the body, Joseph wrapped it in fresh linen and laid it in his own new tomb which had been hewn from a formation of rock. Then he rolled a huge stone across the entrance to the tomb and went away. But Mary Magdalene and the other Mary remained sitting there, facing the tomb.

Celebrant: We adore You, O Christ and we bless You.

All: Because by your holy cross You have redeemed the world.

Reader: The two Marys are signs of faith and hope to us all. They had witnessed a death so violent that its reality could be doubted by no one. Yet they stayed, and though they returned home later, they were back early in the morning to keep watch. It was then that they found the stone rolled away from the entrance to the tomb.

Celebrant: Father, raise up your people as You raised up your Son Jesus. Raise up the weary, the sick, the needy. Raise up the world and all who live on it; raise us up to You. Renew us and give us life, we pray, through Jesus Christ our Lord.

All: Amen.

(The stations are finished; all the candles have been extinguished but the Christ-candle on the altar. After a few minutes pause for silent prayer, the cantor announces a final hymn, "Keep in Mind" by Deiss (WLP). At its conclusion the ministers leave.)

Part IV
The
Easter
Vigil

Wheat Grains Crushed

Michael E. Moynahan, SJ

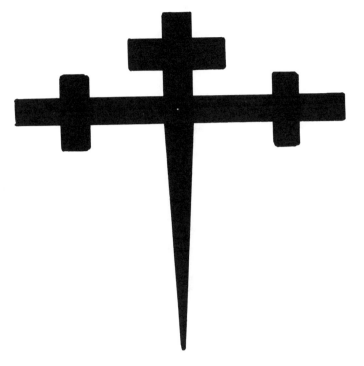

Wheat grains crushed
provide our food.
grape full bunches pressed
become our table drink.
because they do not cling
to what they were,
a wonderful new happening:
our paschal meal.
we who are hungry—
fed;
we who are thirsty—
satisfied;
we who were empty—
filled;
we who were dead—
alive again!
Proudly rising:
new life from old ashes.
death never again the end
only a stop on the journey.
But new things also die
to come again in unimagined ways.
bread broken becomes a meal—
signs us a community.
wine passed around and shared
becomes our cup of blessing.
and when we eat
and when we drink
we remember.
our eyes are opened a little more
and we know:
this is the bread of life,
this is the cup of our salvation.
so we eat,
we drink,
we die,
but most importantly
we rise.
Alleluia!
Come Lord Jesus!
again,
and again,
and again.

Celebrating Jesus' Resurrection With Song

Eileen E. Freeman

For us Christians, the historical fact of Christ's resurrection is the pivot-point around which our lives turn. The living Christ penetrates our lives in innumerable ways, drawing us to the Father through His work in each of us. If Christ had not been raised from the dead, we would be the victims of the cruelest hoax in history (to paraphrase Saint Paul). We would be centering our lives around a practical joke and basing ourselves on a lie. *That* is a horrifying thing to contemplate.

But as it is, Christ has been raised from the dead, raising us with Him to a new life — and that's something to celebrate, to rejoice in and stand in awe of, something to sing about, something to make us shout with joy and gladness and thanksgiving! But after we've sung the *Hallelujah Chorus* and *Jesus Christ is Risen Today*, where do we go? The past ten years have witnessed the writing of many new guitar songs for the Eucharist, but comparatively few of those have been Easter pieces. We need a larger repertoire of Easter music, one that can pry out of us all the joy that the celebration of our resurrection with Christ gives us the right and need to feel. I think we often tend to associate Easter with some future hope for us of heaven and forget that for us, our experience of heaven has already begun in this life. At Easter we are celebrating not only Christ's historical resurrection or our own resurrection on the last day, but our constantly renewed resurrection to new life at every moment of our existence. That's what our Easter music ought to convey, both to us and to our other brothers and sisters in the pew.

The Vigil is the most solemn and important Eucharist the Church celebrates during the year. From the viewpoint of drama and music, very little can compare with the Easter Vigil. The transitions from darkness to light, from death to life, from sin to grace, can be compelling, deeply emotional experiences for us all.

The guitar has always seemed a particularly suitable instrument for the Easter Vigil, for several reasons: 1) The guitar can evoke a quiet and mysterious mood; it can complement the drama inherent in the service of light and in the readings. It is a sensitive instrument for highlighting the atmosphere of awe and mystery which dominates so much of the Easter Vigil. 2) At the same time, the guitar can be joyful and rythmical, practically passionate with feeling. It can almost dance itself right out of one's hand with exultation and joy in the resurrection. 3) The guitar is like a mirror; it catches and reflects the soul of the assembly at worship. It shines back at the congregation the very mood of that congregation. Few guitar arrangements legislate the notes, the strum, the picking pattern the guitarist is to follow. He has to "sense" it. Obviously, since the first mirror-image the guitar reflects is that of the one who plays it, the guitarist needs to be a person of deep faith in the power of the resurrection, or his music will be spiritually dead, it will have no power to strike sparks of light and life from the hearts of the assembly.

Easter Vigil — The Service of Light

Ordinarily the Vigil does not begin with music; the idea that all Masses must start with a hymn is a late idea, and not necessarily a good one. On this night in particular it is fitting that we gather in darkness, silence and expectancy, almost as though, we, too, were in the tomb, awaiting our resurrection. Such a silent beginning gives great power to our acclamation of the new fire and to the cry, "Light of Christ!". This acclamation is rather short, though, and the response, "Thanks be to God" does not always unite the congregation in worship. A good alternative acclamation is a guitar song called *The Light of Christ.*[1] At the three stations when the Paschal Candle is elevated, the congregation can sing the refrain, and the schola can sing a verse. The refrain is simply: "The light of Christ has come into the world."

The water, light and Spirit themes of this hymn make it almost a natural here or at the Baptismal Service later on. The melody is easily learned for singing in the dark, and the refrain may be sung as a two-part canon, if desired. During the Service of Light, whatever music the guitarists perform ought to be memorized; it would detract from the drama of a darkened church to have a light on for the musicians.

Ron Ellis has written an excellent setting of the *Exultet,* available from Raven Music.

Easter Vigil — The Liturgy of the Word

Nine readings are given for the liturgy of the Word at the Easter Vigil. Few churches do all of them, which is somewhat unfortunate, but often understandable. The nine readings bring together all the main themes of salvation history, from the creation of the world to the resurrection of Christ. Not surprisingly, there are responsorial psalms to accompany these readings, to complement and enrich our understanding of them. Good musical settings exist for most of these psalms.

God's creation of the world is the text of the first reading. Psalm 104 is a poetic retelling of creation. Lucien Deiss has the most complete setting of the text, and one of the best musically, *Splendor of Creation.*[2] It adapts extremely well to the guitar in the keys of E minor or D minor, and there are enough verses so the planners of the Liturgy can choose the most appropriate ones. Peloquin[3] has a choral setting of the same psalm, for organ and choir; it is a loud, triumphant work, in contrast to the Deiss piece, which moves well, but is much more meditative. The Grail Psalter[4] has a quiet, somewhat neutral setting of this psalm. Finally, there is a setting, published by Resource Publications,[5] which is also suitable, but a little difficult for a congregation to learn for just a responsorial psalm.

Abraham's sacrifice of his son Isaac has always been seen as a "type" of the sacrifice of Christ on the altar of the cross. The psalm, one of trust in God's providence, is one which the Patristic Church often put in Christ's mouth. It is a serene psalm, and our setting of it ought to reflect that serenity. John Foley's *For You Are My God*,[6] is about the best of the new music I've seen. Not only does it fit the mood of the Vigil well, it also adapts the psalm text carefully, and does no violence to it. Any congregation can easily learn the refrain. As with all the responsorial psalms, the verses should be sung clearly by either the guitar group or a single cantor.

God parts the Red Sea for the Israelites in the course of the third reading from Exodus; the response, also from Exodus, is the triumphant hymn of thanksgiving sung by Moses after their victory over Egypt. The musical directions given in Exodus 15 for singing this psalm indicate that it should be sung joyfully with tambourines (and with dancing!). One excellent setting which follows these 3000 year-old directions is *The Song of Moses*. It is somewhat demanding on a guitar group, but well worth the effort of learning it. Again, the refrain is simple. The setting is very "Jewish"; it suits the text marvelously. See the Music Index for the other settings.

It is more difficult to find good settings for the next few readings than for most. The fourth response[7] is available in a setting by Frank Quinn, O.P., as is Isaiah 12,[6] the response to the fifth reading. Neither of these is particularly a folk setting, but both can be successfully adapted to the guitar if the instrument is played or plucked softly as background while a cantor sings the verses. Both responses are quiet and reflective, and offer a change of pace from the triumph of the Exodus reading is available, called, *Ho Everyone That Thirsteth*. Actually, a good musical setting of part of the fifth reading is available, called, *Ho Everyone That Thirsteth*.[3] It is bright, almost bouncy. Perhaps it could be used as an alternate responsorial psalm, or later on during the Baptismal Rite.

There is one setting for the 6th responsorial psalm, Quinlan's *It's a Brand New Day*[6]. The refrain is a little difficult, if the congregation has never done it before, but if a community is quick to learn, its quick and lightly swinging rhythm can be a successful change of pace.

The seventh reading, from Ezekiel, speaks about cleansing and changing our hearts to love and seek the Lord. Psalm 42, the responsorial psalm, is a rather emotional song. My preference for a setting is that of Mike Fitzgerald. The refrain has the advantage of being simple, and the verses not only adapt the psalm text well, but musically move between A minor and F, a nice touch. I also like Quinlan's setting, *Like a Deer in Winter,* but the refrain is difficult, and the text is not as full as is the Fitzgerald setting. Both emphasize the longing for God which is the essential theme of the psalm.

The epistle for the Vigil is Paul's marvelous statement about our own dying and rising with Christ. Its accompanying responsorial psalm, #118, recurs frequently during the Easter season. It is at this point in the Liturgy that the first solemn proclamation of Alleluia occurs; the Alleluia has been conspicuous by its absence for six weeks by this time. Since it is such an important Alleluia, make sure that whatever setting you do for it is a musically powerful one, a full one, a dramatic on. Quinlan has a setting for the Psalm with an Alleluia response called *Sing a Merry Song*[8]. Its only fault is that it does not take up all the crucial verses of the psalm; for example, the verse "The stone which the builders rejected has become the cornerstone" does not appear. Perhaps you can improvise a verse to round out the psalm. If that stumps you, try singing a familiar alleluia for the refrain, and have someone read dramatically the psalm text, using the chords from your alleluia as a light background. This preserves the musical continuity of such an arrangement. At the Vigil it is not necessary to sing a separate Gospel alleluia. Instead, try singing an Alleluia after the deacon announces the reading, and again at the end of the Gospel.

In addition, remember that the congregation needs a music sheet with words (and music, if possible) for their parts. A separate Easter Vigil pamphlet is a great project for parishes to do, and music companies generally have a license to cover copyright costs for a one-time project such as this.

Easter Vigil — The Liturgy of the Eucharist

By the time we get to the preparation of the gifts, the average congregation, for all its goodwill and enthusiasm, will have just about exhausted its ability to do any more new music. So — instead of putting the assembly in the position of watching the guitar group perform, (a fate worse than death!) use as much familiar, good quality music as you can, provided of course that it focuses on what we are about at the Vigil. An instrumental solo during the preparation of the gifts will enable both congregation and guitar group to recollect their thoughts and pray quietly. If you would like to use a communion meditation, learn *Glorious in Majesty,* a resurrection piece for guitar, recorder and finger cymbals, set to a hauntingly beautiful Jewish tune. It is written in simple four-part harmony with a refrain. For a rousing, triumphant recessional, take a look at Ken Meltz' *He Has Life Restored.*

Choose joyful acclamations and Mass parts; by all means sing the *Holy,* the *Anamnesis* and the *Great Amen.* Take some pains with the *Anamnesis*; this is *the* night *par excellence* to emphasize that "Christ has died, Christ is risen, etc." If the celebrant is a good singer, he may like to try the simple *Doxology*[6] by the St. Louis Jesuits, which can be used with their *Amen* (NAL).

Before the Vigil begins, the lead singer of the group should introduce the congregation to the new music for the celebration. If the *Light of Christ* or some other hymn is being done during the procession with the Paschal Candle, the congregation should be well-rehearsed since they will be singing their part without any light to read by. At the beginning of each responsorial psalm, have the group sing the refrain once, then invite the congregation to sing the refrain; then begin the verses. This should effectively refresh the memory of the congregation on how to sing the refrains, but will not distract them from prayer.

THE HOLY WEEK BOOK

Easter Vigil — Rite of Baptism

During the Rite of Baptism there is room for music, perhaps as the participants assemble, and again after the blessing of the water. See *Springs of Water Bless The Lord* in this book for specially composed music for the baptismal liturgy. Music which takes up the themes of water and light, such as the *Light of Christ,* and *Ho, Everyone,* is also useful. *A Voice Cries Out in the Wilderness[1]* is a hymn which is in the Godspell style and is about Jesus' baptism. Two other excellent pieces are *Alleluia, Alleluia, Give Thanks to the Risen Lord,[1]* and *I Want to Walk as a Child of the Light[9].* The former deserves to be in the repertoire of any folk group; its use is by no means limited to Easter.

If you sing all the things mentioned above as possibilities, you may run the risk of detracting from the solemnity of the Gospel, particularly if your parish does most of the readings. Also, the average congregation will balk at being asked to learn eight or nine new pieces of music at a gulp. So — try singing only every other psalm, or sing them in radically different styles, or use schola on one and cantor on another, or even recite one or two with a guitar in the background, catching the mood of the psalm. If the parish has an organ choir, why not combine for the Easter Vigil and alternate selections between the organ and the non-organ group.

1. *The Light of Christ, Alleluia Alleluia Give Thanks, A Voice Cries Out* are copyrighted by Servant Publications, PO Box 87, Ann Arbor, MI 48407.

2. *Splendor of Creation, He Has Life Restored, Priestly People, All You Nations,* are copyrighted by World Library Publications, 2145 Central Parkway, Cincinnati, OH 45214. They also have an arrangement of *Oh Sons and Daughters.*

3. *Psalm for Pentecost* (Peloquin), *Song of Moses, Ho Everyone, As a Doe* (Fitzgerald), *I am the Bread of Life* and *Glorious in Majesty* are copyrighted by GIA, 7404 S. Mason, Chicago, IL 60638. *The Canticle of the Gift* is copyrighted by ACP.

4. *The Grail Psalter* is published by Paulist Press Deus Books, New York.

5. *Modern Liturgy,* Vol. 3 No. 1, published by Resource Publications, PO Box 444, Saratoga, CA 95070.

6. *You Are My God, Doxology, Are Not Our Hearts, Like a Deer in Winter, It's a Brand New Day* are copyrighted by North American Liturgy Resources, 2110 W. Peoria Avenue, Phoenix, AZ 85029.

7. Settings for the 4th and 5th responsorial psalms are contained in *Morning Praise and Evensong,* edited by William Storey, Frank Quinn, OP, and David Wright, OP, and published by Fides Press, Notre Dame, IN.

8. *Sing a Merry Song, We Long for You, I am the Resurrection, The Lord is My Shepherd* (Quinlan). *The Lord is My True Shepherd* (Repp) are copyrighted by FEL Publications, 1925 Pontius Avenue, Los Angeles, CA 90025.

9. *I Want to Walk As a Child of the Light* is copyrighted by NET Music, Houston, TX.

The Flowers Appear On The Earth

Eileen E. Freeman

"The time of the singing of birds has returned...the flowers appear on the earth." The author of the Song of Songs could not, of course, have known about the Easter Vigil. Nevertheless, the correlation between Easter and the return of Spring is high, particularly in the Western Hemisphere. Easter comes at a time when the promise of life renewed is held up to us in the green buds of trees, in blooming crocuses, pussywillows and daffodils. The sun's warmth melts the mountain snows; and the fallow fields soak up the distilled rays. Spring is the time of warm rains and swallows returning to Capistrano. Spring is the time of Easter.

Between the starkness of Good Friday and the richness of the Easter Vigil there is a whole lifetime of differences. On Good Friday the church is bare, completely devoid of decoration or ornamentation. There are no good "smells" of flowers or incense. Even the sounds are somewhat harsher, plainer. But only a day later, what a change has occurred in the church. White linens and colored cloths, banners, flowers are everywhere. The smells of wax and incense, and above all, flowers fill every part of the church.

The traditional flower for Easter church decoration is, of course, the Easter lily, that creamy, trumpet-shaped flower with the golden center that rides the crest of a dozen green, sword-like leaves. The lilies are usually placed in foil-covered pots behind the altar, below the altar, on the side niches, the pulpit, everywhere. In fact, sometimes it looks as though those lilies are going to take over the church!

Now I do not mean to "knock" the traditional Easter lilies, hyacinths and the like, but I would like to point out a few disadvantages to their exclusive use at Easter. First of all, Easter lilies are expensive, even for churches, which often obtain substantial discounts from florists. The lilies must be forced out of season, since they usually bloom later on in the early summer in most places. If we are not careful, we can find ourselves in the position of spending hundreds of dollars so "Jesus can have the best," while some of our brothers and sisters, Jesus' brothers and sisters, lack the most necessary things. One Easter lily plant could feed a family of five for a whole day.

A second reason why the usual Easter flowers give me some negative feelings is that many people associate lilies with death, not life. The lily is not so much a symbol of purity or virginity anymore. Rather the cartoon character or the television comedian holding a lily on his breast and joking about death has become a frequent association with the sight of the Easter lily. For younger Christians especially, the symbolism seems to be changing slowly but steadily.

Hay fever is a third reason why the traditional lilies and hyacinths bother me. Like many people, I have a mild allergy to strongly scented spring flowers that leaves me sneezing, with a puffy face and watery eyes. Since I am usually the cantor or choir director, this has been a problem to me for years. However, even when I celebrated the Vigil from the pew rather than the sanctuary, I experienced the same problems. Consider how many people in a congregation have hay fever, pollen allergies, asthma, emphysema and the like, which make them acutely uncomfortable as their noses are increasingly assailed by the heavy perfumes of lilies, hyacinths, lilacs, and the like.

The allergic Christian comes to the Vigil bravely, with an array of handkerchiefs ready to hand, and even a nose spray. What should be a joyful celebration is marred by coughing, sneezing fits, etc. Even the back corners of the church are filled with the scents. The elderly, the visually or auditory-handicapped who need to sit near the front of the church, take "refuge" in the rear, where they can neither see nor hear well enough to participate in the celebration as they might like to. The heavy smell even makes a few people nauseous, not because the scent is bad, but because there's far too much of it in too close quarters.

Of course, no matter what we choose to adorn our churches, someone is going to have an allergic reaction. However, since the reaction to lily and hyacinth pollen is quite marked, we ought to consider how we can show the love of Christ to others by toning down our use of the traditional Easter floral church decorations.

We can have an esthetically pleasing sanctuary without having to spend great amounts of money on flowers which cause grief to a large number of people. What we need to do is to look around outside our neighborhoods to see what signs of life there are, and take advantage of them. An old Easter hymn says, "Love (Christ) has come again, like wheat that springeth green." Our Easter flower decorations should make that connection clear.

Although the date of Easter varies, even when it arrives early there is a hint of Spring in the air. In the colder climates people are beginning to believe once more that winter will not last forever. The promise of new life held in one purple crocus or catkin is more than a hundred pots of exotic foreign flowers. We must provide flowers and greenery that are signs to the people who see them.

In the areas of the world where Spring is a real season, and not merely a passageway to summer, early spring is accompanied by crocuses, pussy-willows, cherry blossoms and flowering trees, magnolias, dogwood and grape hyacinth. In later spring the daffodils, tulips, iris and other bulb flowers come up. The trees grow green. Ferns and dandelions, poppies and peonies abound right in our gardens. Even in the desert, cactus and other flowers bloom. We should bring all this into church: in these plants and flowers are *our* signs of resurrection.

In order to have a church full of home-grown blooms, a few things are necessary. Most important is the service of some parishioner with a green thumb who can make things grow. Next is someone with a sense of flower arrangement and composition. Many people learn Japanese *ikebana*, flower arranging. This oriental art can take a bowl, some pebbles, a few iris, and create an arrangement so well balanced and harmonious, that it can transmit that quality to anyone who takes the time to contemplate the arrangement.

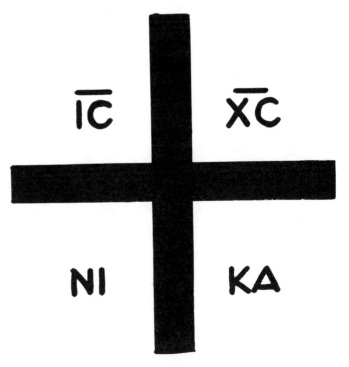

There are two options in arranging plants; using cut flowers in water, or using potted plants. The latter is usually preferred because the flowers last longer. Cut flowers need to be changed at least once a week. Since few spring flowers take kindly to being cut, potting generally works best.

Where to put floral arrangements is an important consideration, especially at the Easter Vigil where there is so much movement. Flowers are generally arranged about the altar, on the steps, flanking the tabernacle or the like. These are appropriate, but we should not forget the other equally important places, the pulpit, the Paschal candle and the baptismal font. We emphasize these with flowers because they are symbols of life to us: the living Word, the new light (made from the wax of bees), the living waters that renew us.

The type and color of flowers that we use will ultimately depend on the area of the country in which we live. But in general there should be variety. Ten vases or pots of iris will get just as monotonous as ten pots of lilies. Different colors and heights of plants in each arrangement is usually best. The plants should be potted in wooden, pottery, china or similar containers. They should not be put into plastic containers, since plastic is not a natural material and will look quite incongruous next to delicate pastel flowers. However plastic pots can be sunk into the dirt of a large tub successfully. This helps avoid the shock of transplanting which sometimes affects plants adversely. A plastic tub can be camouflaged with fabric, barnwood or the like to hide it.

Hanging baskets of ivy, philodendron, ferns and the like can be used to great advantage, if one can mass enough of them. One large fern which dwarfs a living room will be invisible in a church. Several, hanging together at slightly different heights, are much more effective. Often they can be hung from a ceiling beam by thin, strong, wire, or firm commercial hangers temporarily or permanently attached to an appropriate wall. Persuading parishioners to loan their hanging baskets is not hard. Many consider it an honor to have something they can share with their fellow parishioners.

Large floor plants can also be used effectively at the Vigil and during the Easter season. Potted forsythia, azalea, small flowering trees beside the pulpit can create an extremely dramatic effect. Draecaena, dumb cane and rubber plants, are "foreign" shrubs and plants, and many people cannot identify them with their own experience of plants that seem to die only to live again.

A typical large arrangement for the santuary, entrance-way or pulpit might consist of the following:

A large redwood tub, about three feet in diameter.

A blooming yellow forsythia in the center.

Dwarf iris and grape hyacinth surrounding it.

Ivy cascading over the sides.

Moss

In each church there should be one arrangement which is clearly the most important, the paradigmatic composition which gives definition to the rest. Where this principal arrangement is placed depends on the architecture of the church, on what the liturgist wants to emphasize. Where the altar is set far back from the congregation, it is unwise to put large masses of flowers or plants in front of the altar or all over the front of the sanctuary. This creates even more of an artificial barrier between celebrant and congregation. Emphasize, rather, the pulpit or Paschal candle, which are usually placed to the side in the sanctuary. Use smaller, but coordinated arrangements near the altar. Sticking to a single floral theme, such as pussywillows, tulips and cherry blossoms will tie together a sanctuary which is spread out all over the place.

THE HOLY WEEK BOOK

The dogwood is a flowering tree which deserves to be used a good deal more at Easter, since it is one of the few flowers of America which has a Passiontide "legend" attached to it. Most people have heard the legend: how the dogwood was once the tallest tree in the forest, with beautiful white flowers. The Romans used the tree to make crosses with, which mortified the dogwood. However, when Jesus was crucified, He promised the dogwood that He would make the dogwood grow too short ever to be a cross again, and He touched each white petal with a drop of blood red color. It is not difficult to force dogwood to bloom for Easter, if Easter comes too early for it in some locales. The same is true of forsythia.

Because trees and plants live for a number of years, they can often be used for several Easter celebrations. This necessitates planting small trees and bushes permanently in large pots, so they will not need to be dug up each year and replanted. During the remainder of the year they can beautify the rectory or a parishioner's garden. In warmer climates, flowering cactus and succulents and citrus trees can be grown similarly.

Recently the houseplant business has boomed. All over, people are seeing the value of having reminders of life and growth and hope around them. If some horticulturists are to be believed, plants can contribute their own unique empathy to those around them. If plants are used which root easily; ivy, begonia, impatiens, forsythia, pussy-willow; cuttings can be rooted and given to parishioners as living and growing reminders of the Lord's new life, shared by us through his death and resurrection.

A Blessing For Growing Things

This blessing can be done on the day of the Vigil by those who are preparing the church for the evening celebration. It could also be done in homes, since many people decorate their homes with flowers for Easter.

The various arrangements, pots, vases, etc., should be gathered together, as well as those who are decorating the church or home. The leader should have a watering can and a Bible, for the reading.

The blessing begins with an appropriate hymn: "All Things Bright and Beautiful" from the 1940 Episcopal hymnal, "Let All Things Now Living" from the Peoples' Mass Book, a setting of the three young men from Daniel, or Psalm 104 (Deiss (WLP) has a good setting).

Leader: Jesus Christ, You are the life of the world.
All: Praise and thanks be to You forever.
Reader: A reading from the Book of Genesis (1:9-12) God said, 'Let the waters under the sky be gathered together into one place, so that the dry land may appear.' And so it happened. God called the dry land earth; the waters that had been gathered together he called seas; and God saw that it was good. Then God said, 'Let the earth produce fresh growing things, let seed-bearing plants spring up on the earth; let there be fruit-trees reproducing according to their kinds. And so it was. The earth yielded fresh growth and seed-bearing plants; and fruit-trees appeared, each reproducing according to its own kind. And God saw that it was very good. Evening came, and morning came, the third day. This is the word of the Lord.

All: Thanks be to God.
Psalm Response: Psalm 1 (sung or recited).
Leader: Let us pray.
Blessed are You, O Lord our God, King of the Universe, who creates all growing things for your children to enjoy and delight in. The beauty of creation reminds us of your own beauty, and we are filled with joy. Father, we ask that these plants and flowers may be signs to your people of the resurrection of your Son Jesus. May this water which we pour on them to make them grow, be a symbol of the waters of baptism which brought us from death to new life through the death and resurrection of the Lord. (*The leader should water some of the arrangements.*)
All: Amen.
Leader: Blessed are You, O Lord our God, King of the Universe, who has given to us the ministry of caring for these living signs of your evergreen life in us. May we arrange them, display them and tend them in such a way that all who see them will be led to a deeper understanding of the mystery of our salvation. We ask this through Jesus our Lord.
All: Amen.

Fire Upon The Earth — Kindling New Fire

Eileen E. Freeman

We are a strange society when it comes to fire. We send men to the moon, using the most sophisticated technology, but cook our food over barbecue pits; we have modern homes with labor-saving appliances, yet we heat them with fires burning in our basements. It appears that although we don't often think of it, fire is very much a part of our lives. Even on the day when we succeed in making solar energy available to all, we shall still be only reflecting the heat of a huge fire burning ninety-three million miles away from us.

No matter how far away we think we are from the primitive societies who huddle around their campfires, we must still acknowledge a very basic kinship with such groups. We still use fire every time we light a cigarette or turn up the gas. But except for scouts and campers, it seems we have lost the meaning of fire as a symbol. At the most, fire is a symbol of the destruction it can cause when uncontrolled.

One could speculate forever on why we have lost the symbolism of flame and fire. Part of it, no doubt, is that our most basic needs which fire can provide, namely light and warmth, are now usually met without the obvious presence of fire. We do not read by candles or kerosene lamps; we plug in our space heaters when our feet get cold. Another part may be due to the demands of our society. Fire is a symbol of warmth, of spontaneity, of deep emotion, of passion. All of these qualities are rather submerged in today's world, resulting in the loss of fire as a symbol.

A third reason for the loss of fire as a powerful symbol to us is its primitive nature. In the Bible, fire "from heaven," that is lightning, is invested with many powers. It is the Lord's agent of destruction. Yet, paradoxically, the pillar of fire that led the Israelites in the desert is an agent, too, in the Bible, which melts out impurity and leaves behind only pure gold or silver. The ancient view of fire is that it is a very violent thing. We do not like to think about such violent images any more, whether they be the end of the world, the conventional view of hell, or our own "purification" by fire.

For all these reasons, as well as others, we have lost the symbolism of fire that was so special to our ancestors in the faith. The ceremonial blessing and lighting of the new fire at the Vigil means much less to us than to the Christians of long ago. The effects of this loss can be seen in the typical parish during the Vigil. The pastor goes to the back of the church, pours charcoal starter fluid over a few twigs, and applies a cigarette lighter to it.

How depressing this is, how demeaning to the nature of fire! Such a ritual travesty makes fire the slave of mankind, forcing the flame to obey our will, rather than allowing fire to be a "free creature of God," as Saint Francis described it. How can such a fire have any symbolic value? Anyone who sees such a fire being transfer-red from match to kerosene-soaked wood is more likely to think of the last time they tried to get the barbecue started for hamburgers and couldn't get the charcoal to catch, than the creative, destructive, purgative, light and warmth-giving symbol of the Spirit.

Before we kindle the new fire, before we come to the Vigil to share the resurrection with our brothers and sisters, we need to rekindle in ourselves an appreciation for God's gift of fire, a gift so precious that in many societies fire was viewed as divine, a god in its own right. To do this, take about a half-hour when you can get away from everything: people, phones, television. Wherever you go, take a large beeswax candle, (even one of the small tapers for the Vigil will do), and a box of wooden matches. You will also need a candle holder of some sort, and a Bible.

A Meditation on Holy Fire

Go into your room or wherever you plan to make this meditation. Darken the room somewhat. Sit down with the candle on a table in front of you, and take a few minutes to be quiet. Breathe deeply and slowly, concentrating on relaxing. When you feel sufficiently relaxed, take a short scriptural passage such as: "The Light shines in the darkness, and the darkness has never been able to put it out"; or "He will baptize you with the Holy Spirit and with fire." Close your eyes and say it slowly several times, trying to synchronize it with your breathing.

After you have done this, open your eyes. Take one of the safety matches and strike it on the side of the box. Watch that brief spark carefully; it is the basis of both a candle flame and a forest fire; the same spark ignites not only the furnace in our basements, but all the stars in the universe as well. Imagine that you have never seen a spark before. It comes from friction — two things rubbing against each other. What about the frictions of daily life...? Notice how the sparks cause the tip of the match to catch fire.

Now light the candle; it takes a moment — the wick is still cold. It is hard to catch the fire of the Spirit when our hearts are cold. Blow out the match and focus all your attention on the candle. Look closely at the flame, at its colors, its ever-changing size and dimensions. Fire is versatile, changeable. Now it is orange, now yellow, now with a bluish tinge. Relax; let the flame look at you, too. Watch how the candle wax is drawn up into the wick; how the heart melts it even before the flame touches it; how hot wax melts the cold wax around it. What is fire made of; is it animal, vegetable or mineral; solid, liquid or gas; or none of the above?

Now you should try to *become* the *flame*. Imagine that you are the fire, that you are waving and flickering or burning steadily. What causes you to flare up? You are drawing the wax up into yourself, melting it, vaporizing it. The wax gives up its life to you, and you turn it into

— what? Like the flame, like Jesus, you become a mediator, through you the wax becomes light, warmth. God created you on the first day, to give light to the world, and set you in the heavens. You gather men and women who are stumbling in the dark; you are a beacon of safety. You give them light by which they can recognize each other. You protect them from wild animals, who are afraid of the light you give. You warm the frozen body and spirit. Because of you, people come together to shut out the cold, to share a meal. You are fire; your heart is burning; your eyes are flames. You must be gentle in your touch, or you will hurt others. But some things must be burned; palms must be turned to ashes; selfishness is dross to be purged.

Look at the shadows you cast around the room. Now you are a bonfire, bringing a great number of people out of the darkness and cold. You are light, you are warmth, you are companionship, you are Spirit, Mediator. You are the heart of Jesus Himself.

Take as long as you need to renew your acquaintance with Sister Fire, to familiarize yourself with this symbol, archetype of life. Don't rush; just be quiet and peaceful, and let the Spirit teach you whatever She wants to about fire.

Practical Considerations

Making the symbol of fire real to a typical congregation requires some planning, but with a little care, it can help them make sense of what surely must seem somewhat strange. It is really essential that the blessing of the new fire should take place outside. Even in the innermost of inner-city parishes, surrounded for miles by cement, a real fire can be kindled outside on the steps or sidewalk, even if it is in a barbecue grill.

Most people use charcoal starter or kerosene to soak the wood for the fire. This not only creates an unpleasant smell, but is totally unnecessary. Any fire, if it is laid properly, can catch from a match, or even from a spark itself. Perhaps laying the new fire and lighting it is a job for the parish scout troup. As a former scout, this author can testify that scouts learn how to set a proper fire. It is not important that the congregation watch while the fire is started, although many will be around to watch. If you are fortunate to have a dirt playground or a lawn for the fire, then dig, or have the scouts dig a fire pit. It should be a foot deep and about five feet in diameter. The outside should be lined with brick or stone.

There are still people who have the knack for starting a fire from flint and steel or from friction. If your scout leader or another parishioner can do it, then let them. It's not necessary, but it's a nice touch and more symbolic of how everything seems to have inside it a potential flame just waiting to burst through.

If this approach is not practical, then use a large outdoor barbecue with a fire of wood inside it. Again, keep some water handy. Make as big a fire as you can safely make. People must be able to see each other in its light, and warm some of the outdoor chill by its warmth, or they will never begin to understand what fire can be.

Bad or cold weather is often people's excuse for not kindling the new fire out-of-doors. Short of a blizzard or a hurricane, this objection is hardly valid. After all, fire is meant to guard against cold. If it is rainy, put up a tent roof for the people; once a fire is going, it can usually withstand a moderate rain. The more serious problem seems to be wind, not weather. There is a certain symbolism lost if the Paschal candle is blown out in the wind while the procession is going on. To avoid this, use a small clear-glass globe that fits over the top of the wick. This is usually all that is needed.

The blessing of the new fire shows us that fire can be a real sacramental for us, a sign of God's power living in our midst. Whoever is the celebrant ought to have a speaking voice that will project in the open air without a microphone. The whole point is lost if people cannot hear what is going on.

The blessing of the new fire should not begin until it is quite dark outside. There is no point in proclaiming Jesus Christ as the light of the world, if it is still daylight or twilight outside; the symbolism is not there. Depending on both geography and the date of Easter, the Vigil may well have to be scheduled for a different time each year. The most symbolic time to kindle the new fire is at midnight, when the world around us is quiet, and the light of the Paschal candle does not have to compete with automobile headlights. But since few parishes can begin their Vigils that late, at least let us resolve not to begin until the sky is really dark.

Let the new fire become for us a symbol of the spark of new life, struck into our hearts when we first believed, and fanned into flame by the action of the Spirit in our lives. Let the Spirit make us passionate men and women, warmed by the one Fire, and enlightened by the one Light, Jesus Christ.

The Light Of Christ

Eileen E. Freeman

Of all the visible symbols of Easter, the Paschal candle lit by the new fire is by far the most important. The senses of sight, smell and touch all combine in us to make our experience of the Light of Christ a vivid one. We can see the candle and the flame, red contrasting with white; blood and passion mixed with triumph and tranquility. We can smell the burning wax from the Paschal candle and our own smaller candles. We can feel the warmth of the flame.

During the whole of the Easter season, the Paschal candle is with us whenever we celebrate together in the Lord's name. The candle reminds us that Jesus is the one light that the darkness has never overcome. Even during the rest of the year the Paschal candle is lit during baptisms as a sign of Christ's gift of life to us.

The candle is a powerful sign of our unity in the Body of Christ. As the candle is carried in and we light our candles from its one flame, we are reminded graphically that in Jesus, who is the world's Light, we become the light of the world ourselves. The symbolism of the Paschal candle is carried out not only in our small candles, but also in the candles which are given to the newly baptized.

Since the Paschal candle is so important, it is essential that the candle we use be truly impressive, or it will have little or no sign value. The fact is, in many parishes, the Paschal candle is nothing more than a large altar candle stuck into a floor stand, or even a plastic or wax cylinder into which is inserted a small candle or votive for effect. Both are poor excuses for the real thing.

The usual reason for a tiny Easter candle is that a large one plus a stand to put it in is too expensive. In fact, a commercial candle about three feet high and two inches thick plus a stand can cost over two hundred dollars. However, by economizing on expensive Easter lilies or the like, in most cases the money could be found. Any Paschal candle less than the above dimensions is not likely to last throughout the entire Easter season without burning down to a mere nub.

For those parishes who either haven't the money to spend on commercial candles, or who would like to try their hand at decorating one themselves, there is an alternative to the usual type of Paschal candle, a home or locally-made one.

Most large towns and cities have at least one craftsperson in them who makes candles. Perhaps even a parishioner has the skill and can be "volunteered" to try to make a candle for the parish Easter season. Or perhaps the parish could sponsor an interested parishioner through a class in chandlery at a local craft store. Very often a craft store will offer free classes in various types of arts, provided that the student purchase the necessary supplies from the store.

To make a candle four feet high and four inches in diameter, about 20 pounds of wax will be needed, as well as good quality wicking. Traditionally, church candles are made of beeswax, or are at least predominately beeswax. There is a good reason for this. Beeswax is not only naturally fragrant, but is a natural material, unmixed with modern chemicals. However, beeswax burns with greater speed than candles made only partially with beeswax, or with other commercial wax. Moreover, beeswax is hard to obtain from commercial suppliers, who prefer other waxes because they mix with dyes and scents easier than beeswax. However, if otherwise unavailable, one can melt down ordinary church candles. Every parish should have a box in which to save the stubs of altar candles when the candles are changed. The wax can be melted in the top of a double broiler, after the wicks and any bits of charcoal adhering to the stubs have been removed. It can then be stored in blocks in a cool place until needed.

This is not the place to go into directions for the making of Paschal candles, since the skill cannot be learned merely from reading an article. However, there are a few things that may facilitate the process. It may be difficult to locate a candle mold four feet by four inches. If so, one can go to a large hardware or plumbing supply store and purchase four feet of aluminim heat piping or plastic piping. Both of these can be cut in half lengthwise with some ease, and bound around again with electrical tape or twine before the wax is poured. A bottom for the mold can be made from a large food can. It is also possible to dip a candle of some length and width, but this requires both skill and equipment beyond the range of most people.

The preparation of the Paschal candle, if it is being made by hand, should be done at the very beginning of Lent, if not before. It may take some experimenting to get the right mold, or to decide on whether to use all beeswax or a combination of beeswax and commercial wax. If a new stand has to be made, this will also take time.

The Paschal candle is usually decorated in a particular way, with a cross, the numerals of the year, and the Alpha-Omega monogram. These designs may be done in any way that suits the artist, but they should be done in such a way as to be clearly visible to the majority in the congregation. Colors which stand out at a distance should be used. Grains of incense are traditionally stuck into the extremities of the cross to represent the wounds of Christ. It is difficult to stick small pins into natural grains of incense; the incense crumbles readily. It is easier to use part of a cone of commercial incense; there are numerous brands available. In any case, the candle should be prepared to receive the pins with the incense on them, by having holes already started in the candle in appropriate places.

The Paschal candle should not be painted with any other symbols; it is a symbol itself and needs no others. However, horizontal bands or some repeating design can often be used to highlight the traditional designs. Since many paints do not adhere well to a wax surface, the artist will need to experiment. Acrylics and other thick paints seem to work best.

Hopefully, there will be some baptisms taking place at the Easter Vigil. Since each one being baptized will be given a candle during the ceremony, it is fitting that they be made especially for the occasion. The fact is that most baptisms are still infant baptisms, and therefore most stores offer candles with religious designs in either pink or baby blue, depending on whether the candidate is a baby boy or girl! While this may be at the worst mere foolishness at a child's baptism, it is sheer idiocy when the baptized is an adult catechumen.

Fortunately, candle molds up to fourteen inches long and four inches wide are regularly made. It should not be difficult to provide a substantial candle for each person to be baptized. These candles may be painted with the same design used on the candidate's new white robe, or they may be decorated to recall the Paschal candle itself. The idea is that the newly baptized Christian should have something to burn during Easter and on other occasions to recall his or her baptism and new life in Christ.

The stand usually made for Paschal candles is designed for a fairly thin candle. It is also a modern affair, often rather insubstantial and easily knocked over. The following are some suggestions for a stand to accommodate the type of candle described earlier in this chapter.

The stand is basically made of brick with green plants hanging from it. It can be constructed on a movable platform, if desired. Needed will be a three foot length of pipe, just wider than the Paschal candle to be inserted in it. The bottom of the pipe is bolted, welded or glued with cyano-acrylic glue to a metal plate the size and shape of the stand. On this plate, surrounding the candlestick, ordinary red bricks, (the type with four to six holes), are alternated in staggered rows, allowing about two or three inches space between the inside of the brick and the candlestick. The bricks should be mortared for strength. When the bricks have been built up to the level of the top of the candlestick, the space is filled with dirt. Sterile planting medium mixed with peat moss should be used. This planter-stand is then planted with trailing plants such as philodendron and various types of ivy. Small plants are used at random in some of the holes in the bricks; they can be watered from the brick holes immediately above the ones in which they are planted.

The use of live plants to decorate the Paschal candle is a very refreshing sort of ornament. The fact that the plants are living and growing things speaks to all of us who are trying to live and grow in Christ; it gives us hope that the seeds planted at our own baptism will bear fruit.

Because this stand and planter for the Easter candle is quite heavy, it should either be placed in a permanent spot, or the bottom should have casters or glides of some kind. This may necessitate making the base of heavy plywood rather than metal. The individual ought to modify the design as desired. A certain amount of maintenance will be needed. The plants unlike cut flowers, will need to be watered and occassionally fertilized. These plants may be blessed along with the flowers for the church on Saturday.

After the candle is inserted into its holder, the total height will be between seven and eight feet. This is a size which will clearly be visible throughout the church. When the cantor stands beneath it to sing the Exultet, when the catechumens are baptized in its light, it proclaims to all that "Jesus Christ is the Light of the world; a Light that no darkness can extinguish!"

O Felix Culpa

Eileen E. Freeman

If the Exultet had never existed, it would be necessary to invent it. The solemn chanting of the Paschal Praise is the most dramatic, emotion-filled prayer of the entire Church Year. It has a literary and artistic quality that causes it to rank among the finest poetic compositions of all time. The Paschal candle may be the radiance of Christ illuminating the world, but the Exultet is liquid light and faith turned into music.

When we gather around the Paschal candle to hear the great prayer of praise, our hearts are stirred at the incomprehensible depths of the Father's love for us. The Paschal Praise reminds us of our inestimable worth to God, who gave up his Son to redeem a world of "slaves." The boldness of the Church, which in a stunning hyperbole can even call the sin of Adam a "felicitous fault, a truly necessary sin" is understandable, when we consider what a joy and privilege it is to know Jesus as Lord and Savior.

The Christian community, gathered together in the dead of night to keep vigil, spiritually and psychologically enters into the womb of creation. The ancients believed that each year the world was threatened with a return to chaos; and that only the death and resurrection of their god could bring the monster that represented chaos down and bind him for another year. Those "gods" were only shadows of the reality which Christ accomplished once for all in his own person. We who stand holding our small candles are, as it were, witnesses to the re-creation of the world, of the seasons, of divine order. The awesome terror of Good Friday, when the monster seemed to have overwhelmed Christ on the cross has passed. Christ, the archetype of a thousand lesser heroes, has "descended into Hell" to fight the Enemy on his own ground, and vanquish him forever. The Paschal Praise, of course, does not herald a new resurrection, much less accomplish the old; Christ died once for sin and is now at the right hand of the Father. But for us, who must still do daily battle, the Paschal Praise proclaims with all possible surety that Christ has been raised from the dead, victorious, and that, in Him, our victory too is assured. The Paschal Praise is the Lord's voice speaking to us from a burning bush.

The images of darkness and light, of battles fought and victories won, of chaos struggling with divine order for possession of the world are what Carl Jung called the collective unconscious. Whether transmitted genetically or through a million subtle and psychological echoes, the archetypes of death and resurrection have been deeply ingrained in us. The Exultet proclaims not only Christ's resurrection, and our own with Him, but renewal of each tree and flower waking from winter rest, the renewal of sun's warmth, of robins returning and swallows flying back to Capistrano, and monarch butterflies journeying back from Mexico; the renewal of the whole earth around us. This celebration has been at the heart of every civilization that has ever added anything to our beliefs and attitudes. The whole religious life of the ancient Near East, from which sprang our spiritual ancestors, the Jews, was based on this alternating dance of life and death, fertility and sterility.

It is hard, almost impossible to put a name to this odd and restless thrill that the Exultet stirs up. St. Paul says that at such times, we hardly know how to pray, "but the Spirit of God prays within us with yearnings too deep for words. And God, who searches the depth of our hearts, knows exactly what the Spirit means." If the gift of tongues is a way of letting that Spirit-prayer bubble up on our lips, then of all times, the chanting of the Exultet is bound to be a suitable catalyst.

If our death and resurrection with Christ is the pivot on which the rest of our faith turns, then we have a pastoral obligation to make sure that the turning mechanism, namely the Exultet, has no "rust" or "squeaks" in it. All the mystery and joy can be taken from the proclamation if the cantor is ill-prepared or a poor singer; if the inherent dramatic possibilities of the Exultet are ignored. If all eyes in the church are not riveted on the Paschal candle and if all ears are not opened to and drinking in the words of the Paschal Praise, then a liturgical tragedy has taken place. We must minister to our brothers and sisters the richness of our heritage.

The Exultet: Creating an Artistic Whole

Whoever is going to chant the Exultet should know about it by the first week in Lent. As with any actor, even one taking a ministerial role, a great deal of rehearsal needs to be done. This rehearsal cannot usually be left until Holy Week itself, since the week is already quite full of services, rehearsals, activities, etc.

The most often asked question is: Who should sing the Exultet? The best answer is: Whoever can sing it best. The rubrics allow great leeway in selecting the cantor. Liturgically speaking, the ideal is to have the parish deacon sing the Exultet. However, few parishes have deacons, and even fewer of them can sing. A priest can sing the Exultet, but again, the question of celebrants with good voices is an important one. Very few priests, even those with good, strong, pleasant voices know anything about proper breathing and phrasing; and for the Exultet to be sung well, it requires a singer who knows both. It is better to find a parishioner, man or woman, who can sing the Exultet surpassingly well than to have a priest or deacon who can only do a mediocre job.

Like the Word of God, the Exultet is a proclamation. It is designed to be listened to; the congregation ought not to be following it along in books or missalettes, except for the very few so hard of hearing that a book is a pastoral necessity. The Exultet should not be printed in any Holy Week folders that a parish may want to make up. Since the Exultet will be heard, someone should work with the singer to make sure his or her diction is crystal clear.

There are two forms given for the Exultet; a longer and a shorter one. The longer form should always be chosen. There are sound liturgical reasons for this. The Exultet recapitulates our entire salvation history, from the time of Adam. It gives us our spiritual roots, delineates our heritage. The readings do this, too, in a fuller way. But unfortunately very few churches use the full set of readings. Most do the Exodus reading, perhaps an Isaiah reading, and then the Epistle and Gospel. We need to hear the complete Exultet to make up for what we are not hearing, but should be hearing in the full set of readings.

Aesthetics

The cantor and the Paschal candle are designed to be an artistic whole during the Paschal Praise. They should both be together. The cantor is generally standing almost under the candle, which provides light to read by. (Since the Exultet is read by candle-light, this is another compelling reason for having six weeks to practice it and almost learn it by heart.) Ideally the candle should be large enough and thick enough to create a towering, dominating focal point in the church. The stand should be tall and impressive. A funeral candlestick with a large altar candle in it is a poor excuse for a Paschal candle! In most churches the cantor will need to sing from the podium or pulpit so as to be seen and heard. For maximum visual effect, the pulpit should be draped or hung with cloth. This does not mean a banner; banners often have words on them; but the candle and Exultet can speak for themselves. Rather a plain white or gold drape is very effective. The cantor must be vested, either in plain alb and cincture, or with dalmatic if a deacon is available who sings well.

It would be foolish to go to all the above mentioned effort, and then have the cantor sing from xeroxed sheets of paper. If the words are to be highlighted, they should be sung from as visually attractive a book as possible. They can be clipped inside a Lectionary. In this age of craftspeople, it should not be too hard to find someone who can tool and gild a leather Lectionary cover for a reasonable cost. The importance of making the Exultet (not to mention the Word of God itself!) a pleasing sight cannot be overemphasized.

Another possibility is one which goes back to ancient times, and was suggested to the author by the Rev. Clifford Howell's book, *Preparing for Easter* (Liturgical Press; Collegeville, Minn.). The Exultet was read from a large parchment scroll rather than from a book. "As the deacon sang from it, he had to unroll it; and the part which he had used hung down from the front of his lectern in the sight of the people. And so there were

drawn on it, upside down to the deacon so as to appear the right way to the people, various pictures corresponding with the parts being sung". A parish artist who knew something of the technique of illuminating manuscripts, could be commissioned to produce such a scroll, which could then be used from year to year.

Parchment paper is readily available in well-stocked art supply stores, as are lettering pens, drawing ink, and suitable painting media, gilt and the like. The paper will need to be at least twelve inches wide; the edges of sheets can be glued together with a flexible cement until a length of about six feet is reached. However, it is much easier to work on each sheet separately and only join them together when they are finished. A wooden rod, stained, with tassels on each end, should be glued to each end of the roll, so that it will roll easily and hang flat over the lecturn.

The artist will need to draw a number of pictures. They should be simple enough as to be clearly visible; the use of gold and silver paint will catch the light from the candles and glitter impressively.

Some possible pictures are:
An angel with a trumpet, for the first "Rejoice" section
A rayed sun, for the second "Rejoice" section
A figure leaping, for the third "Rejoice" section
A jeweled cross for "Christ has ransomed..."
A lamb, for "This is our passover feast..."
Stylized waves of water, for "This is the night... holiness."
A broken chain, for "...Christ broke the chains..."
An apple, for "O happy fault"
An empty tomb, for "Most blessed of all nights..."
Interlocked wedding rings, for "..Heaven is wedded..."
A flame, for "Accept this Easter candle..."
A large star, for "May the Morning Star..."
Alpha and Omega, for the doxology.

The artist will have to work with the parish's minister of music when it comes time to copy the music notation for the Exultet. As a general rule it is always better to write the text first and fit the music over it, than to write the music first, and squeeze or stretch the text to accommodate the music. For the cantor, reading the words and music from a text printed with large characters will be an asset in dim lighting. However, it is hoped that the cantor will know the words and music well enough that the scroll (or the book) will serve as merely a reference point.

The triangle formed by the Paschal candle, cantor and pulpit is a very pleasing one, and one that attracts attention. If the Paschal Praise is allowed to be visually exciting and vocally dramatic, then it will draw people into its sphere by itself, or rather, by the power of the Spirit. This is the Spirit of Him who raised Jesus from the dead, who prays within us, and through the Easter Vigil leads us to the Father.

Come To The Water: Proclaiming The Risen

by Eileen E. Freeman

One of the things we tend to forget about our yearly celebration of the resurrection is that it begins with a *vigil*. The word itself comes from Latin. In its original language and as it was used by the Church "vigil" means "to stay awake at night." By its very nature the word implies staying awake beyond the normal hours. Thus, an evening service that begins at eight and ends at ten can only be called a vigil in a loose sense, since the average adult includes those hours in his or her waking time.

More than any other aspect of the Easter Vigil, except perhaps the proclamation of the Exultet, the Liturgy of the Word reminds us that the Mother of Feasts is supposed to be a vigil. There are seven readings, an epistle and a gospel, plus eight responsorial psalms. The seven readings present important moments of salvation history to us. The first three readings deal with sacred history: accounts of creation, the promise to Abraham and the Exodus event. The remaining four are all from the prophets. They focus on timeless promises and words of the Lord: renewal of the covenant, coming to the water, God as fountain of wisdom, God sprinkling Israel with clean water. All of these passages manage to include themes of washing and cleansing, and are especially appropriate since the Vigil is the paradigmatic example of the time when baptism should take place. The epistle makes the connection between the Old Testament readings and the meaning of Christian baptism. The gospel account of the resurrection makes clear the purpose of the other readings.

This structure is important when a parish is deciding which readings to use at the Vigil. Unlike votive and special occasion masses, which offer a wide variety of choice from which a single reading is chosen, the Easter Vigil by its very nature, if not by rubric, demands more than three readings.

Few parishes are able to use all the readings. Pastoral reasons are usually cited as the main reasons. It is true that to add the remaining readings would lengthen the Vigil by at least twenty minutes. However, the Vigil is designed for mature Christians, who on this one occasion should be able to handle the additional readings.

If a parish simply cannot use the full complement of readings for the Vigil, it is important to select readings from each of the two sections. The Exodus reading, of course, must be done. The passage of the Israelites through the Sea of Reeds prefigures every Christian's passage from death to life in the waters of baptism. As for the prophetic readings, the fifth reading, from Isaiah is probably the least difficult to understand. It is an invitation from God to come closer to Him and know Him better. However the seventh reading and the sixth, which refer to the Exile, bridge the gap from sacred history to theology more clearly.

Another possibility in planning the readings for the Vigil is to sing one of the readings rather than have it spoken. For example the text of the fifth reading is the subject of both "Ho! Everyone That Thirsteth" (GIA) and "Come To The Water" (NALR). A choir or groups might sing one of these settings, or the congregation might join in on a verse or refrain. Such singing has a long tradition behind it. We know from early church documents like the *Hymns Of The Lord's Rest* that the Christian community sang hymns of encouragement for the catechumens who were to be baptized that night.

One can also combine readings to some extent. This is particularly true of the four prophetic readings. The script that follows gives one such example of a Liturgy of the Word for the Easter Vigil.

Word

Come To The Water

This catena of readings is designed to be accompanied by slides, but it may be done effectively without them. The reading requires three adult readers who can proclaim a text dramatically. They should be vested in albs, and their scripts should be clipped inside three lectionaries or identical red folders. Gold or white folders could be used as well. They should sit in the sanctuary. When it is time for them to begin, they go to the foot of the altar and bow, then take their places: one at the pulpit, one at the cantor's stand on the other side of the sanctuary, and one on the top altar step. Each must have a microphone. The church should be darkened, except for spotlights on the three readers. If the places marked for responsorial psalmody are used, then the lights in the body of the church can be raised during the singing, but only if the congregation actually needs to read from a sheet or book. If they sing by rote, then keep the lights dim.

Slides for this presentation can be easily made or obtained. There are two kinds of slides: views of sunlight and clouds, and views of water. The different kinds of sunlight and clouds correspond to the readings from sacred history. Whether the slide scene is bright or cloudy, whether the sun is setting or rising, the events of sacred history are mirrored in terms of good and evil. Slides from nature can be used to accompany the creation reading. Mountains and sheep can be added for the selections from the Abraham reading. The water scenes are used during the prophetic section. The slides should range from the merest trickle of water from a faucet to pounding ocean surf. In between are slides of creeks, inlets, streams, rivers, lakes, torrents, falls, seas and oceans, etc. Scenes of dry lakes, arroyos, icebergs can also be used.

Only suggestions for slides can be made here. Each planning team must be able to think and adapt creatively.

In addition to slides, music may be used. Some suggestions are given the the script. It is usually best to tape the music beforehand onto a quality machine, and have a person watch the machine in case the speakers slow down or pick up the pace.

Script

(Total darkness, except for Paschal candle. First Reader may use a penlight. Music: Ligeti, 2001: Space Odyssey.)

Part 1: The Pentateuch

Reader 1: When God first made the earth and sky, the world was a formless waste. Deep and still, the darkness covered the abyss. And the Spirit of God brooded over the waters. Then God said, "Let there be light!" And there was light.

(Turn spotlights on the three readers. Turn on projector. Suggested slide: sun rising over the ocean, no visible land.)

Reader 3: God saw how good the light was, and so He separated the light from the darkness. He called the light "day" and the darkness He called "night."

(Suggested slide: moon over the same ocean scene.)

Reader 2: Thus evening came and morning followed, the first day.

Reader 1: Then God said, "Let there be a dome in the middle of the waters." And so there was.

(Suggested slide: sky shot of clouds.)

Reader 2: Thus evening came and morning followed, the second day.

Reader 3: Then God said, "Let all the water be gathered together, so that dry land may appear." And so it hap-. pened.

(Suggested slide: aerial shot of coral atoll.)

God called the dry land "earth" and the water "sea." And He said, "How good it is!"

Reader 2: Then God said, "Let the earth bring forth all kinds of seed and fruit bearing trees." And so it was.

(Suggested slide: fruit trees, etc.)

And seeing them, God said, "How good this is!"

Reader 3: Then evening came and morning followed, the third day.

Reader 1: Then God said, "Let there be lights in the sky to separate day from night, to give light to the earth, and to mark the passing of days and months and years. And so it was.

(Suggested slides: moon and stars, or a comet, or nebula, or the sun, perhaps in eclipse.)

And when He had set them in their places, God said, "That's good."

Reader 2: Evening came and morning followed, the fourth day.

Reader 3: God said, "Let the sea be filled with living creatures, and let birds fly throughout the sky." And so it happened.

(Suggested slides: various fish and birds.)

God created all kinds of sea monsters and all sorts of birds, and He blessed them, saying, "Be fertile, multiply, and fill the water and the skies."

Reader 2: Evening came and morning followed, the fifth day.

(Suggested slide: a school of fish or flock of birds.)

Reader 1: Then God said, "Let the earth bring forth all kinds of living creatures, beasts wild and tame, large and small." And so it was.

(Suggested slide: collage of animals.)

Reader 2: Then God said, "Now I will create a man and a woman after my own image. I will give them dominion over the earth, and sky and the sea and over all the creatures in them. And so it was.

(Suggested slide: close-up of a male hand clasping a woman's hand. Music: something classical, such as the "Ode To Joy" by Beethoven.)

Reader 1: God looked at everything He had made and He was delighted at how good it all was.

Reader 2: Thus evening came and morning followed, the sixth day.

Reader 3: This is how the earth, the sky and the sea and everything in them were created. And when the seventh day came, God took a rest from all the work He had accomplished.

(Suggested slides: several scenes showing the growth of humanity, a single farmhouse, a hamlet, a village, a town, a city street done with telephoto to "crowd" things together. The responsorial psalm may be sung here, if desired. Some musical settings are suggested in "Celebrating Jesus' Resurrection With Song," in this section.)

Reader 1: Much, much later, God decided to test the humans he had made, to see whether or not they remembered Him. He spoke to one of them.

(Suggested slide: hill or mountain with its top shrouded in clouds. Suggested music: "Night On Bald Mountain.")

Reader 3: Abraham!

Reader 2: Here I am, Lord.

Reader 3: I want you to take your son Isaac, your only child, whom you love so deeply, and go to the land of Moriah. When you get there I want you to kill him and make a burnt offering of him to me on a mountain I will show you.

(Suggested slide: darker clouds, thunderheads.)

Reader 1: And Abraham left the next morning with his son Isaac to do as God had commanded him. After three days' journey they reached the place. Isaac turned to his father.

Reader 2: Where is the lamb for the sacrifice, Father?

Reader 3: God will provide the lamb, my son.

(Suggested slide: violent storm in the desert.)

Reader 1: When they reached the top of the mountain, Abraham laid the firewood upon the altar. Then he bound his son Isaac and laid him on top of the wood. He took his knife in hand and prepared to slay his only child.

Reader 2: Abraham! Abraham!

Reader 3: Who is calling me?

(Suggested slide: storm receding.)

Reader 2: I am the Lord, the God of your ancestors. Stop! Do not harm the child; do not lay a hand on him. Now I see that you truly are devoted to me, since you did not withhold your only son from me.

Reader 1: As Abraham looked around after the Voice, he saw a ram caught in a thornbush. He took the ram and he sacrificed it to the Lord as a burnt offering in place of his son Isaac.

(Suggested slide: sun, rainbow. Suggested music: "Morning" from Peer Gynt Suite by Edvard Grieg.)

(Suggested slide: Egyptian pyramids, sand dunes.)

Reader 2: Many years later, the descendants of Abraham, like the ram God had provided for sacrifice, were caught in the thornbush of Egypt. In their distress they cried out to the Lord, and He heard them.

Reader 3: He said to Moses,

Reader 1: Lead my people out of the land of Egypt and bring them into the Promised Land.

Reader 2: But Lord, how shall we cross the Sea? Surely we will drown.

Reader 3: Have I not told you to trust me? Tell the Israelites to go forward. As for you, stretch out your staff over the waters and the sea will be split in two. You will all cross on dry ground. Then, when these stubborn Egyptians follow you, I will make the sea waters come together, drowning Pharaoh and his chariots.

(Suggested slide: the cracked bottom of a dry lake.)

Reader 1: The pillar of cloud, which had been leading the Israelites, now moved behind them to block them from the sight of Egypt. As Moses stretched out his staff, the waves parted and dry land appeared. Soon the Israelites were safely on the other shore.

(Suggested slide: huge ocean waves breaking on shore.)

Reader 2: But Pharaoh and all his soldiers were drowned, as the Lord himself had promised. And Moses and the Israelites sang this (a) song to the Lord, while Miriam led the women in the dance:

(If the responsorial psalm is sung at this point, either by the congregation or by the choir, do not use the word in parentheses. If no psalm is being done, use the parenthesized word.)

Part 2: The Prophecies

(Suggested slide: either a fountain or an oasis in the desert. Suggested music: "Water Music" by Handel or music for harp. In this version the fifth reading precedes the fourth as set up in the Vigil liturgy. If the psalm to the Exodus reading is sung, do not sing the fifth reading which begins this section. If the psalm is not sung, the Isaiah 55 reading may be sung. If the reading is not sung, proceed with the spoken version. Fifth reading: Isaiah 55.)

Reader 1: All you who are thirsty, come to the water! You who have no money, come, get your bread and eat it. Come, drink wine and milk for free!

Reader 2: Why spend your hard-earned money for fake food?

Reader 3: Why give up your wages for imitation drinks that cannot quench your thirst?

Reader 1: Come, hear me.

Reader 2: Listen to what I have to say.

Reader 3: Pay attention to my words, and you will live.

Reader 1: Seek the Lord now, while he may still be found, Cry out to him, while he is still near.

(At this point the song "Seek The Lord" by Roc O'Connor, SJ (NALR) may be sung instead of the following dialogue. Suggested slide: fountain or geyser.)

Reader 1: Turn to the Lord, for he is merciful; Return to the fountain of living water, for he is generous with his forgiveness.

(Suggested slide: rainstorn in the desert.)

Reader 3: For just as the rain and snow fall from the sky, and do not return until they have watered the earth, so my word, too, is a source of life. It shall not return to me empty, but shall do my will, achieving the purpose for which I sent it.

(Suggested slide: well, cistern. Sixth reading: Baruch 3.)

Reader 1: My people, why do you still prefer to lower your buckets into a dry well? Why do you choose broken cisterns that contain no water?

Reader 3: You have forsaken the fountain of wisdom, you are dirty and covered with dust. You are foolish, my people; you wash yourselves in dust and you think you are clean.

(Suggested slide: waterfall. Seventh reading: Ezechial.)

Reader 2: Come to the water, children; let me wash your dust away. Let me pour clean water upon you and cleanse you from all your sins. Let me wash away your stony hearts and give you hearts of flesh. Let me put my spirit within you, that you may keep my words.

(The following section may be sung. Suggested version, "Though The Mountains May Fall," by Dan Schutte, SJ, NALR. If it is not sung, continue with the dialogue. Suggested slide: rainbow. Fourth reading: Isiah 54.)

Reader 2: I am the Lord, your redeemer; I call you to come back to me. Once I hid my face from you, but no more. Once I turned away in anger, but never again.

Reader 3: Let us make a new covenant together, a covenant that will last forever, just as in the days of Noah, when I swore that the waters would never again cover the earth.

Reader 1: There! I have sworn it! Though the mountains leave their place, though the very hills be shaken, my love will never leave you, nor my covenant of peace be shaken.

Reader 2: Come to the restful waters; refresh yourselves beside the quiet stream.

(Suggested slide: peaceful brook, grassy bank.)

Reader 3: Draw your water joyfully from the springs of salvation.

(Here the dialogue ends. However, the music should continue. The lights on the readers should be turned off; and they should leave quietly. For the next two or three minutes, show additional slides. These should start with a tiny pond or creek, and become successively larger bodies of water, until they finally empty into the ocean. The whole effect should be one of peace and refreshment. Alternatively, while the slides are being shown, have a soloist sing Psalm 42, the responsorial psalm for the last reading.)

New Ideas For The Easter Vigil

Michael E. Moynahan, SJ

Because of the length of the Easter Vigil and the many ceremonies attached to it, certain parts of the Vigil are easily ignored, accidently by-passed in planning the Vigil. With so many readings, it is easy to ignore the Gospel as "just another reading." During the excitement of baptism, the Litany and Profession of Faith can be overlooked. The whole Eucharistic Prayer and the Breaking of Bread can become anti-climactic.

Lest any of these things happen, here are some ideas for celebrating different parts of the Easter Vigil. Included are: the Gospel Narrative arranged for various parts, forms for the Litany, ways of professing faith, a Peace Rite and a Fraction Rite.

Easter Vigil Gospel Proclamation

The Easter Gospel, although short, lends itself to a narration in parts. Three readers are needed: Narrator, Angel, and Jesus. If one wishes to dramatize the story, two guards and two women will also be needed. The story lends itself to dance or mime quite easily.

Narrator: A reading from the Good News according to Matthew. After the sabbath, and towards dawn on the first day of the week, Mary of Magdala and the other Mary went to visit the sepulcher. All at once there was a violent earthquake, for the angel of the Lord, descending from heaven, came and rolled away the stone and sat on it. His face was like lightning, his robe white as snow. The guards were so shaken, so frightened of him, that they were like dead men. But the angel spoke, and said to the women:

Angel: There is no need for you to be afraid. I know you are looking for Jesus, who was crucified. He is not here, for He has risen, as He said He would. Come and see the place where He lay; then go quickly and tell his disciples, "He has risen from the dead and now He is going before you to Galilee; it is there you will see Him." Now I have told you.

Narrator: Filled with awe and great joy the women came quickly away from the tomb and ran to tell the disciples. And there, coming to meet them was Jesus.

Jesus: Peace be to you!

Narrator: And the women came up to Him, and falling down before Him, clasped his feet. Then Jesus said to them:

Jesus: Do not be afraid; go and tell my brothers that they must leave for Galilee; they will see me there.

Narrator: This is the Gospel of the Lord.

158

THE HOLY WEEK BOOK

The Litany

One of the main disadvantages of the litanies, especially the Litany of the Saints, is that the saints mentioned in it are often foreign to our experience. We know a little bit, or we think we do, about Mary and Joseph, about St. Francis and a few others, but most of the names of the list fail to hold our attention. Here is a new version of the Litany of the 'Saints' both in general terms and for those who in their lives were peacemakers.

Deacon: My brothers and sisters, as we prepare to renew our Baptismal vows, let us ask Christ and the saints of heaven to intercede for us.

Deacon: Lord, have mercy.

All: Lord, have mercy.

Deacon: Christ, have mercy.

All: Christ, have mercy.

Deacon: Lord, have mercy.

All: Lord, have mercy.

Deacon: Let us remember all those in times past whose lives have helped make us who we are today.

(The response to each line of the Litany is "Pray for us.")

Abraham and Moses
Isaiah and Jeremiah
Holy Mary, Mother of the Lord
St. Joseph and St. John the Baptist
St. Peter and St. Paul
St. John the Evangelist and St. Mary Magdalene
All patriarchs, prophets, disciples and evangelists
St. Joan of Arc and St. Thomas More
Dietrich Bonhoeffer and Anne Frank
St. Mugagga and the Christian martyrs of Uganda
Martin Luther King
All martyrs and blood witnesses
St. Clare and St. Francis of Assisi
St. Ignatius of Loyola
St. Francis Xavier
St. Stanislaus Kostka
St. Benedict and St. Elizabeth Seton
John Roncalli and St. Thomas a'Becket
All peacemakers
St. Gregory the Great and Fra Angelico
Dante and Michelangelo
Gerard Manley Hopkins and C. S. Lewis
Teilhard de Chardin
All poets, musicians and artists
All men and women of science
All holy and heroic men and women
(pause)

(The response to the next set of petitions is "Lord, save your people.")

Lord, be merciful
From all evil
From every sin
From everlasting death
By your coming as a man
By your death and rising to new life
By your gift of the Holy Spirit
(pause)

(The response to the next set of petitions is: "Lord, hear our prayer.")

Be merciful to us
Give new life to us who renew our baptismal promises
Bless all of us, our families and friends
(pause)

(Repeat the "Lord have mercy" which began the Litany.)

If desired, other names can be added to the Litany, such as: Johann Sebastian Bach, St. Theresa, John Henry Newman, Alfred Delp, Thomas Merton, John and Robert Kennedy, Dag Hammerskjold.

Renewal of Baptismal Vows

(1)

Celebrant: Baptism is not a once-for-all event only. It is initiation into a community of faith in which the pattern of dying and rising again with Christ is the enduring rhythm of life. Every eucharist is, in this sense, a renewal of our baptismal promises. Every experience of sin or failure or diminishment, every experience of forgiveness, success, or growth makes us feel this rhythm and invites us to a stronger and steadier and more committed discipleship.

Do you promise, then, to seek the good life for your sisters and brothers everywhere, rejecting sin and living in the freedom of God's children?

People: We do.

Celebrant: Do you promise to work at building the human family, rejecting the idols of money and property and color and class and position?

People: We do.

Celebrant: Do you promise to seek peace and live in peace, in one human family, rejecting Satan's prejudice and nationalism and all barriers to unity?

People: We do.

Celebrant: Do you believe in Jesus Christ, his Son, our Lord and brother, whose life and death and resurrection stand before all of us as a saving way and truth and life?

People: We do.

Celebrant: For those of you who have made covenant with the Lord and the Christian Community through religious vows, as special ministers within the Church do you promise to continue your service to the church at large and to the whole of humanity through the Church?

Religious: I do!

Celebrant: Do you promise through your vows of poverty, chasity and obedience to be a faithful witness to the world of the mystery and strength of Christ's love?
Religious: I do!
Celebrant: For those of you who have made covenant with one another and with your children through marriage vows, do you promise your continued support and love for your faithful married partner — to continue to serve in health or sickness, in difficult and easy times, in the face of one another's weaknesses and failings?
Married People: I do!
Celebrant: Do you promise your continued service and love to your children — in helping them become mature men and women, growing through Christ our Lord?
Married People: I do!
Celebrant: God, the Father of our Lord Jesus Christ, has given us new birth, assurance of new beginnings, fresh starts each day, and has forgiven all our sins. He is faithful; his love will never end. It is with confidence then, that we pray to Him in the words that Jesus taught us:
People: Our Father *(sung)*

Signing With Water

(The deacon instructs the congregation that at this time each is to sign his neighbor with the water which has been blessed in the Baptismal Font. Several goblets filled with that water are passed around. The sign of the Cross on the forehead symbolizes the sealing of each one's covenant.)

(2)

Celebrant: Friends, we have blessed this water to recall our baptism. In baptism, we died with Christ; in baptism we also rose with Him to a new life. When we were baptized, God extended to us a share in his life and love. But our baptismal commitment did not take place once and forever. We renew our baptism whenever we celebrate the Eucharist, seek forgiveness for our sins, or simply turn to God in prayer. God's love always reaches out to encompass us.

Tonight as we celebrate the mystery of Christ's death and resurrection, let us again commit ourselves to a life lived in the love of God, just as we did on the day of our baptism.

Do you reject the evil in the world, the evil that separates races, nations, individuals, the evil by which people turn from their brothers and sisters to seek only their own good, the evil that lets men and women live in poverty of body or soul, to cry out in anguish without being heard? Do you reject this evil?
People: We do.
Celebrant: In faith, then, do you accept God's love and join Him in bringing harmony and justice to the human family?
People: We do.

Celebrant: Do you believe that God is the Father of all that exists, that he created our world and all the worlds by his almighty power, that He made us as well, to love Him and be loved by Him?

People: We do.

Celebrant: Do you believe that God loves us so much that He gave us his only Son, Jesus, who became a man, a brother to us all, who out of love gave himself over to human suffering and human death?

People: We do.

Celebrant: Do you believe that Jesus rose from death and thus brought the triumph of his Father's life and love to us all?

People: We do.

Celebrant: Do you believe in the Holy Spirit, who dwells within us and calls us together in the Church?

People: We do.

Celebrant: Do you believe in God's forgiveness of sins, the resurrection of the body and everlasting life in the love of God?

People: We do.

Celebrant: God, the all-powerful Father of our Lord Jesus Christ, has given us a new birth through water and the Holy Spirit, and forgiven all our sins. May He also keep us faithful to our Lord Jesus Christ forever and ever.

People: Amen *(sung)*

Peace Rite

It is proper for the greeting of peace to be more elaborate during the Easter Vigil than is usually done during the year. The fact is, we are celebrating in a particularly intense way, that Jesus has made peace between us and the Father. This makes us more aware of the need to be at peace among ourselves. The following rite is taken from the Syrian Liturgy.

First Celebrant: God and Lord of all that is, make us worthy of this hour, unworthy that we are, for You have our interests at heart. Cleanse us from all deceit and hypocrisy, that we may be united one to another by the bonds of peace and love. May we draw strength and holiness from knowing You, through your only Son, our Lord and God and Savior, Jesus Christ. Blessing be yours, and his, and your holy, all-holy, life-giving Spirit's, now and forever.

Second Celebrant: Let us stand and pray peacefully to the Lord.

First Celebrant: You are the God of peace and mercy, of love and compassion and kindness: You and your only Son and your all-holy Spirit, now and forever, age after age.

People: Amen.

First Celebrant: And now, let us share this holy Paschal flame, as a sign of that radiant love and affection that is the Risen Savior in our lives.

Fraction Rite

During the breaking of the Bread before the Communion procession begins, the Lamb of God is usually sung. However since the Lamb of God was originally a litany designed to cover the time it took to break up the Eucharistic bread in earlier times, we may adapt it to our needs. This fraction prayer may be accompanied by soft instrumental music, if desired.

Wheat grains crushed
provide our food.
grape full bunches pressed
become our table drink.
because they do not cling
to what they were,
a wonderful new happening:
our paschal meal.
we who are hungry—
fed;
we who are thirsty—
satisfied;
we who were empty—
filled;
we who were dead—
alive again!
Proudly rising:
new life from old ashes.
death never again the end
only a stop on the journey.
But new things also die
to come again in unimagined ways.
bread broken becomes a meal—
signs us a community.
wine passed around and shared
becomes our cup of blessing.
and when we eat
and when we drink
we remember.
our eyes are opened a little more
and we know:
this is the bread of life,
this is the cup of our salvation.
so we eat,
we drink,
we die,
but most importantly
we rise.
Alleluia!
Come Lord Jesus!
again,
and again,
and again.

Michael E. Moynahan, SJ

Springs Of Water, Bless The Lord

Christian Rich

During the past decade, Catholic Church musicians have concentrated their efforts on music for the Eucharistic liturgy. In many places this has borne fruit in liturgical celebrations that are both aesthetically pleasing and musically prayerful. Many talented persons have composed music for the Eucharist that blends the voices of cantor, congregation, choir and celebrant in various combinations producing worship that is truly "praise to the Lord." We need only look at the multitude of Mass settings, acclamations, hymns, psalms, and choral works for the Eucharistic liturgy along with the attention given it in workshops, conferences, and publications to see that this has been the priority as the re-establishment of healthy and prayerful musical experiences continue. It is now time to turn some of these efforts and concerns towards the other sacramental celebrations. Most important of these is The Rite for Christian Initiation.

Because of the long tradition of private, "uncelebrated" baptisms, hidden in some dark corner of the church without the participation of the community, there was little need for baptismal music and as a result none was composed. Now, with the new rite's emphasis on the participation of the faithful and the restoration of Initiation to its proper place, namely the Easter Vigil, the need arises for music that will both enrich the celebration and be an assent on the part of the faith community to the sacramental actions.

Christian Initiation during the Vigil provides many opportunities for song. This article will explore these possibilities and offer various ways for their implementation, so that the rite may be celebrated in a full and reverent manner.

Music for the Easter Vigil Initiation rite can be divided into the following:
1. Litany
2. Blessing of Water/Acclamation
3. Baptism/Acclamation
4. Sprinkling of Water

The Litany

As the candidates stand on the threshold of sharing in the death and rising of Jesus, the Christian community, in readiness to receive them, invokes Christ and his saints in a solemn gesture of prayer. This litany, an old and venerable prayer of the Church, not only gathers together the supplications of the community into one repetitive prayer but serves to remind us that the Church, welcoming its new members, is a Church that transcends the boundaries of time and place.

Properly done, the Litany can set an atmosphere of anticipation as the candidates await their passage. It should always be sung, preferably with a *trained* cantor in dailogue with the congregation. Pulse and drive should be its characteristics and slow tempo avoided. Traditional chant versions of the Litany seem to work best and can be found with some modifications in the Sacramentary, most missalette worship aids, and in the more complete hymnals (i.e. *Worship II* GIA). Slight adaptation of the Litany to include local church patrons and the patrons of those to be baptized is desirable. The choir should rehearse the Litany beforehand so that they may reinforce the people's response.

Blessing of Water/Acclamation

The Blessing of Water is the most significant prayer in the Rite. Following the Jewish *berakah*, a blessing form of the Eucharisitc prayers, it should be enriched in a similar fashion by sung acclamation on the part of the community.

The prayer begins with an epiclesis in which three references are made to water in the Old Testament: creation, flood and Exodus; and three New Testament references: Baptism of Jesus, water and blood flowing from his side on the cross, his command to "Go teach all nations, baptizing in the name of the Father, and of the Son, and of the Holy Spirit." Following this, the celebrant continues in a text closely parallel to the Eucharistic prayers:

Blessing of Water
Father, look with love upon your Church and unseal for it the fountain of baptism. By the power of the Spirit give to the water of this font the grace of your Son.

Eucharistic Prayer For Reconciliation
Father, look with kindness on your people gathered here before you: send forth the power of your spirit so that these gifts may become for us the body and blood of your beloved Son, Jesus the Christ.

After the gesture of touching the water with his right hand, the celebrant continues with two petitions: 1) sending of the Spirit upon the water, and 2) newness of life for those to be baptized. A short doxology concludes the prayer and the faithful give their assent with an Amen.

Because of the solemn character of this prayer it should be sung in the style of the chanted prefaces. Musical notation for it can be found in the Sacramentary. For the community's affirmation, the same Great Amen used later in the Liturgy of the Eucharist would be appropriate here. This duplication will also serve to emphasize the close relationship of the two sacraments.

Two alternative forms of this prayer are given in the Rite (389). These prayers are interspersed with short acclamations for the faithful in a manner like the Eucharistic Prayers for Children. These prayers allow for a more active role on the part of the worshipping community. To implement the singing of these prayers, a setting is given below for the second one. The celebrant sings each sentence of the prayer to the simple formula. The community responds each time with the acclamation and concludes with the Amen.

Christian Rich

Celebrant:

Father, God of mercy, through these waters of baptism you have filled us with new life as your very own children.

Acclamation
All:

Christian Rich

Bless-ed be God.____ Ho - ly His Name.____ Al - le - lu - ia!____

Amen
All:

Christian Rich

A - men, A - men, A - men.

As an acclamation to the Blessing of Water the Community sings:

Springs of water bless the Lord
Give him glory and praise forever.

This acclamation can be easily intoned by the cantor or choir and then repeated by the people. If your congregation learns new material slowly, the text can well be adapted to a melody of a refrain or acclamation from the existing repertoire. This form of musical recycling can prove quite helpful for those once a year acclamations that occur during the Triduum liturgies. However, one should guard against overworking one particular melody. The Sacramentary provides a chant-like melody for this text which might be difficult to get into the hands of the people. Worship II has a setting and follows the music for the Litany. Another follows:

THE HOLY WEEK BOOK

Cantor/Congregation   Christian Rich

Springs of wa - ter bless the Lord, give him glo-ry and praise for-ev - er.

The Baptism and Acclamation

If it is desirable to solemnize the actual baptism in song, a setting using the Easter Alleluia is provided here. The number being baptized will help determine whether this option is used.

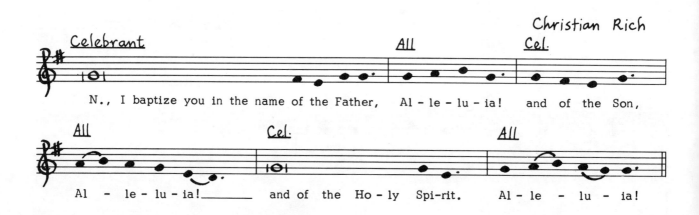

Christian Rich

Celebrant   All   Cel.

N., I baptize you in the name of the Father, Al - le - lu - ia! and of the Son,

All   Cel.   All

Al - le - lu - ia!_____ and of the Ho - ly Spi-rit. Al - le - lu - ia!

After each baptism the people sing a short acclamation voicing their acceptance of the catechumen into the Christian community and praising God for her or him. If the above sung baptismal formula is used then this acclamation should be deleted. The new rite for Christian Initiation gives twelve texts for use as acclamations here (390). Musical settings for the complete texts have been published by the *Composers' Forum for Catholic Worship*, #CF73-108 (CFCW). These settings serve a diversity of musical needs by offering settings for both the organ and guitar idioms. It should be noted that these acclamations along with the other liturgical text found in 390 — two New Testament Hymns and Songs of the Ancient Liturgies — are available through CFCW and mark the most significant contribution to music for the Baptismal Rite to date.

The settings below follow the familiar cantor-intone congregation-repeat structure.

Blessed be God who chose you in Christ. God is love; he who lives in love, lives in God. Hap-py are those who have washed their robes clean, washed in the blood of the Lamb!

The final component of the Baptismal Liturgy of the Vigil is the renewal of baptismal promises by the faithful. After this has been completed the people are sprinkled with the blessed water as they sing a song that is either baptismal in character or a song of praise. The hymn "All Creatures of Our God and King" (tune: *Lasst Uns Erfreuen,* text: Francis of Assisi) has become traditional in many churches. This hymn calls upon all creation to praise its Maker with a multitude of Alleluias. The beauty of the moment seems to be perfectly expressed in verse three: "Thou sister water pure and clear, make music for the Lord to hear, Alleluia!" An alternate verse for this hymn is given in Hymns for Baptism and Holy Communion, Contemporary Worship 4 (Concordia Publishing House, St. Louis, MO). This text by Roger Lauren Tappert is specifically baptismal and could be sung as a first verse with the St. Francis text following. Other appropriate songs at this time are Lucien Deiss' *There is One Lord* from *Biblical Hymns and Psalms,* Vol. II (World Library Publications); S. Suzanne Toolan's *Ephesians Hymn* from *Living Spirit* (available through G.I.A., G-1625); Alexander Peloquin's setting of the chant *Vidi Aquam* published under the title *Prayer* from *Celebration of Presence, Prayer, and Praise* (G.I.A., G-1925); also many of the CFCW *Seven Songs from the Ancient Liturgies* by S. Theophane Hytrek (CF 71-103).

Names and addresses of Publishers referred to in the text:
Composer's Forum for Catholic Worship
The Composer's Forum was dissolved in 1976. Many of the songs published by this organization are made available through G.I.A. Publications, Inc.
Concordia Publishing House
3558 South Jefferson Avenue
St. Louis, MO 63118
G.I.A. Publications, Inc.
7404 South Mason Avenue
Chicago, IL 60638
World Library Publications
2145 Central Parkway
Cincinnati, OH 45214

Clothed In White Garments

Eileen E. Freeman

"Then one of the elders asked me: 'Who are these people clothed in white?' I said to him, 'You know the answer to that, Sir.' He replied, 'These are they who have survived the great trial. They have washed their robes and made them white in the blood of the Lamb.'" (Rev 7:13-14).

In John's vision, the chosen people of God stood before the throne wearing long white robes and holding palm branches. The white was a sign of their worthiness to stand in God's presence; the palms, signs of their victory over great trials.

In the church today we think much less in terms of victory and worthiness than the early Christians did. Children are baptized into the Body of Christ without ever making the choice of becoming Christians for themselves. Adult catechumens who need to be baptized are relatively few, except perhaps in the "missionary areas." White is no longer the symbol of purity and worthiness that it used to be; in fact, for large parts of the world's people, white is a sign of deep mourning and always has been.

In the ancient world, the changing of garments meant the assuming of a new identity. When David put on Jonathan's cloak and armor, he ceased being a simple shepherd (1 Sam 18). When a Roman boy became a certain age, he put on the toga and became a man. Similarly when a newly baptized Christian puts on the "white robe," he or she becomes a "new creation." The early Church generally baptized by immersion; the candidate was quite often baptized naked. Needless to say, the actual baptism was accomplished with some degree of privacy. The white robe which the candidate received served not only as a symbol of an identity change, but also as necessary clothing.

We rarely baptize adults by immersion nowadays, although the practice has begun to return to Church usage. Even when we do, it is not necessary to clothe them; rather, the donning of the white garment retains only its symbolic meaning.

If adult baptism is the norm of the Church, then the symbols of baptism should be employed on an adult level. However, it is not uncommon to see an adult baptized being given a "white garment" which is nothing more than a small strip of cloth suitable only for being placed around the neck of a baby (which also makes minimal sense). There is no sign value for an adult or even for the parents and relatives of an infant in such a "white robe." It is so severely truncated as to be useless.

The difficulty with obtaining some type of large white robe for an adult has been both the fact that adults differ in size; and that the few commercial robes available are expensive and, because of their commercial nature, impersonal. The decorations usually put on baptismal robes have begun to get excessive; candles, water pitchers, crosses, fishes, waves all appear on the same garment, each trying to say what the robe itself and the rite are designed to say. We must not proliferate symbols, at Baptism or any other place, or the significance of the important ones will be inevitably obscured.

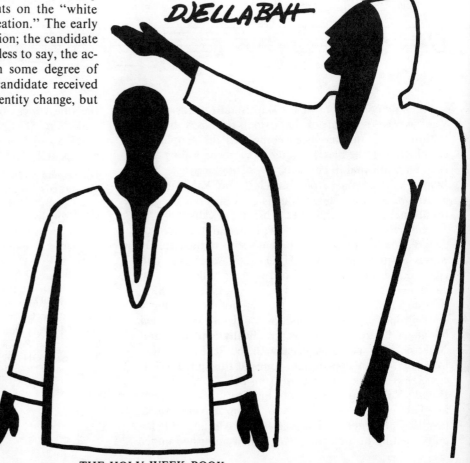

DJELLABAH

DASHIKI

THE HOLY WEEK BOOK

With a little adaptation, a number of commercial patterns and clothing styles are admirably suited to being used as baptismal garments. There are eight basic styles which have lines that look well on almost anyone. They are: the caftan, poncho, bathrobe, tunic, kimono, dashiki, night shirt and choir robe (cotta). Most of these are ethnic types of clothing from Africa, Japan and Mexico. Depending on the type of fabric used, a full garment which either substitutes for street clothes or which covers them can cost between three and twenty dollars.

The caftan is a full length garment with very simple sleeves, and is among the easiest kinds of garments to make. A single bedsheet can be used quite inexpensively and elegantly. The caftan is designed to substitute for street clothes. The one baptized who receives it will need a place to change into it. Some easy caftan patterns are: McCall's 5386, 5354, 5286 (for girl's or very short people); Butterick 3384, a more tailored caftan for smaller sizes; Vogue 1643, containing patterns on caftans, tunic, vest, 9374 and 8869 in larger sizes for men. Some of these are hooded caftans, others have collars. The caftan, like all these designs, looks well on men as well as women, and if not decorated in too "fussy" a pattern, is well accepted by them.

The poncho is a sleeveless garment that fits over the head. It may have a collar or hood. Some poncho patterns readily available are: McCall's 5027, Simplicity 7183 with a matching dress pattern as well which makes a nice outfit for ladies size 8-18; Vogue Very Easy 9588 with hood. The poncho can be easily pulled on over the head without the necessity of changing one's clothes. Women seem to prefer the poncho to men,

The robe pattern which works best is the wrap-around style, with or without a fabric belt-tie. The sleeves are usually narrow, and there is a collar. Again, the robe can be donned over street clothes. McCall's 3738 is a useful pattern which fits nearly all sizes.

The tunic or tabard is shaped rather like the large monastic scapular, but has ties on either side to keep the garment from flapping around. It is a fairly short garment, rarely extending as far as the knees. It is collarless, and is slipped on over street clothes. Tabard outfits for women are increasing in popularity. One pattern for the tabard tunic is McCall's 3845, which is called an apron, but works well for either men or women.

The kimono is rather like the robe pattern mentioned above, but is tailored a little differently, and can be made either as a slip-on garment, or a substitute for street clothes. Simplicity 5685 is a relatively easy pattern to make.

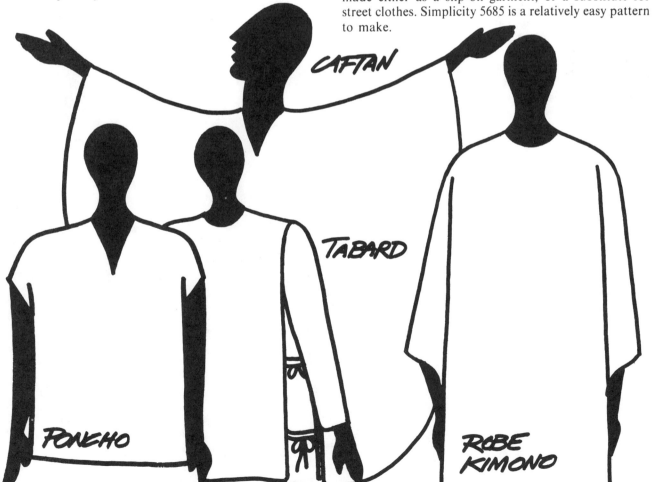

The djellabah and dashiki are both garments of African origin. The former is a full length robe with a hood and wide sleeves. It must be changed into. The dashiki is a hip length garment with very full, long sleeves and no collar, but split at the neck. Men very often prefer this style because they can be baptized in their shirt sleeves and then put this on over their shirts. McCall's has a djellabah pattern, which is easy to make, while Simplicity 6864, 7996 (for knits) patterns make excellent dashikis.

The night shirt pattern by Butterick, 3879, makes a very good complete outfit. It has a bonus in that it comes with transfers in a "fish" motif. Since the Fish, or ICHTHUS, is an ancient Christian symbol often associated with baptism, it is convenient to have it here.

Butterick makes about the only pattern for choir robe surplice. This garment has less usability than the others, because of its clear connection with church services. However, those who prefer this sort of "over the head" garment can use Butterick 3194. The pattern is not regularly stocked in fabric stores, and usually needs to be ordered.

Some of these patterns can be worn quite well as ordinary garments, making the tradition that the newly baptized wore their white robes for a week after Easter a viable possibility once again. They work well because they are the ordinary clothes patterns of millions of people in the world. The present patterns, based on either the priestly stole or the chasuble, are not really clothing, and look very artificial; even more so when they are wrapped around the necks of babies.

The material for these garments should, of course, be white unless the one baptized is Oriental or comes from a tradition in which white is associated with funerals. There are different shades of white, ranging from a pure dead-white, to off-white or eggshell. A white in acrylic or polyester is a shinier white than white wool or linen or 100% cotton, the natural fibers. Actually there is something about the natural fibers that is often more pleasing than synthetics. The white robes of Revelations were probably seen as linen ones, while Egyptian cotton was known all over the ancient world. Modern processes have made linen and cotton that are virtually crushproof and stain-repellant. The cost of using natural fabrics is often higher than white polyester or other synthetics, but the additional sign value afforded by linen or cotton should not be overlooked. The patterns described above require anywhere from two yards for the tabard to five or six for a flowing caftan.

Some small decorations or colored borders can make one of the above baptismal robes look unusually striking. Since the robes have their own symbolic value, and ornamentation is strictly that, even when it uses a religious motif. Wide embroidered ribbons with cross, flower, fish motifs are available in well-stocked fabric stores. With a little ingenuity, however, one can embroider one's own motifs. For example, a pattern of sea waves in three shades of blue around the sleeve ends of a robe or djellabah, or a fish motif on the neck of a dashiki looks quite striking.

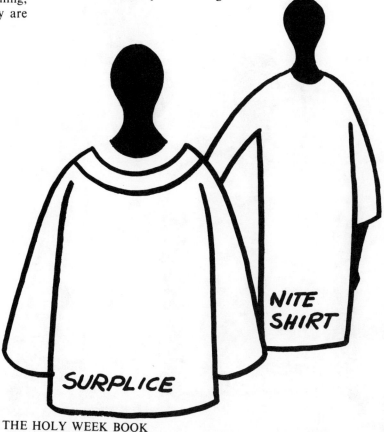

NITE SHIRT

SURPLICE

THE HOLY WEEK BOOK

The following patterns are suitable for embroidery on baptismal garments for adults. Some of the patterns are repeating ones, like the waves; others may be used singly or as repeating patterns. To transfer them to a garment, the following steps should be followed:

1. With tracing paper, trace the outline of the design desired.

2. Tape or staple the tracing paper to the top of a similar sized piece of transfer paper available at fabric stores. Transfer paper has an ink on the back that is printed by pressure on cloth, but which washes out.

3. Put the fabric to be marked on a hard, flat surface, and line up the cloth with the transfer.

4. Trace over the design on the tracing paper with a sharp pencil. The design will appear on the cloth and may then be embroidered.

For these designs, crewel wool should be used which is preshrunk and color-fast. Interesting textures can be obtained by mixing different kinds of threads. It is best not to use more than one pattern on any one garment, not to use any words, and not to use the design to excess. With a little care, those baptized at the Easter Vigil will be a sign of Christ's promise of a new life not only to themselves, but to the rest of the Christian community as well.

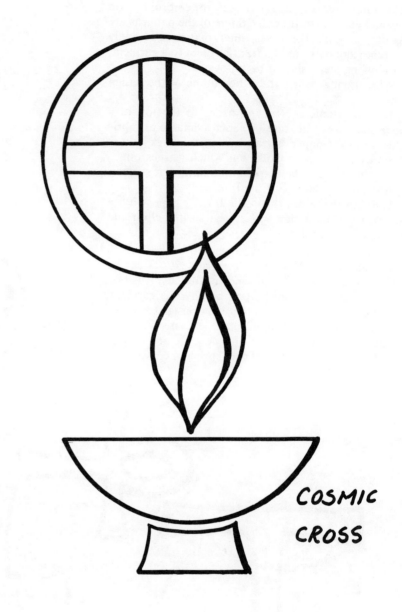

COSMIC
CROSS

JAPANESE WAVES

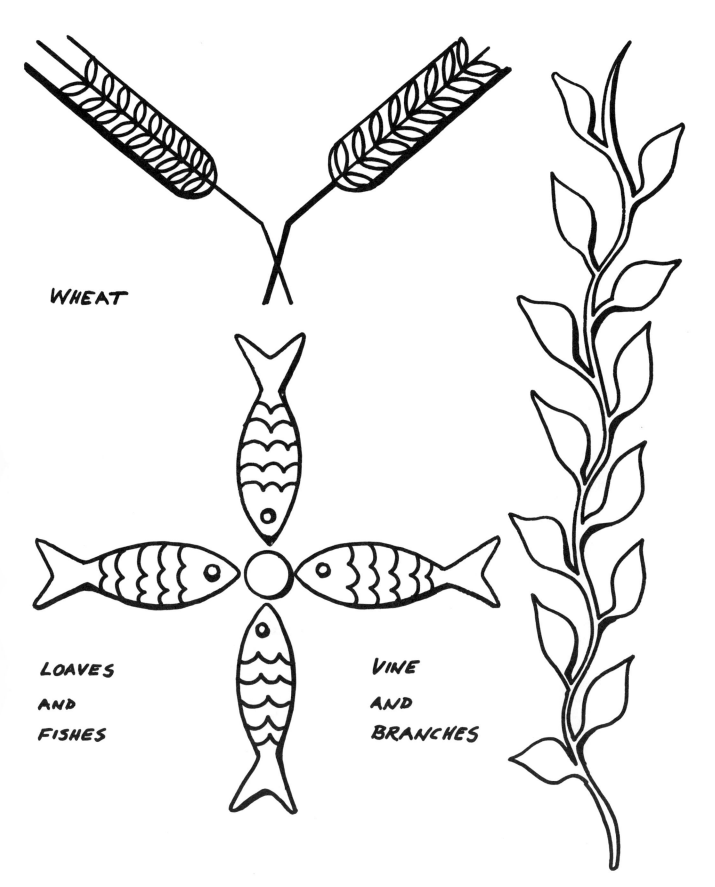

WHEAT

LOAVES
AND
FISHES

VINE
AND
BRANCHES

Love Is Come Again: A Song Drama

Eileen E. Freeman

The seasonal pattern is deeply ingrained in us; it is part of our blood, perhaps even part of our genetic make-up. There is a bio-rhythm in each of us that responds to the changes of the year, whether we live in a climate that has four distinct seasons, or whether we live in the tropics where there are only two. When winter comes, we greet the first snow like children on holiday, but when the winter outstays its welcome, we look for spring with an almost physical pain of longing.

In the ancient Near East which gave birth to the ancestors of Jesus, the two main seasons of the year were ushered in with great ceremony. The warm, rainy winter, when the crops grew abundantly, was a sign that all should rejoice in the continuation of life. The torrid, bone-dry summer, when all vegetation withered and died, was accompanied by fasting and mortification, as though humans wanted to die themselves along with the vegetation, as though they wanted to become part of the yearly cycle of life, death and rebirth.

Because most of us live in climates where new growth and life coincide with the time of the Resurrection, we have made an important identification of the two. English is almost the only language that names the time of the Resurrection after "Spring" rather than "Passover." Easter originally meant "Spring," while our more learned term, "Paschal-time," means Passover."

In the ancient world, there was usually a god of springs, of new growth and plant life. During the growing season this god or goddess lived on earth, giving life and fertility. During the torrid season it was believed that the god of heat and sterility had temporarily vanquished the spring god, bringing drought to the land. For us, the shadow has become reality. All those gods were only faint and obscure preshadowings of Christ. Christ is our God, a God of life. But, as Saint Paul tells the Near East-minded Christians, "Christ, having died once, dies no more: death has no dominion over Him. The death He died, He accomplished once, for all."

Thus, for us, even though the flowers and plants die over the winter, it does not mean that Christ dies again. Christ does not rise from the dead every time we celebrate Easter. It is we who "rise" again, we who are still bound to the cycle of the seasons. The new life of Spring is a type, a parable of Jesus' resurrection nearly two thousand years ago. Jesus told his followers plainly, "Unless the grain of wheat falls into the ground and dies, it remains but a single grain."

There is a carol, set to an old French tune, which perfectly expresses the relationship of Jesus' resurrection to the seasons; it is called "Love is Come Again." With a little effort it can be presented as a part of either the Vigil or the Easter season. Particularly when the Vigil is celebrated in its entirety, it can be used in place of the psalm after the seventh reading, from Ezekiel. If slides are being used elsewhere in the Vigil, they could be used here, with scenes of newly growing plants, seedlings first pushing through the ground. One could take an ear of wheat from its sowing to its reaping. Or perhaps an interpretive dance can be performed in the sanctuary area.

In either case the congregation will be watching what is going on. They could be taught the refrain easily, without their needing to look at the words. A small group can sing the verses, clearly, so they can be understood. Because of the antique character of the tune, it may be better to accompany the carol with guitar and recorder than with organ. However, if the congregation is going to sing the entire hymn, an organ accompaniment will work better.

Here is the text and music for "Love is Come Again." It is not too difficult to sing. The key of *e*-minor seems to work best.

THE HOLY WEEK BOOK

J.M.C. Crum

In moderate time

French

1. Now the green blade ris - eth from the bur-ied grain,
2. In the grave they laid him, Love whom men had slain,

1. Wheat that in dark earth ma - ny days has lain;
2. Think - ing that nev - er he would wake a - gain,

1. Love lives a - gain, that with the dead has been:
2. Laid in the earth like grain that sleeps un - seen:

Refrain

Love is come a - gain, Like wheat that spring-eth green.

3. Forth he came at Easter, like the risen grain,
He that for three days in the grave had lain,
Quick from the dead my risen Lord is seen:
Love is come again, etc.

4. When our hearts are wintry, grieving, or in pain,
Thy touch can call us back to life again,
Fields of our heart that dead and bare have been:
Love is come again, etc.

Adapted with permission from the Oxford Book of Carols.

Hymns Of The Lord's Rest

Eileen E. Freeman

In the early Church, Baptism and the death and resurrection of Christ were inseparably linked. Normally the catechumen was baptized at the Easter Vigil so that the symbolism of dying and rising with Christ would be most clearly evident. For the catechumen, full initiation into the Christian Mysteries was the crown of his or her life, the most important experience possible except perhaps for martyrdom. To become a baptized Christian in the second century usually meant that one experienced a complete change of lifestyle. Christianity was against the law in many places, and Christians were often stripped of their property, families, citizenship, health, jobs, and even their own lives. It was not a step to be taken lightly.

Today in many parts of the world, the same holds true. To be a baptized Christian in Russia, or China, or Uganda or other countries, is still dangerous. However, in America and the free world, the Christian commitment has often become merely another thing to do or organization to join. An infant is brought to the parish church, and the commitment to Christ and His Church is made in that infant's name by others, using a rite, which until recently was done in a back corner of the church building.

The revised rite for the Easter Vigil encourages the administration of Baptism as an extremely important and integral part of the Vigil, just as it was in the early Church. It provides for community participation in the sacrament, for singing of hymns and rejoicing.

To that end, *The Hymns of the Lord's Rest* are included here. These hymns, sometimes called the "Odes of Solomon," were written by an anonymous Christian during the second century of the Christian era. They form, in fact, the earliest Christian hymnal known. The melodies have not survived, but the words make it clear that the work is a hymnal for Baptism. The poems recall the joy of the catechumens as they first grasped hold of eternal life and turned to Jesus the Light. Some scholars have suggested that the hymns were appointed to be sung during the Lent preceding the catechumen's baptism.

Much of the language of the hymns is highly symbolic, poetic and rhythmical in an Easter fashion. Images of light, rest, flowering and bearing fruit, peace, flowing waters, crowns predominate; nowhere does the darkness of sin and sorrow intrude.

The author of the Hymns believed that he was composing them by the power of the Holy Spirit; that the Lord was speaking to the Christian assembly through his mouth. To compose sacred music, one had to have received a prophetic gift from God; it was not a task one could decide to do *ad lib.*

For centuries this treasury of baptismal images was lost; even since its rediscovery few liturgists have been aware of it, since it is written in Syriac, a beautiful but obscure Semitic language closely related to Aramaic, Hebrew and Arabic. The translations available are difficult to obtain.

The present translation is offered here in the hope that it will inspire liturgical composers to reset some of the Hymns to music so that the Christian community can once again use them to celebrate their own Baptism into the death and resurrection of Christ. In the meanwhile, they can be used as liturgical meditations, accompanied by some simple stringed music. I say stringed, because in the early church these hymns, if accompanied, would have been set to a plucked or strummed instrument such as the *kinnor* or *kithera*, harp or lyre. This translation is meant to be a faithful one, but not always a literal one. The hymn titles are the work of the translator. A very few hymns in bad textual shape or containing images too far removed for the average congregation to understand have been omitted.

Many centuries have passed since the *Hymns of the Lord's Rest* were composed, but they still speak to the Body of Christ today. Like our brothers and sisters of long ago, who have gone before us marked with the sign of faith, we, too, are in need of entering into the Lord's rest.

The first hymn
Evergreen
Like a wreath the Lord encircles my head,
  never shall I be without it.
Woven for me the wreath of Truth,
  Your branches blossoming upon me;
Not like the withered wreath without flower;
You live upon my head and have blossomed
  bountifully upon me.
Your fruits have ripened to perfection:
  Their nectar is salvation.

Hallelujah!

THE HOLY WEEK BOOK

The second hymn
Love Is A Circle Of Life

I am clothed in the Lord's love;
    And his many members are with Him,
    And I am dependent on them,
    And He loves me.
For how could I have learned to love the Lord,
    Had he not loved me from the first?
Who can discern love but the beloved?
I love my Beloved totally,
    And where he rests, there am I as well,
    No stranger to Him;
For the Most High and Merciful is not a jealous Lord.
United to Him am I, the Lover has found the Beloved.
Because I love Him that is the Son,
    I shall become a son;
For truly whoever is joined to the Immortal One
    Shall be immortal,
And whoever delights in the Life
    Will become living
Through the Spirit of the Lord,
    Which has no falsehood in Her,
    Which teaches the children of men to
        know His ways.
Be wise and watchful and understand.
Hallelujah!

The fifth hymn
A Firm Foundation Forever

O Lord, I praise You because I love You.
O Most High, never desert me, for my hope
    is in You.
Freely did I receive Your grace,
    Help me to live by it.
Persecutors are sure to come,
    But let them not see me.
Cover their eyes with a cloud of darkness,
    Let them grope in the pitch-dark night.
Give them no lamp to lighten their way,
    So that they can never capture me.
Let their plotting be foolishly fashioned,
    Whatever they plan falling on their own
        heads.
Though they devised treachery,
    They were beaten,
They were defeated,
    Although they were mighty.
They readied their wickedness,
    But were made weak.
Therefore my hope is with the Lord,
    And I will not fear.
And because the Lord is my salvation,
    I will not be afraid.
Since He is the crown upon my head,
    I shall not be shaken.

Even though the world should be shaken and shattered,
    I shall stand firm.
And though all things visible perish,
    I will not die,
Because the Lord Himself is with me,
    And I am with Him.
Hallelujah!

The sixth hymn
The Living Stream Of The Spirit

As wind glides through the harp and the strings speak,
So the Spirit of the Lord speaks through my members,
    And I speak by the power of His love.
He destroys everything alien,
    That all may be from the Lord;
For so it was from the beginning,
    And will be until the end,
So that nothing shall be in opposition,
    Nothing rise up against Him.
The Lord multiplied knowledge of Him;
    He was zealous that everything
    Grace-given to us should be known.
For the sake of His Name He gave us the
    gift of praise;
Our spirits praise His Holy Spirit.
A stream has spread abroad,
    Becoming a river great and wide;
It carried away all things,
    Shattered them,
    Brought them to the Temple.
All men's efforts to restrain it were in vain,
    Even the makers of dams failed;
So it spread over the face of all the earth,
    Filling the deepest valleys.
And all the thirsty drank their fill,
    Thirst was conquered and quenched,
For the drink was a gift from the Most High.
How blessed are the ministers of that drink!
    Who have been entrusted with His water.
They have cooled the parched lips,
    And stirred the torpid mind.
Even those on the point of death
    They have given new life.
Limbs which had collapsed utterly,
    They have restored and lifted up.
They gave strength for their coming,
    And light for their eyes,
Because everyone recognized these ministers
    As the Lord's own,
And lived because of the flowing water
    That is eternal Life.

                                    Hallelujah!

The seventh hymn
I Will Sing Of His Mercy To Me

As anger is to wickedness,
  So is joy to the Beloved,
  Fruiting freely in all seasons.
My joy is the Lord and my road leads to Him;
  How beautiful is this path I travel!
The Lord Himself helps me along the way;
Generously has He shown Himself to me
  in simplicity,
His kindness diminishing his dreadfulness.
He became like me, so that I would accept Him,
His form was like my own, that I might
  Clothe myself with Him,
And I trembled not when I saw Him,
  Because of His graciousness to me.
He took on my nature, so that I could understand Him,
And my form, that I might not turn away from Him.
The Father of knowledge
  Is the Word of knowledge.
He is wiser than his works, He who created wisdom.
And He who created me from the abyss of un-being,
  Already saw the pathways of my life.
On account of this He was merciful towards me
  and gracious,
And allowed me to petition Him that I might
  benefit from his Sacrifice.
For He alone is incorrupt,
  The Perfection of the worlds and their Father.
He has allowed Him to appear to His own,
  So that they might acknowledge Him that made them
  And not suppose that they made themselves.
He has set his way towards knowledge,
  He has widened it and lengthened it,
  And made it completely perfect;
He has set over it the traces of His light
  from beginning to end
For He was served by Him, pleased by His Son.
Through his salvation He will possess everything:
  The Most High will be known by His holy ones,
Those who announce to those who have the "songs of
  the coming of the Lord"
That they may go forth to meet Him and sing to Him
  with joy and the many-toned harp.
The Prophets shall go before Him,
  And they shall praise the Lord for His love,
  Because He is near and keeps watch over all.
And hatred shall vanish from the earth
  As knowledge of the Lord dawns upon it.
Let the singers chant the mercy of the Lord Most High,
  And let them sing their songs before Him;
Let their heart be like the daylight,
  And their peaceful voices like the majestic
  beauty of the Lord;

And let nothing that breathes
  Fail to sing and understand,
For He gave a mouth to all His creation,
  So that they might praise Him.
Confess His might and acknowledge His grace.
                                    Hallelujah!

The eighth hymn
Joyful Words of Life

Open, break open your hearts and exalt the Lord,
And let your love bubble up from your heart to
  your lips
So that you may bear for the Lord the fruit of a
  holy life.
Speaking with watchful care in His light.
Rise up, stand straight, you who were once brought low;
Speak out, you who lived in silence, ephphetha;
You who were despised, now be held in high esteem,
  For you Righteousness has been raised on high.
The Lord's right hand is with you to help you;
A time of peace is prepared for you,
  Before your war may begin.
    Christ speaks:
Hear these true words, accept the understanding
  that is a gift from the Most High:
Your flesh may not comprehend what I am going to tell you,
Nor your outer covering what I am about to show you.
Keep my mystery, you who are kept by it,
Keep my faith, you who are guarded by it,
And understand my knowledge, you who know Me in truth.
Love me with devotion, you who love,
For I turn not away from my own, because I know them.
Before they even existed, I acknowledged them,
  And imprinted a seal on their faces.
I fashioned their members and opened my fountains
That they might drink my holy and life-giving milk.
I am pleased with them and not ashamed of them,
For they are my craftsmanship, the strength of my thought.
Who can stand against my work or not be subject to them?
I willed and moulded mind and heart, and they are mine.
At my right side I have placed my chosen ones,
And my righteousness goes before them;
Never shall they be deprived of my Name;
  It is with them always.
    The Odist speaks:
Pray and increase, and dwell in the love of the Lord,
For you are loved in the Beloved,
  Guarded by Him who lives
  Saved in Him who is salvation,
And you shall be found incorrupt in all ages
On account of the Name of your Father.
                                    Hallelujah!

The tenth hymn
Conversion

The Lord directs my mouth by His Word,
   And opens my heart by His Light.
His immortal life He has caused to live in me,
   And has allowed me to proclaim
      the fruit of His peace;
To convert the lives of all who desire to
   come to Him,
And to make captivity captive and bring it
   to freedom.
      Christ speaks:
I took courage and grew strong and captured the world;
It became mine to the glory of God Most High.
And the nations which had been scattered
   were gathered together,
And my love for them brought Me glory,
And they praised Me in the high places.
For I set the traces of light on their heads,
And they walked according to my life and were saved,
And they became my people forever.
                                    Hallelujah!

The eleventh hymn
Ever-Spring In Paradise

My heart was pruned that its flower might appear;
   In it grace grew tall
   And produced fruits for the lord.
The Most High pruned me by his Holy Spirit,
   Laid bare my deepest heart to Him
   And filled me with his love.
And his pruning became my salvation,
And I ran in the Way, in His peace, in the
   Way of truth;
From beginning to end I received His knowledge.
I was established on the Rock of Truth
   where He had placed me,
And murmuring streams touched my lips,
   Sprung generously from the fountain of the Lord.
And so I drank and became inebriated
   with the living water that never dies,
And my inebriation did not cause foolishness;
   Rather, I abandoned stupidity altogether,
And turned toward the Most High, my God,
   And was enriched by his kindnesses.
And I rejected worldly folly,
   Stripped it off and cast it behind me;
And the Lord covered me with a new robe,
   And possessed me by His light;
And from above He gave me rest undying,
   And I became like a land that blossoms
      and rejoices in its fruits.
And the Lord is like the sun upon that land.

My eyes were enlightened,
   My face drank in the dew,
And my breath was refreshed by the pleasant
   fragrance of the Lord.
He took me to his Paradise,
   In which lies the fullness of the Lord's delights.
I gazed on blooming and fruiting trees,
   Crowned by a natural crown.
Their branches sprouted continously;
   Their fruits were always shining.
Their roots sank deep into the soil of
   an immortal land,
While a gladsome stream watered them
   And flowed round about them in the land of
      eternal life.
Then I adored the Lord in His magnificence, saying:
"Blessed are they who are planted in your land,
"And who have a place in your Paradise,
"And who grow as your trees grow,
"And have passed from darkness into light.
"Behold how fair are all your laborers,
   They do good works and turn
   From evil towards your recreation.
"When they were planted in your land as trees,
   They turned away from bitterness.
"Everything has become your 'Remnant',
   An everlasting memorial for your faithful ones.
"Your Paradise spreads out farther than the eye can see,
   Yet there is nothing barren in it;
   Everything is filled with fruit.
"Glory be to You, O God,
   The joy of Paradise forever."
                                    Hallelujah!

The twelfth hymn
Out Of His Mouth: Truth

He has filled me with truthful words,
  So that I might proclaim Him;
And like flowing waters, truth flows from my mouth,
  And my lips declare his fruits.
He caused knowledge of Him to bubble up in me,
Because the mouth of the Lord is the true Word,
  And the entrance of his light.
The Most High gave Him to his generation,
  Those who interpret his beauty,
  And who tell of his glory;
  Those who confess his divine plan,
  And who preach his mind,
  And who teach his works.
How ineffable the subtlety of the Word!
Like his utterance, so also is his swiftness and
  his sharpness,
For without limit is his progression.
He never falls, but remains upright,
  And no one can follow his descent or his way.
As his work is, so is his advent,
  For He is the Light and Dawning of Thought.
It was by him that the Ancestors learned to speak
  to each other.
And those that were dumb acquired language.
From Him came love and equality,
  And they told each other of that which was theirs.
They were stimulated by the Word,
  And came to know Him who created them,
  Living together in perfect peace.
For the Most High spoke to them by his mouth,
  And his explanation prospered in them;
For the dwelling place of the Word is the human race,
  And his truth is love.
Blessed are they who through Him have seen all things,
  And have known the Lord in his truth.
                                          Hallelujah!

The thirteenth hymn
Mirror Of Perfection

Behold, the Lord is our mirror,
  Open your eyes, see their reflection in Him,
And learn the contours of your face.
Then sing praises to his Spirit;
And wipe the dirt from your face,
  And love his holiness and put it on.
Then you will stand unblemished in his sight at all times.
                                          Hallelujah!

The fourteenth hymn
Teach Me To Sing

As the eyes of a boy are toward his father,
So are my eyes, at all times, to you, O Lord;
From you come my consolation and delights.
Do not turn your mercies away from me, O Lord,
  Take not your kindness from me.
Stretch out to me your right hand always, O Lord,
  And be my guide until the end according to your will.
Let me be pleasing before You for your glory's sake,
  Because of your Name let me be saved from the Evil One.
Let your gentleness dwell with me, O Lord,
  And the fruits of your love as well.
Teach me the Hymns of your truth,
  That I may bring forth fruits in You.
And open to me the harp of your Holy Spirit,
  So that with every note I may praise You, O Lord.
And according to the abundance of your mercies,
  So grant this to me,
For You are sufficient for all our needs.
                                          Hallelujah!

The fifteenth hymn
Sol Invictus

As the sun is the joy of those who seek its dawning,
  So my joy is in the Lord.
Because He is my Sun
  And his rays have lifted me up.
  And his light has dispelled all darkness from my face,
I obtained new eyes from him,
  And I have seen his holy day.
I obtained new ears and have heard his truth.
Thought and knowledge I have acquired,
  And have lived fully in Him.
I repudiated the way of error and went towards Him,
  And received abundant salvation from Him.
He bestowed it on me generously;
  He made me according to his excellent beauty.
I put on incorruption through his name,
  And took off corruption by his grace.
Death has been destroyed at the sight of my faith,
  And Sheol has been vanquished by my word.
And immortal life has arisen in the land of the Lord;
  It has been proclaimed to his faithful ones,
And been given without measure to all who trust Him.
                                          Hallelujah!

The sixteenth hymn
Music Is Prophecy

As the ploughman is concerned with the plow,
As the captain is concerned with the ship's rudder,
    So my concern is the praise of the Lord in
        His Hymns.
My art and my ministry are in his Hymns,
    Because his love has fed my heart,
    And his fruits He has poured into my heart.
My love is the Lord;
    Therefore I will sing to Him.
For I receive strength when I praise Him,
    And I have faith in Him.
I will open my mouth,
    And his Spirit will speak through me,
(Telling of) The glory of the Lord and his beauty,
The work of his hands, the labor of his fingers,
For the abundance of his mercies,
    And the strength of his Word.
For the Word of the Lord investigates the unseen,
    And reveals his thought.
For the eye sees his works, the ear hears his thought.
It is He who made the earth so broad,
    And placed the waters in the sea.
He stretched out the heavens and fixed the stars,
And He established creation and set it up;
    Then He rested from his labors.
So created things run in their appointed courses,
    And accomplish their tasks unceasingly and
        without fail,
And the host of heaven is subject to his Word.
The sun is the reservoir of the light,
    The reservoir of darkness is the night.
For He made the sun to give light to the day,
    But night brings darkness over all the earth.
And by their appointed portion, one from another,
    They complete the beauty of God.
There is nothing outside of the Lord;
    Before anything came to be, He was;
And the worlds were created by his Word
    And by the thought of his heart.
Praise and honor to his Name.
                                    Hallelujah!

The twentieth hymn
All Priesthood Is A Garland

I am a priest of the Lord
    And Him I serve as a minister;
To Him I offer the oblation of his Thought.
For his thought is not like the world's,
    nor is it material,
Nor is it like that of those who worship in the flesh.
The oblation of the Lord is righteousness,
    And purity of heart and lips.
Offer your inmost heart completely,
Restrain your compassion from running roughshod over others,
    and oppress no one.
Never purchase a servant, even a foreign one,
    Because he is a person like yourself.
Do not seek to deceive your neighbor,
    Nor deprive him of his only cloak.
But rather be clothed with the Lord generously,
    And come into his Paradise,
And make for yourself a garland from his tree.
Then put it on your head and be joyful,
    And recline where He rests.
For his glory will go before you,
    And you shall receive his kindness and his mercy,
    And be anointed in truth with the praise of his
    holiness.
Praise and honor be to his Name!
                                    Hallelujah!

The twenty-first hymn
How Great Is My Happiness

I raised my arms on high,
    Because of the compassion of the Lord.
Because He had loosened my shackles from me;
    My Helper lifted me up according to his compassion
        and his salvation.
And I took off the robe of darkness,
    And put on the garments of light.
I myself acquired members,
    And in them there was no sickness or affliction
        or suffering.
And abundantly helpful to me was the Thought of the Lord,
    And his eternal friendship.
And I was lifted up in the light,
    And I walked before Him.
And I was constantly near Him,
    Ceaselessly praising and confessing Him.
He made my heart overflow,
    It bubbled up on my lips.
And on my face was revealed the exultation
    of the Lord and his praise.
                                    Hallelujah!

The twenty-sixth hymn
The Hymn Of The Lord's Rest

I poured out praise to the Lord,
  Because I belong to Him;
And I will sing his holy Hymn,
  Because my heart belongs to Him.
For his harp is in my hand,
  And the Hymns of his Rest shall not be silent.
I will call to Him with all my heart;
  I will praise and exalt Him with all my members.
For from the East as far as the West is His praise,
  From the South to the North, His thanksgiving.
Even from the mountain peaks to the valleys,
  Is His perfection.
Who can write the Hymns of the Lord,
  Or who can be worthy to sing them?
Or who can train himself for life,
  So as to save himself?
Or who can force the Most High
  to speak from his mouth?
Who can interpret the wonders of the Lord?
Though the interpreter will pass away,
  Yet what was interpreted will remain.
It is enough to perceive and be content.
For the singers stand in serenity, like a river,
  Like an increasingly gushing spring,
That flows to the relief of those who seek it.
                                        Hallelujah!

The twenty-seventh hymn
I Am The Cross

I stretched out my hands,
  And praised my Lord;
For the expansion of my hands
  is His emblem,
And my trunk,
  The upright cross.

                                        Hallelujah!

The twenty-eighth hymn
In The Shadow Of Your Wings

As the wings of doves protect their nestlings,
  And the mouths of nestlings are toward their mouths,
So also are the wings of the Spirit over my heart.
My heart ceaselessly refreshes itself and leaps for joy,
  Like the baby that leaps for joy in its mother's womb.
I trusted, therefore, I was at rest,
  Because He in whom I have trusted is trustworthy.
How greatly He has blessed me;
  So I have given Him all my love;
And the dagger shall not separate me from Him,
  nor the sword.
Because I am prepared for disaster,
  even before it comes,
  And I have been placed on his immortal side.
Eternal life embraced me and kissed me,
And from that life the Spirit proceeds with me;
  And it cannot die, because it is Life itself.
                                        Hallelujah!

The twenty-ninth hymn
All His Enemies Are But Dust

My hope is the Lord,
  I shall not be put to shame in Him;
For He made me according to his praise,
  And gave to me according to his grace.
Because of his mercies He lifted me up,
  And because of his great honor He exalted me.
And He raised me up from the depths of Sheol,
  From the mouth of death He snatched me.
And He humbled my enemies,
  And He justified me by his grace.
For I confessed my faith in the Lord's Messiah,
  And acknowledged that He alone is Lord,
Therefore He revealed to me his sign,
  And He led me on by his light.
And He invested me with his mighty scepter
  That I might subdue the treacherous nations,
  And break the power of the powerful.
To make war by his Word,
  And to take the victory by his power.
And the Lord overthrew my enemy by his Word,
  And he became dust scattered by the wind.
And I gave praise to the Most High,
  Because He had magnified his servant,
  The child of his handmaid.

                                        Hallelujah!

The thirtieth hymn
Living Waters

Draw water for yourselves from the flowing
    fountains of the Lord,
Because they have been opened for your benefit.
Come, all you thirsty, and drink,
    And rest beside the fountain of the Lord.
For its water is refreshing and sparkling,
    And continually renews your life.
Sweeter than honey is its water,
    The bees' honeycomb cannot be compared to it;
Because it flowed from the lips of the Lord,
    Its essence from the Lord's own heart;
And it rushed down boundless and invisible,
    And until it was set in the Middle,
        mankind knew it not.
Blessed are they who have drunk from it,
    And have refreshed themselves with it.
                              Hallelujah!

The thirty-first hymn
Christ The Passion-Ate

Deep ravines vanished before the Lord,
    And the darkness was dissipated at his appearance.
Falsehood fled and vanished because of Him,
    And scorn found no way in the wilderness,
    For it was drowned in the truth of the Lord.
He opened his mouth and uttered grace and joy,
    And He sang a new song to his Name.
Then He lifted up his voice to the Most High,
    And offered to Him all who had become sons and
        daughters through Him.
And his face was vindicated,
    For his holy Father granted his request.
        Christ speaks:
Come forth, you who have been afflicted; you shall
    receive joy now.
Be self-possessed in grace and take hold of immortal
    life for yourselves...
They condemned me when I stood up,
    Although I was guilty of no evil.
Then they divided my garments as their booty,
    Although I was not in debt to them for anything.
But I stood fast and held my peace and was silent,
    So that I might not be disturbed by them.
I stood as unmoved as a granite cliff,
    Which is continuously pounded by walls of waves,
        yet abides.
And I bore their bitterness for the sake of humility,
    That I might redeem my people and teach them;
    That I might not bring to nought the promises
        made to the Patriarchs,
To whom I was promised for the salvation of their
    descendants.
                              Hallelujah!

The thirty-second hymn
Heart-Felt Joy

To the blessed ones, joy springs from the heart,
    And light, from Him who lives in them;
    From the Word of Truth, who is self-originate;
Because He has been strengthened by the sacred power of
    the Most High,
And He remains unshakeable forever.
                              Hallelujah!

The thirty-fourth hymn
Still, Small Voice

No path is too hard for the simple heart,
    No barrier can defeat upright thoughts,
    No whirlwind can stir the depths of the enlightened mind.
When one is surrounded by pleasant countryside,
    Nothing in him is divided.
The mirror of that which is above,
    Is that which is below.
For everything is from above,
    And from below there originates nothing—
    Although the foolish believe differently.
Grace has been revealed for your salvation;
    Believe and live and be saved.
                              Hallelujah!

The thirty-fifth hymn
More Than Shade To Me

The dew of the Lord sprinkled me with serenity;
    And caused a cloud of peace to rise over my head
    So that it might always guard me;
    And it became my saving.
Everyone else was distressed and afraid,
    The smoke of judgement poured from them,
But I was tranquil in the Lord's care.
More than shade was He to me,
    More than a standing-place.
I was carried like a child by its mother,
    And He gave me milk, the dew of the Lord;
And I was enriched by his favor,
    And I rested in his perfection;
And I spread out my hands towards the Lord,
    Turned my face to the Most High,
    And I was redeemed for Him.
                              Hallelujah!

The thirty-sixth hymn
Carried In the Spirit

I rested on the Spirit of the Lord,
    And She lifted me up to heaven.
She caused me to stand in the Lord's high place,
    Before his perfection and his glory,
Where I continued magnifying Him by the composition
    of his Hymns.
        Christ speaks:
The Spirit brought me forth before the face of the Lord,
And because I was the Son of Man, I was named the Light,
    The Son of God,
        because I was the most glorious of all that had ever
            been glorified,
        and the greatest among the great ones.
According to the greatness of the Most High, She made me,
    And according to his newness He renewed me.
And He anointed me with his perfection,
    And I became one of those who stand near to Him.
And my mouth was opened like a rain of dew,
And my heart bubbled over with righteousness.
And I approached in peace,
    And I was established in the Spirit of Providence.
                                            Hallelujah!

The thirty-seventh hymn
Peace Flowing Like A River

I stretched out my hands toward my Lord,
    And to the Most High I lifted up my voice,
And I spoke with the lips of my heart,
    And my voice reached Him and He listened to me.
His Word came towards me,
    In order to give me the fruits of my labors.
And He gave me rest by the grace of the Lord.
                                            Hallelujah!

The thirty-ninth hymn
Walking On The Waters

Raging rivers are like the power of the Lord;
    They hurl headlong all who scorn it.
They entangle their paths and frustrate their crossings.
They weigh down their bodies and destroy their life.
For they are faster than lightning, faster by far.
But those who cross them in faith shall not be disturbed.
Those who walk on them without fault shall not be shaken.
Because the Lord's mark is on them, a sign which is the
    Way for those who cross in the name of the Lord.
Therefore, clothe yourselves with the name of the Most
    High and know Him,
        And you shall cross without danger;
        Even rivers shall obey you.
The Lord has already gone before you, bridging them
    by his Word;
    He walked over them, crossing them on foot.
His steps stood firm on top of the waters and did not sink,
    But were like a wooden beam built upon Truth.
On This side and that the waves lifted their heads,
    But the footsteps of our Lord Messiah stand firm,
And neither swallowed up nor destroyed.
A way has been established for those who cross after Him,
    For those who are faithful to the path of his faith,
    And who adore his Name.
                                            Hallelujah!

The fortieth hymn
His Song Is Life

As honey drips from the comb,
    And milk from the mother who nurses her child,
    So is my hope in You, O my God.
As a fountain gushes with water,
    So my heart bubbles over with praise of the Lord,
    And my lips give Him praise.
My tongue is sweetened by his anthems,
    And my members are anointed by his Hymns.
My face rejoices in exalting Him,
    And my spirit leaps in his love;
    My very nature shines with joy in Him.
Let those who are afraid trust in Him,
    And redemption shall be assured in Him.
For immortal life is his to give,
    And those who receive it are incorruptible.
                                            Hallelujah!

The forty-second hymn
He Descended Into Hell

I stretched out my hands and prayed to my Lord,
For the expansion of my arms is his symbol,
And my body is the upright Cross,
    That was raised high on the way of the Righteous One.
        Christ speaks:
I became of no account to those who knew me not,
I was hidden from those who did not possess me,
And I will dwell with those who love me...
All my persecutors have died,
    Though they sought me, hating me,
    Because I myself am Life.
But I arose, and am with my own,
    And will speak through their mouths,
For they, too, rejected those who rejected them;
So I threw over them the yoke of my love.
Like the arm of the bridegroom around his bride,
    So is my yoke over those who know Me;
And as the wedding feast is spread out by the
    parents of the couple,
        So my love is spread out abroad by those who
        believe in Me.
And I was not rejected,
    Although I was considered to be so.
And I did not perish,
    Although they supposed I had.
Sheol saw Me and was shattered,
    Death ejected Me and many with Me.
I was vinegar and gall to it;
    And I went down to its very depths.
Death let go its hold on my head and feet,
    Because it could not endure my face.
And I made a congregation of the living
    among its dead,
        And I spoke to them with living lips
        So that my word would not be unprofitable.
And those who had died ran toward Me.
    And they cried out and said,
    "Son of God, have mercy on us,
    "Deal with us according to your kindness,
    "And bring us out from the bonds of darkness,
    "And open the door to us,
        By which we may come forth to You,
    "For we see that the death we endure has no
        hold on You.
    "May we also be saved with You,
        Because You are our Savior."
Then I heard their voice,
    And I placed their faith in my heart,
    And my Name upon their head,
Because they are free and they are mine.
                        Hallelujah!

A Resurrection Vigil For The Lord's Day

John A. Melloh, SJ

The Paschal Vigil is celebrated by the whole Church, as described in the respective liturgical books. 'The vigil of this night is so important,' says St. Augustine, 'that it is called The Vigil as if demanding exclusively for itself a term which is common to the rest.' 'We spend that night in vigil, the night on which the Lord rose, and began for us in his own flesh that life where there is neither death nor sleep. Therefore, as we sing in our long vigil to him who has risen, so we will reign with him in life without end.'
The General Instruction on the Liturgy of the Hours, par. 70.

Sunday is the Day of the Lord. It is special. It is different. It is not a weekday. It is not within the ordinary weekly time cycle; it is outside the experience of the time of the week, the day in and day out routine. Recall how on Sunday, only "Sunday" clothes were worn; remember how one remained dressed up on Sunday, just because it was Sunday — the day was somehow special; think back to the special Sunday breakfasts (feasts in themselves!) — delightfully communitarian-familiar meals, full of rejoicing — shared by the family after the Sunday Eucharist. Sunday is really "outside of time" as it were.

Sunday is the day for celebrating the Meal of the Kingdom, the Eucharist. It is the day when we gather as the assembly of Christians to proclaim to one another our belief in the Resurrection of the Lord, to praise and thank the Heavenly Father for his gift of His Son to us, to listen attentively to the Word of God and to allow His Spirit, that Holy Presence, to move us to bless and eucharistize in the name of Jesus. Sunday is the day for celebration *par excellence*. It is the day when the Christian community must celebrate and only Eucharistic celebration expresses fully the joy-filled shared faith of this Pilgrim People.

The primitive Church, the early Christians, celebrated the eucharistic meal each Sunday: with joy and reverence, with holy fear and festive awe, they assembled on the Day of the Lord, to celebrate a weekly Easter. The Resurrection of the Lord — the culmination of passion and death — and the memorial of this great and wonderful deed of God the Father is celebrated; it becomes the focus for gathering together and is the reason for offering Eucharistic Prayer.

The weekly Easter, the Day of the Lord, was so special that there developed the practice of preparing for so special a day. A time of preparation, of praying together, of watching and waiting — of keeping vigil — grew up in Christian communities. A vigil or night-watch, resplendent with paschal themes, preceded the celebration of the Eucharistic Meal. This vigil was a weekly commemoration — with all the potency that that word "memorial" can contain — of the day of the Resurrection of the Lord.

It was a time for the faithful to gather, to wait for the coming of the Lord, to stand before the God of all Creation and to pray for coming of the Kingdom: Maranatha! To emphasis and concentrate on this mystery of passion, death, resurrection, and second coming, the assembly ritualized that moment of waiting and expectancy; thus, the Vigil of the Lord's Day.

We are all acquainted with the Great Vigil of Easter, the Paschal Vigil, the "Mother of all Vigils," as Augustine termed it. This is the archetype of the weekly Resurrection Vigil of the Lord's Day. The paschal flavor of the Resurrection Vigil is captured and ritualized as the community celebrates in joyful and holy waiting.

Allow me to make some of the theoretical considerations a bit more practical by describing one possible structure for a Resurrection Vigil, for celebrating the weekly Easter. Four parts of the service are identifiable: The Service of Light, The Service of the Word, the Service of the Baptismal Water, and the Maranatha. I shall detail each of the elements in the service.

(From the Paschal Vigil the custom grew in different Churches of beginning certain solemnities with a vigil, especially Christmas and Pentecost. This custom is to be preserved and encouraged according to the special traditions of each Church...)
The General Instruction, par. 71.

The Service of Light

The presiding minister (the one who exercises the presidential ministry, the one who calls the community to worship) enters the assembly with the lighted Paschal Candle and proclaims that Jesus is truly Light of the World. All respond to the proclamation and join in the singing of a Hymn of Light, as the Paschal Candle and other candles are lit. Then the presiding minister sings the blessing prayer, thanking God for the gift of light, both natural and supernatural.

The Service of the Word

In order to prepare ourselves as a community, to be able to hear the Word of God proclaimed in the assembly, we set the tone by praying the psalms. Alleluia antiphons help to make the psalmody more paschally oriented; the alleluia adds Easter spice. The Psalter collects — prayers prayed after a good chunk of time is spent in silent prayer — conclude the psalms and call the group to common prayer.

The Word of God is read in two sections: a reading from the Acts of the Apostles, specifically from one of the primitive sermons of Peter or Paul. A period for silent reflections follows in which we can digest the Word of God, that Bread of Life which nourishes the soul.

The Gospel account is always one of the accounts of the Resurrection of the Lord. It is preceded by the singing of an Alleluia with some verses and accompanied by the incensation of the Book of Gospels.

The Service of the Baptismal Water

The presidential minister sings the blessing prayer for water. All then participate in the action of symbolic renewal. A variety of actions is possible: each member may come forward, dip one's hand into the water and sign oneself; the water may be poured over the extended hands of the members of the community. During this action a litany of praise to Jesus Christ is sung. The action is concluded with a collect prayed by the president.

The Creed may be used to conclude the service: the profession of faith is an affirmation of the Christian life begun by Baptism. Likewise, on occasions, the verbal renewal of the Baptismal promises may be fitting.

The Maranatha

The final section of the Vigil service is fully eschatological in character. The community prays the Lord's Prayer, praying for the coming of the Kingdom of the Lord. Then the Maranatha (Come, Lord Jesus) is prayed. This may take the form of a simple sung proclamation or may be sung according to a more elaborate musical setting. The intent is to focus directly on the sense of waiting for the Lord, for His Second Coming and waiting for the celebration of the Meal of the Kingdom, the Eucharist, to be celebrated on the Lord's Day.

In order to make the above delineation of the elements of the Resurrection Vigil of the Lord's Day more concrete, I shall give an example of one Vigil Service

Glory to your holy Resurrection, O Lord! Today the whole creation, heaven and earth and the deepest abysses of the earth are filled with joy. Let the whole universe celebrate the Resurrection by which we are strengthened.

Glory to your holy Resurrection, O Lord! Yesterday I was buried with you, O Christ! Today I rise with you in your Resurrection. Yesterday I was crucified with you: glorify me with you in your kingdom.

Glory to your holy Resurrection, O Lord! Christ is risen from the dead! He has crushed death by his death and bestowed life upon those who lay in the tomb.

Glory to your Resurrection, O Lord! Jesus is risen indeed, as He had foretold: He has given us eternal life and abundant mercy.

—Third Ode. Easter Canon of John of Damascus. *Byzantine Daily Worship*, Easter Sunday, page 849.

The Service of Light

The joy, the sense of exultation should fill the Christian assembly as the Resurrection Vigil is celebrated. The Church is darkened, as the people gather around eleven p.m. or twelve midnight; there is but a bit of light, enough to find one's way around. After the assembly has gathered, the lights are all extinguished and the people remain in darkness for a while. The church should experience the darkness of sin, the darkness of the world; they should wait with expectancy for the coming of the Christ.

Then the presiding minister carries in the lighted Paschal Candle and proclaims in song:

V. Jesus Christ is the light of the world.

The people respond in song:

R. A light that no darkness can ex-tin-quish.

Other candles in the church are lighted and the church is illumined; if candlelight suffices (if for example, the people have individual candles, it may suffice), the electric lights are not used.

As the other candles, lamps are being lit, the Light Hymn is sung. Lucien Deiss' *Joy-Giving Light* (WLP) is appropriate, as is Suzanne Toolan's *Walk In Light* (GIA)

After the lighting of the lamps accompanied by the singing, the presiding minister proclaims the blessing prayer. (If a presbyter presides, it is good praxis if a deacon assist him; it is the deacon who proclaims the Light Preface.) Keep in mind that there is really no restriction concerning the presiding minister: in families, either parent may preside; in religious communities, the superior should preside; in special parish groups, the president of that group is a logical choice for presiding.

The Service of the Word

All are seated (and the individual candles are extinguished if they have been used). A psalm is sung responsorially. In this service Psalm 92 is sung: the cantor sings the antiphon and all repeat it. The cantor will sing the verses and the assembly repeats the antiphon after the verses. (Such a method eliminates the necessity of hymn book, lengthy music practices, and generally ungratifying results in psalm-singing.) At the conclusion of the psalm, there is a pause of significant length for silent prayer; then the presiding minister prays the following collect.

Let us pray. Heavenly Father, Lord and King of the Universe, we bless and praise your name, for your goodness to us. Reign over our hearts and minds that we may watch and pray for the coming of your Kingdom. Glory to You and to your only Son, and to the Spirit, now and forever.

All respond: Amen!

All are seated again for the second psalm. Lucien Deiss' *All You Nations* (WLP) is sung in the same responsorial manner. Again, a pause for silent prayer follows the singing and a collect concludes the period of quiet.

Let us pray. God our Father, we praise You for your mighty deeds. We thank You for your great wonders and ask that You lead us to your Kingdom where You live and reign with your Son, united in the Holy Spirit, one God, forever and ever.

All respond: Amen!

The first Scripture reading (Acts 4:8-12) is then read. The lector moves to the lectern, bows as a sign of reverence toward the Word of God and proclaims the lesson.

A period of silence follows, to be broken only by the singing of the Gospel *Alleluia*. All stand as the Alleluia is sung with accompanying verses; during the singing, the Book of Gospels is incensed. Lucien Deiss' *Wonderful and Great* is sung as the Alleluia. Then the Gospel is proclaimed and a sung *Alleluia* expresses the community's joy at hearing the word.

After the *Alleluia* at the conclusion of the Gospel, a homily may be preached. The homily calls the community to reflect on the great mystery of the Resurrection—the Paschal Mystery of the death and resurrection of the Lord—and our own living out of that mystery in our lives as Christian believers.

The Service of the Baptismal Water

The blessing of God for the gift of water, that water which is a symbol of death and also of life, is sung. As the assembly advances toward the baptismal font or toward the vessel containing the water (a large crystal punch bowl serves well!) the Canticle from Philippians is sung responsorially. The singing accompanies the ritual washing: the cantor may repeat verses 1-3 as often as necessary and concludes with verse 4 when all have approached the font. The following collect is prayed:

Let us pray. Father, we stand before You as the children of adoption, born again in the image of Christ your only Son. As You have given us this new life by water and the Spirit, and have forgiven all our sins, we give You thanks and offer You our praise and adoration through Christ our Lord.

All respond: Amen!

The Maranatha

The Lord's Prayer is prayed in song by the entire ecclesial body; it is introduced by the presiding minister. Then the president proclaims:

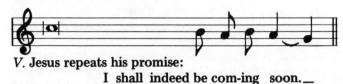

V. **Jesus repeats his promise:**
I shall indeed be com-ing soon.__

This final eschatological proclamation is answered by the people:

R. **A - men! Come, Lord Je - sus!**

Then the Maranatha is sung; Lucien Deiss' melody is fine for the conclusion of the service. As verse 4 begins, the minister(s) exits in silence.

The Day of the Lord has begun! Alleluia! Amen!

THE HOLY WEEK BOOK

MUSIC SECTION

It Behooves Us

Antiphon (stately)

Sr. Suzanne

But it be-hooves us to glo — ry in the cross of our
Lord Je-sus Christ; in whom is our sal — va — tion, life and res-sur-
rec — tion, by whom we are saved and de-liv — ered._____

May God have pi-ty on us and bless_____ us._____ May he let his
face shine up-on us and may he be gra-cious to us,_____ and
grant to us his peace._____

THE HOLY WEEK BOOK

Cry Out With Joy

Antiphon

Sr. Suzanne

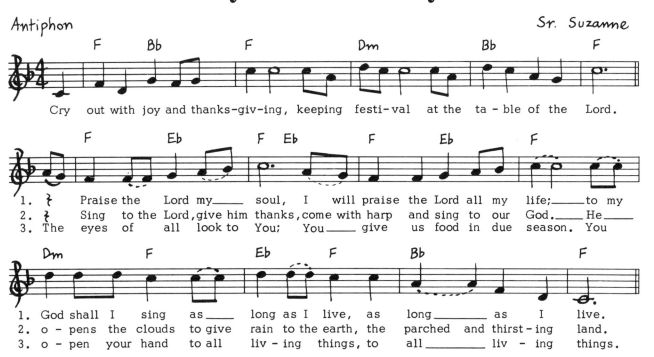

Cry out with joy and thanks-giv-ing, keeping festi-val at the ta-ble of the Lord.

1. 𝄽 Praise the Lord my____ soul, I will praise the Lord all my life;____to my
2. 𝄽 Sing to the Lord, give him thanks, come with harp and sing to our God.____He
3. The eyes of all look to You; You____ give us food in due season. You

1. God shall I sing as____ long as I live, as long_____ as I live.
2. o-pens the clouds to give rain to the earth, the parched and thirst-ing land.
3. o-pen your hand to all liv-ing things, to all_____ liv-ing things.

Holy Thursday Entrance Hymn

Sr. Suzanne

Tenor Solo

Come, let us pre - pare _____ the Pass - o - ver. _____

Flute or keyboard instrument

Tenor solo - slowly and quietly

You will find a room, _____ spa - cious and fur - nished. It ___ is ___

here you shall pre - pare _____ and here that I am to cel -

THE HOLY WEEK BOOK

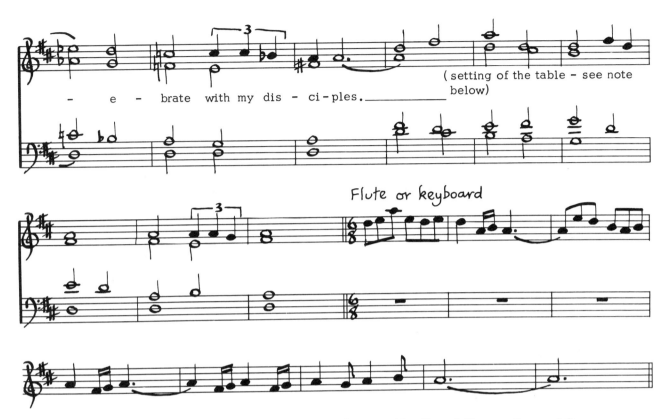

(setting of the table – see note below)

– e – brate with my dis – ci – ples._____

Flute or keyboard

The altar table is ceremoniously set with altar cloth, candles and flowers.
This may be done simply or in stylized dance. This or similar keyboard or
flute and guitar music may be extended during this action.

Like A Lamb

Sr. Suzanne

Like a lamb led to the slaugh-ter, like a sheep dumb before its shear-ers._____

No guitar

1. Sure – ly he has borne our guilt. Sure-ly he has borne our guilt.
2. Look now on the Lamb of God. Look now on the Lamb of God.

1. Ours the sor – rows he has car-ried, he has car – ried._____
2. Look on him who takes a-way the sins___ of the world._____

Used on Good Friday as a response during the reading of the Passion.

Reproaches

Slowly and Quietly

Sr. Suzanne

O my peo-ple, what have I done un-to you? or in what have I of-fended you? Answer me, O an-swer me.

1. Be - cause I led____ you____ out of the land of Eg - ypt. You have pre - pared a cross for your Sav-ior.
2. I o - pened the____ sea____ be - fore you, and you have opened my side with a lance.
3. I gave you wa-ter of sal-va-tion from the rock,____ and you gave me vine-gar to drink.
4. I gave you a____ roy - al scep-tre, and you gave me a crown of thorns.
5. With pow - er____ I____ lift - ed you up,____ and you have hung me up-on____ the cross.

Refrain

Cantor:

Ho-ly God,_____ Ho-ly Might-y One,_____ Ho-ly Im-mor-tal

Congregation:

Ho-ly God,_____ Ho-ly Mighty One,_____

one, have mer-cy on us._____

Ho-ly Im-mor-tal one, have mer-cy on us.

THE HOLY WEEK BOOK

Procession Of Light

Strong and rhythmical

Sr. Suzanne

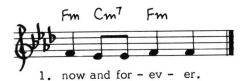

1. Je-sus Christ is ri - sen, Sing his vic-tory song. Share his love and share his light

1. now and for - ev - er.

2. Jesus Christ is Lord of all,
   Sing his victory song.
   Share his love and share his light
   Now and forever.

3. Alpha and Omega
   Sing his victory song.
   Share his love and share his light
   Now and forever

4. Come in joy before him,
   Sing his victory song.
   Share his love and share his light
   Now and forever.

5. Come to the waters,
   Sing his victory song.
   Share his love and share his light
   Now and forever.

Use of the song:

Processional song (from the place of Reading to the place of Eucharist.

Select words from the readings chosen for the Vigil so that the processional
serves as a transition and as a way of praying the readings.

Add simple descants, hand instruments, etc. with each verse so that there
is a sense of growing excitement and joy.

Use hand bells (F and C) on the strong beats of each measure.

THE HOLY WEEK BOOK

Renewal Of Baptismal Promises

Cantor and Congregation   Sr. Suzanne

With each congregational response, add voice
parts and instruments.
(See below for samples.)

The Merchant's Carol

English Traditional
Rather quick

Frank Kendon

1. As we rode down the steep hillside, Twelve merchants with our fair - ing, A
2. Be - neath the ol - ives fast we rode, And loud - er came the shout-ing: "So

1. shout a-cross the hol - low land Came loud up - on our hear - ing, A
2. great a noise must mean", said we, "A king, be - yond all doubt - ing!" Spurred

1. shout, a song, a thous-and strong, A thous-and lust - y voic - es: "Make
2. on, did we, this king to see, And left the mules to fol - low; And

1. haste", said I, I knew not why, "Je - ru - sa-lem re - joic - es!"
2. near - er, clear - er rang the noise A - long the Kid - ron hol - low.

Adapted with permission from the Oxford Book of Carols.

THE HOLY WEEK BOOK

My Dancing Day

Traditional

1. To - morrow shall be my danc - ing day: I would my true love
2. Then was I born of a vir - gin pure, Of her I took flesh - ly

1. did so chance To see the leg - end of my play, To call my
2. sub - stance; Thus was I knit to man's na - ture, To call my

Refrain

1. true love to my dance: Sing O my love, O my
2. true love to my dance:

love, my love, my love; This have I done for my true love.

Adapted with permission from the Oxford Book of Carols.

Friday Morning

Words & music by Sydney Carter

1. It was on a Fri - day morn-ing that they took me from the cell, And I saw they had a car-pen-ter to cru - ci - fy as well. You can blame it on to Pi - late, You can blame it on the

2. You can blame it on to Ad - am, you can blame it on to Eve, You can blame it on the ap - ple, But that I can't be - lieve. It was God that made the De - vil And the Wo - man and the

3. Now Bar - ra - bas was a kill - er and they let Bar - ra - bas go. But you are be - ing cru - ci - fied For noth - ing here be - low. But God is up in heav - en And he does-n't do a

4. To hell with Je - ho - vah, to the car - pen - ter I said, I wish that a car - pen - ter had made the world in stead. Good - by and good luck to you, Our ways will soon di -

THE HOLY WEEK BOOK

1. Jews, you can blame it on the Dev-il, It's God I ac-cuse. It's
2. Man, and there wouldn't be an Ap-ple If it wasn't in the plan. It's
3. thing: with a mil - lion ang-els watching, and they never move a wing. It's
4. vide. Re - mem-ber me in heaven, The man you hung be-side. It's

God they ought to cru-ci-fy In - stead of you and me, I said to the

V. 1, 2, 3

car-pen-ter A hang-ing on the tree.

V. 4

hang-ing on the tree.

THE HOLY WEEK BOOK

Mary's Wandering

German
Rather slowly

1. Once Ma - ry would go wan - der - ing, To all the land would run,____
2. Whom met she as she journeyed forth? Saint Pet - er, that good man,____

1. That she might find her son, that she might find her son.____
2. Who sad - ly her did scan, who sad - ly her did scan.____

Fa-Burden to Verses 4 & 7

4. 'Too well, too well I've seen thy son; 'Twas by a pal - ace gate,____

Most____ griev - ous was his state.'____

Most____ griev - ous was his state.'____

Most griev-ous was his state, most griev - ous was his state.'____

Adapted with permission from the Oxford Book of Carols.

THE HOLY WEEK BOOK